The
Prairie
W.A.S.P.

There was an old man of Saint Bees,
Who was stung in the arm by a wasp,
When asked: "Does it hurt?"
He replied: "No it doesn't,
I'm so glad it wasn't a hornet".

Sir W. S. Gilbert

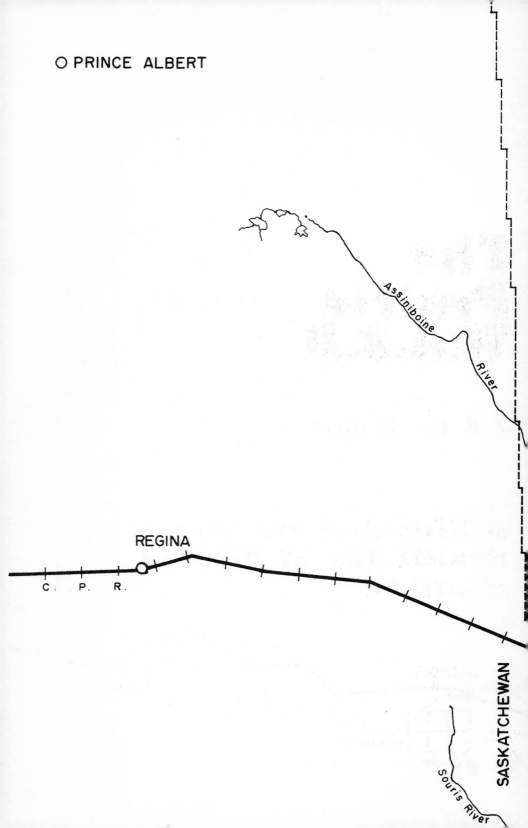

O PRINCE ALBERT

Assiniboine River

REGINA

C. P. R.

SASKATCHEWAN

Souris River

The Prairie W.A.S.P.

J. A. D. Stuart

A History of the Rural Municipality of Oakland, Manitoba

BRANDON

WINNIPEG

River

JRIS

WAWANESA

RM. OF OAKLAND

Red

Published by The Prairie Publishing Company, Winnipeg.
Graphic Design by Jill Brooks
Printed in Winnipeg, Canada, by Wallingford Press Ltd.

To MANITOBA in its 100th year

Foreword

The publication and study of books on history is a natural effect of centennial celebrations. Buildings, useful or otherwise, may be erected to mark dates, but seldom recall much except the date, not necessarily the reason for it. In and since 1967 hefty volumes have been published or promised on Canadian history, but mainly they edge in content to events of political interest and illuminate the personalities of eminent politicians.

Actually all history begins with local history. There were "squatters" in Western Canada, living in comparative comfort on their own productivity long before government surveyors showed up, putting in pegs of wood or iron to mark range, township, section and even quarter-section lines, whereby the resident might acquire a guaranteed "title". History always begins with local history, and for that reason I am happy that so many accounts of so many of our local districts have been and are being published; they lay emphasis on the point that history begins with people, their struggles against circumstances of soil, locality, weather, in order to lead the good life.

Sixty years ago, when I first came to southwest Manitoba, there were still many first generation pioneer settlers around. I cultivated their friendship and learnt the story of their difficulties and conquests. In my own turn I lost myself in the bush of the Turtle Mountain, twice nearly froze to death, and kept myself warm by using an old-style buck-saw with tiring vigour.

And so it is with pleasure that I commend this book which deals with the early settlement of a part of central Manitoba which I know fairly well. It should be in the living room of every house in the area with which it deals, and be read by others who can never experience the same happiness of achievement in this age of electricity, gasoline engines and paved roads.

> T. C. B. Boon, B.A., D.D.,
> Archivist to the Ecclesiastical
> Province of Rupert's Land.

Introduction

Historical writing has not been the same since we have been shown that all communication is affected, and in fact altered, by the medium in use at any given period.

It might even be suggested that the printed word in its ordinary format is so much a prisoner of the nineteeth century and of the assumptions of that century that it is not a suitable vehicle for presenting a complete picture of any area or community during that period.

Since our own climate of thought grew out of the last century (even if it has often been in the form of a reaction), it stands to reason that the very habits of our mental process may tend to obscure certain vital aspects and prejudices of our Victorian ancestors.

Accordingly, in this work, rather than present simply a standard written record of a locality, the author has attempted an integrated statement with all parts contributing to the whole. The text is relatively orthodox, but has been interspersed with literary selections and other material designed to give the reader immediate contact with the thought processes of the people in the narrative. It is hoped that in this fashion, rather in the manner of newer cinema technique, the reader may be enabled to obtain a comprehensive picture of the life and times.

Readers of British extraction whose ancestors settled in this country may gain a truer appreciation of their cultural heritage, or at least should be reminded of long dead or forgotten relatives. The book should give all readers a better understanding of "English Canadians".

W. H. Brooks,
St. Paul's College,
University of Manitoba.

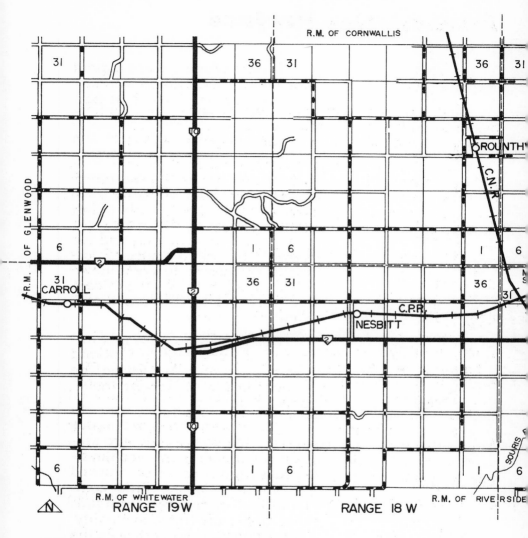

R.M. OF CORNWALLIS

31   36   31   36   31

ROUNTH'

C.N.R.

R.M. OF GLENWOOD

6   I   6   I   6

R.M.

31
CARROLL   36   31   36   31

C.P.R.
NESBITT

6   I   6   I   6

SOURIS

N
R.M. OF WHITEWATER   R.M. OF RIVERSIDE
RANGE 19W   RANGE 18 W

R.M. of Oakland

Preface

If North America was a giant dartboard, the Rural Municipality of Oakland would be part of the bull's-eye.

Here, in the middle of the continent, it's easy to dream.

An essentially flat horizon— broken by bluffs of hardy trees and gently rolling hills that glow beautiful blue shades in the clear air—lifts one's gaze up and far away into the distance. Enormous sky seems to come down all around, while the magnificent sunrises and sunsets are a preview of paradise.

But there's no heaven without hard work, and in Oakland material comfort hinges on the annual hustle to harvest thousands of acres of grain.

The system of gravel roads carving the countryside into sections of square miles was developed so grain could be trucked to elevators in the little communities on the two railroads that criss-cross the municipality. These branch lines were once the sole economic link with world markets.

Today, paved highways tend to bypass the local elevators. With business greatly diminished, the little communities have shrunk in size and influence. One such village folded up some years ago, and for the rest it's probably just a matter of time.

Nearly all the men in the area are, or were, farmers. If the crops are good, many own new cars; and perhaps take pleasure trips. Others drive older models, and can't for the life of them see much sense in traipsing around. Then there are those who believe the only place for money is in the bank. And, of course, there are some who do things they can hardly afford—such as younger fellows gambling on the big mortgages needed to start up fresh in these days of costly farm machinery and steep land values.

The citizens of Oakland also have in common that friendly foe they both fight and depend on, the sub-Arctic weather. Short summers with light rainfall and fierce hail or thunderstorms are a headache. As for the long winters, there's still something a bit too true in the old yarn about the prairie farmer who saw a blizzard heading towards his barn. It is said he grabbed a couple of boards, ran to a knoll a few feet in front of the barn, stood the boards up on end, and held them together tightly. When the wind finally had stopped, he turned around, and found that the damage wasn't half as bad as it might have been. The wooden wedge had split the blizzard, and the barn was only missing two corners!

This book, however, isn't simply the story of a typical chunk of prairie.

Oakland is blessed with a better than average location near the junction of two rivers in the heart of a prosperous grain and mixed farming region.

Moreover, the municipality belongs to that vast riddle among nations, the Dominion of Canada; and its history is woven into the Canadian experience.

Two centuries ago—before kilts scaled a cliff and drove the fleurs-de-lis off the Plains of Abraham—Indians wandered across Oakland mumbling prayers taught them by a brave missionary from New France.

Oakland later was the scene of keen competition when a daring group of Montreal merchants tried to steal an empire of furs from "the Governor and Company of Adventurers of England trading into Hudson's Bay".

About the time Yankee doodles sulked home from the border battles of Queenston Heights and Chateauguay, food was shipped from Oakland to help save Lord Selkirk's newly arrived Red River colonists from starvation.

Although some of these early events are included, what follows is primarily a history of Oakland municipality from 1879 to 1889—the settlement period.

Men and women came to Oakland from various places and for more than one reason; yet, almost without exception, they shared a strong British background. Not afraid to live with conviction, they brought to this part of the Canadian West that remarkable blend of common sense and idealism which gave the British Isles power and glory around the globe in the last century. And with the same spirit as the farmer who held up the boards and defied the blizzard, they accepted the challenge of building Christian homes in strange surroundings.

Publisher's Note

Readers who may be unfamiliar with the land survey system used in southern Manitoba are advised to consult the first item of the appendix.

Contents

Shenanigans Before the Storm

Beaver hats!

That's what the British Lords of Trade meant in 1763, when they dryly informed King George III: "The most obvious Benefit acquired by the Cessions made to your Majesty is the Fur & Skin Trade of all the Indians in North America."[1] In the seventeenth and eighteenth centuries "the vogue for the big hats with the rolling brims was more than a fashion . . . it was a mania. To appear without one of the elaborate affairs of felt, plumes, jewels, braid and embroidery was to be quite hopelessly out of style".[2] Consequently, after Quebec fell, Wolfe's jubilant countrymen wasted no time investing in the wilderness of their newly-won continent. And, thenceforth, Oakland was on the map.

Year after year, century upon century, Manitoba had been the home of roaming wildlife and primitive peoples. Not until Captain Thomas Button planted a British flag and wintered at the Nelson River mouth in 1612 did the first harbinger of modern European civilization arrive on

1

the scene. "Behind the voyage stood the chivalry and wealth, and indeed the royalty, of England, committed to the discovery of a North-West passage to the Orient . . ."[3] Other English explorers followed: Baffin, Foxe and James, for example—names prominent on a map of the Canadian Arctic.

English interest in finding an Arctic route to the Far East then waned, and was not rekindled until the late 1660's. By that time the explorations overland from New France of Pierre-Esprit Radisson and his brother-in-law, Médard Chouart, Sieur des Groseilliers—the first coureurs de bois known to have sought furs in what is now Manitoba —had received some English backing. This link resulted in the incorporation by King Charles II of the Hudson's Bay Company in 1670.

The "Honourable Company" was granted the sole right to trade in furs and fish, administer justice, erect buildings and otherwise control the lands that drained into Hudson's Bay. The vast chartered territory was called Rupert's Land in honour of the Company's first governor, Prince Rupert.

Oakland, situated near the junction of the Assiniboine and Souris rivers, is part of the territory claimed by the English throne in 1670. Because the English were too busy competing with the "frog-eating French" elsewhere in North America, gaining nationality scarcely mattered for a hundred years or so. When, in time, the Hudson's Bay Company had to defend Rupert's Land from a series of commercial assaults, the area of the lower reaches of the Souris was in the thick of the fray.

Meanwhile, Oakland's earliest recorded contact with Europe apparently resulted from the explorations of Pierre Gaultier de Varennes, Sieur de la Vérendrye. Hearing that the Sioux Indians spoke with a Chinese-sounding accent, the native of New France hoped they would show him a route to the Far East.[4] Instead the Sioux massacred his eldest son, his missionary, and twenty-two men in 1736.[5] After a number of discouraging years, he was paddled back to New France physically and financially exhausted.

2

Yet la Vérendrye achieved more than is generally realized. The chain of fur posts which he and his followers established, close to the sites of Winnipeg, Portage la Prairie, and Dauphin, and at other points, was a precedent that eventually led to the entry of Manitoba into the Canadian Confederation. Although there is no proof la Vérendrye saw Oakland, it seems a missionary involved in this push westward did. More than fifty years later Indians at the Souris mouth could still repeat short prayers in the French language.[6]

The influx of British funds and supplies to the former New France following the Treaty of Paris in 1763 greatly invigorated the far inland fur trade that la Vérendrye had pioneered. Shortly thereafter Montrealers occupied three positions on the Assiniboine—the closest to Oakland being Pine Fort, where Pine Creek empties into the larger river. These posts became part of a daring plan to destroy the Hudson's Bay Company's influence in the West after these and other traders organized themselves into the North West Company.

Being approximately on a line between the buffalo plains south of the river and good fur grounds to the north, the posts doubled as food supply depots and bases for trade and exploration.[7] Thus the Nor'Westers gambled on gaining control of the lands drained by rivers running towards Hudson Bay. The older company would then languish or, better still, leave "The Bay" altogether, and its rivals from the St. Lawrence could exploit the ocean route to the Prairies which the French before them had coveted for years.

By 1790 the beaver population of the present Brandon-Winnipeg region was virtually depleted, whereupon the Nor'Westers shifted their prime trading operations a couple of thousand miles away to the Peace River country. Owing to their proximity to the buffalo plains, this move greatly increased the importance of the Assiniboine River posts, because the North West Company brigades depended on pemmican for food on the long return trip from Lake Superior to Athabaska and Great Slave lakes in one season.

3

As competition obliged the Hudson's Bay Company to send men farther and farther inland, this long-lasting Indian preserve of dried buffalo meat, fat, and sometimes berries, also became their staple diet. Soon they, too, relied on the thundering, bellowing herds of southern Manitoba. The subtrade in pemmican was one of the main factors which induced both companies to plant posts near the junction of the Assiniboine and the Souris.

Montrealers moved into the district first. In the summer of 1793, an independent operator set up shop about two miles west of the Souris mouth, leaving Ronald Cameron in charge, and the North West Company stationed a man called Augé immediately upriver from Cameron's post not long afterwards. Third to arrive was Donald (unaffectionately nicknamed "Mad") MacKay of the Hudson's Bay Company.

According to his journal, MacKay reached the Souris mouth early in October with three boats, two canoes, and nineteen men. He stopped to pay his respects to the two Canadians, Cameron and Augé, before commencing operations, but his welcome was none too cordial:

> I heard that some Stone Indians arrived on the other side [of the river]. I went to our Crafts [boats] at the same time the Canadians [were] running over & taking everything from the Indians. I entered one of their tents & was presented with six pieces of meat, I then returned back and the most part of the Indians followed me, & began to trade [for] Brandy in particular . . . all the men up the whole night watching the Crafts . . .[8]

The next evening Cameron and Augé visited "to excuse themselves for last night's misconduct in running before the Indians . . ."[9] They may have hoped to persuade MacKay to trade somewhere else. If so, they failed. MacKay well appreciated the tactical advantage in being located near buffalo grounds among the Canadians; and warned the Nor'Wester Cuthbert Grant, Sr., (then trading near what is now Togo, Saskatchewan) in a letter a few days later: ". . . I am fully persuaded that that old spirit

4

of opposition so notoriously known to some individuals is not yet Extinguished . . . [but you cannot prevent the Hudson's Bay Company] . . . from coming to their own undoubted rights to oppose any intruder that may come from Canada".[10]

Step number one in opposing the "intruders from Canada" was to erect a warehouse "to secure the Company's property". A man stood sentry over the trade goods, while the rest either collected stones for the foundation or squared timber. But not without a labour dispute. Two men, supposed to have been throwing stones from the edge of the river up onto the bank to dry, fetched only thirty small stones during a four-hour period. As punishment, MacKay cut off their ration of grog; whereupon William Corrigal, one of the slackers, grew so insolent that MacKay was "in a passion to strike him with a willow I had in my hand". For his rudeness, Corrigal was placed off-duty until he apologized; and it was three days before the culprit begged his master's pardon.[11]

This altercation notwithstanding, the warehouse soon was completed, and the next project was to erect the trader's house. It was very cold on October 16, the day the foundation was laid, when MacKay wrote in his journal: ". . . . at 5 p.m. I baptised the house and called it Brandon House [and] treated the men with Grogg to drink the Companys health & success".[12] The treat apparently warmed the men's muscles, because the two-storey building progressed well—too well, as far as the opposition was concerned.

Early in the afternoon of the 23rd, a gang of Canadians commenced cutting wood within twenty yards of the spot where the house was under construction. When MacKay protested, they threatened to fell wood right at his doorstep, if they so wanted. "I said should they attempt that, that they would return with broken bones", MacKay claimed. One of the Canadians then advanced "as if he meant to make a blow at me with his hatchet" and MacKay vowed to shoot in self-defence if he came any closer. The fact that James Moar, who was with MacKay, ran for cover shows the situation was momentarily tense.[13]

The following day the Canadians again began cutting wood nearby as an excuse to spy on Brandon House; MacKay and all hands therefore "cut a track to divide our ground from theirs" as a "last warning". Since the rival fur traders wished to avoid coming to blows, this rough survey brought the incident to a close, and the Hudson's Bay men were able to proceed with the task of completing the house before winter set in.

The men did not regard the fast approach of frigid weather as any reason to work seven days a week. The roof of MacKay's dwelling was finished on November 3, a Sabbath; yet not without "much difficulty with the men for working on Sunday", he reported. Possibly the feeling they were being exploited prompted the men to disobey their leader on November 5 (Guy Fawkes Day). "This being the day so much distinguished for a holly day I ordered the men to burn a pope [an effigy of the Pope?] in the face of all the Canadians", he noted. " . . . the men did not wish to do so I relinquished my Idea, as it might create something of Consequence . . ."[14] Or maybe the men simply knew better than to insult the faith of the Canadian voyageurs, most of whom were French-speaking Catholics?

Besides, MacKay had other things on his mind than repaying the Canadians for the wood-cutting episode. On December 23, he twice was nearly stabbed by an Indian who drank two quarts of brandy, then refused to trade for them.[15] What was more serious, the Canadians were stampeding the buffalo away from the neighbouring plains— in an effort to starve out the Hudson's Bay Company, MacKay believed.

Also, towards the end of January, 1794, his men again became peevish. MacKay had ordered the completion of some odds and ends of work before the majority of his party set off to establish a post farther up the Assiniboine, but their departure was delayed on several occasions when saws kept mysteriously breaking. MacKay was sure that the men purposely were damaging the saws to sabotage the impending expedition. Although he felt obliged to throw a farewell party when the expedition was at last ready to depart, this was his exasperated comment: "after

6

every thing was ready I gave the men a treate [yet] it would puzzle the greatest philosopher of this Age to hummour these men for realy they are a set of loons".[16]

Life was somewhat quieter at Brandon House after the group left to trade elsewhere, except that MacKay was constantly pestered by intoxicated Indians fighting and demanding brandy, and occasionally killing themselves in the process. On February 27, about thirty natives, already under the influence of North West Company rum, appeared at MacKay's demanding brandy, with nothing to barter in return. "I was under the necessity to give some, being Almost at war with them", lamented MacKay, "the Canadians setting them on to get Brandy from the English-men".[17] The next day he put his foot down and declared there would be no more free brandy. Luckily the unruly visitors went to sleep and calm was restored.

Intoxicated Indians were one of the hazards of com-peting against the Canadians who poured liquor "like water so as to make the Indians come to them". MacKay may have solved this problem partially by having the men enclose the main buildings with a stockade as soon as the weather warmed up.[18]

Spring break-up meant packing pemmican, patching boats, and preparing gear for the trip down the Assiniboine that annually marked the close of the trading season. Yet Mad MacKay would hardly have lived up to his hot-head reputation if he had not tried to finish the season one-up on the opposition. His golden opportunity to do so, he thought, came on the evening of April 23 when he spotted the Nor'Wester Augé heading up-river to trade with an Indian who had debts outstanding at Brandon House.

With the probable pretext that Augé was unethical in dealing with an Indian on whom the Hudson's Bay Com-pany had a claim, MacKay waited until his rival returned and challenged him on the subject. When Augé didn't reply, MacKay threatened to shoot; and, his threat having no effect, finally did fire a shot. (Augé later maintained he had been shot at; MacKay said he had only shot into the air as a warning!) The following day MacKay was

7

attacked by three of Augé's Indians in the upper storey of his house, but managed to throw them downstairs.[19]

Repercussions came early in May when Cuthbert Grant, Sr., and a group of Nor'Westers reached the Souris mouth heading east with the winter's trade. Hearing Augé's side of the story, his friends were determined to teach MacKay a lesson. On May 8 they called at Brandon House—ostensibly, just to be sociable; and, according to MacKay, a "merry evening" was had by all. Acting as the perfect host, he saw his guests part way home and, in doing so, innocently fell for Grant's invitation to join them at the Canadian post for a glass of wine. Alas! It was nothing but a ruse. The Canadians detained him against his will to force him to apologize to Augé. Through the next day and night MacKay was held captive, but he refused to ask Augé's pardon, despite a threat made on his life. Finally he was released on the morning of the 10th.[20]

The conclusion of this curious affair was in tune with the whole season's mock-heroic skirmishes. MacKay was so pleased to recover his freedom that he invited the Nor'-Westers to breakfast at Brandon House before continuing their journey down the Assiniboine. And they, who had imprisoned and intimidated him for two nights and a day, graciously accepted.

Mad MacKay may indeed have been slightly mad and even somewhat dangerous;[21] but he was the right man in the right place. Not that those who worked for him thought so. They ignored his orders, and took vindictive pleasure in smashing his crockery and losing his luggage. Worse still the London Committee of the Hudson's Bay Company considered his escapades nothing short of disgraceful, and in 1794 he was transferred to a post of lesser importance.[22]

The difficulty was that the wealthy eighteenth-century businessmen on the London Committee were benevolent gentlemen whose judgment was distorted by the illusion that the Canadians could be handled with kid gloves. MacKay, being a former Nor'Wester, knew it was time to start talking a tougher language. To him goes the credit for suggesting the English company use the Albany River as a means of regaining power in southern Manitoba[23]—the region from which Indians carried furs to Fort Albany on James Bay in the days before la Vérendrye and the French broke into the market; and he wisely convinced his superiors to locate in the vicinity of the Souris Plains.

It was a decade or so before the Hudson's Bay directors fully realized that whoever controlled the pemmican supply would win the great struggle for fur trade supremacy in the West.

REFERENCES:
1. Hamilton, Robt. M., 1965, Canadian Quotations and Phrases, p. 86. McClelland and Stewart Ltd., Toronto.
2. O'Meara, Walter, 1960, The Savage Country, p. viii. Boston.
3. Morton, W. L., 1957, Manitoba: A History, p. 4-5. Toronto.
4. Hutchison, Bruce, 1955, The Struggle for the Border, p. 89.
5. Morton, W. L., op. cit., p. 27.
6. Harmon, Daniel W., 1957, Sixteen Years in the Indian Country: The Journal of Daniel Williams Harmon, 1800 - 1806. Edited by W. Kaye Lamb, Toronto.
7. Morton, W. L., op. cit., pp. 37-38.
8. MacKay, Donald, Brandon House Journal for October 7, 1793, microfilm reel 1M16 of Hudson's Bay Company records, Public Archives of Canada, Ottawa.
9. Ibid. for October 8, 1793.
10. Ibid. for October 16, 1793.
11. Ibid. for October 11-15, 1793.
12. Ibid. for October 16, 1793.
13. Ibid. for October 23, 1793 and Taylor, R. L., 1966, p. C3, July issue of The Western Producer, Saskatoon.
14. Ibid. for November 3-5, 1793.
15. Ibid. for December 24, 1793.
16. Ibid. for January 27, 1794.
17. Ibid. for February 27, 1794.
18. Ibid. for March 17, 1794.
19. Morton, Arthur S., 1939, History of the Canadian West to 1870-1, p. 434. Thomas Nelson and Sons Ltd.
20. MacKay, Donald, op. cit. for May 8-10, 1792.
21. Rich, E. E., 1959, History of the Hudson's Bay Company, 1670-1870, Vol. II, p. 182. London.
22. Ibid.
23. Ibid. pp. 181-183.

Clenching
the Kid Gloves

Brandon House was established at a critical time in British history. The same year, 1793, the French guillotined a Louis, and declared the war on Britain which lasted until the rout of Napoleon at Waterloo. Not long before, civilian refugees and veterans of regiments loyal to the British Crown had sought sanctuary from George Washington's rebels in what is now Canada. Meanwhile, back across the North Atlantic, poor Scottish crofters, forced from their homes by bayonets, clubs, fire, and sheep, also knew the sadness of exile.

Prince Charles Edward Stuart's defeat at Culloden Moor having sounded the death knell of traditional Highland society, the sons of the clansmen shipped overseas to fight for the British Government or to toil in the Canadian fur trade—like the Frasers so prominent in the dramatic conquest of Quebec, and the MacKays who ran the trading posts in the vicinity of Oakland. Later many of these roving Scots returned to find their native valleys deserted, their families scattered to accommodate great flocks of Cheviot

11

sheep, and the lairds preoccupied with profiting from the sale of wool and mutton to the industrializing regions of the Lowlands and of England.

Among those displaced by this craze for sheep-rearing were the Kildonan parishioners in the shire of Sutherland, a wild piece of territory almost as far north as one can travel in Scotland. Evicted from their small holdings, they faced the choice of gravitating to a Glasgow slum, becoming herring fishermen, or emigrating; and a number of the younger men and women proudly risked a fresh start in the settlement Lord Selkirk then was planning on the bank of the Red River.

Lord Selkirk, a large shareholder in the Hudson's Bay Company at the turn of the eighteenth century, was one of the first to see both the crime and the possible good which might come of the Highland agricultural clearances and of similar events in Ireland. Realizing that emigration from Scotland and Ireland could not be stopped, Selkirk persuaded the Company to grant him land for a colony at the forks of the Red and Assiniboine rivers. To his mind, the prospective colony could help both to deflect the flow of emigration from the United States to British North America and to serve as the wedge needed to split the Nor'Westers' growing hold in southern Manitoba.

The colony was intended to produce food to supplement the pemmican purchased from the natives, to furnish prairie-bred men to work for the Company, and to be a home for retired Company servants and their dependents. Most important, the colony would confirm the Hudson's Bay title to Rupert's Land, which the traders from Montreal disputed by actual occupation.[1]

By that time the British company acknowledged that Mad MacKay had been right about the necessity of adopting more aggressive tactics against its opponents. It had decided to concentrate the new offensive in the Red-Assiniboine trading zone—particularly around Brandon House, a key to the Nor'Westers' supply system.

In 1811, the Hudson's Bay Company hired a group of tough Irishmen to defend its rights in North America

12

—men they thought would not hesitate to swing back in answer to the Montrealers' bullying. Not least, it consistently blocked the North West Company's bid for a port on Hudson Bay. Without an ocean route to the rich, far-inland, fur country, the Canadians were finally obliged to give in.[2]

The planting of the Selkirk settlement was a slap in the face for the Nor'Westers. The philanthropic speculator was given a grand estate called Assiniboia—roughly the Red River country south to the watershed of the Missouri and the Mississippi, east to the head of Rainy River, with a northern line along the Rainy and Winnipeg rivers to the middle of Lake Winnipeg, and westward across Lake Winnipegosis to the source of the Assiniboine. Oakland was part of this tract, as were the lands on which the North West Company depended for pemmican to feed its brigades from Lake Winnipeg to Athabaska.

As a result of losing control of the Red River area, and not having the Hudson's Bay Company's advantage of a cheaper ocean route to the centre of the continent, the Nor'Westers found their backs to the wall. The two fur companies had been co-existing fairly peaceably in the Assiniboine basin before the arrival of the Red River colonists in 1812, and Selkirk wanted things to remain that way. Instead, the stage was set for the fur traders' pemmican war of 1814-17, in which the Oakland area was involved almost from the beginning.

Early in January, to help alleviate the problem of food shortages at the Red River colony, Selkirk's Lieutenant-Governor Miles Macdonell issued an edict banning the export of pemmican from Assiniboia. When messengers from The Forks arrived at Brandon House to announce the news two days later, the master there accepted a copy of the proclamation; but the Nor'Wester in command across the river at Fort la Souris declared the decree illegal, and refused to allow a copy to be nailed to his gate.[3] Likewise the Nor'Westers ignored the proclamation when the time came to ship out their surplus of pemmican. To enforce his decree, Macdonell had a boatload of pemmican seized near the Forks in May, and more was confiscated in June.

13

The North West Company, in turn, began stockpiling the dried meat at Fort la Souris until enough men had been mustered to fight their way past the Red River colony, if need be; and it soon became apparent that trouble was inevitable—especially after Macdonell ordered the Nor'-Westers themselves to leave Assiniboia.[4] The clash came the following spring.

The manoeuvres of the fur traders' war may seem insignificant compared to the great battles of history. Nonetheless, it was hardly child's play when the frustrations and tensions of that tremendous commercial competition culminated in a showdown. Fighting blood came to the fore in the French-speaking Metis, and Scots heard again the call of the days when it was a disgrace to die of natural causes in the Highlands. Also involved were Englishmen with that famous stubborn streak and Irish, who are inclined to have quick tempers. With some relief, therefore, one reads of a love affair blooming in Oakland against the background of raids, counter-raids, and bluffing backed by knives and pistols.

As much as Mad MacKay was a thorn at Brandon House, his niece Bethsy was a rose; and her presence there during her brother John Richards MacKay's mastership of the post was a boon for the young traders of the Assiniboine basin. Before the outbreak of hostilities, the traders usually confined their shenanigans to the commercially crucial spring and fall of the year. "During the long winters the rivalry would become only a concealed watchfulness, and there would be much visiting back and forth, exchange of books, long hours of talk and, when a visit from another post gave occasion, night-long dancing and revelry. As [John Richards] MacKay had as housekeeper his sister Elizabeth, the bachelors of the North West Company often drifted down to the Hudson's Bay trader's post and spent long hours by the fire, smoking their pipes and talking with the men—but really there to enjoy the company of the woman".[5]

One such bachelor was the very eligible, young Nor'-Wester, Cuthbert Grant, Jr., then stationed near the spot where the Qu'Appelle empties into the Assiniboine. Of

14

course, no one knew in those days that Grant would soon lead the Metis nation of the Prairies against the Red River colony. Certainly not Bethsy. All she understood was that, of her many admirers, he alone made the struggle for survival in the wilderness worthwhile. And her affection was returned. Before bloodshed ended the comings and goings of the traders, Grant often visited Brandon House.

Bethsy was sent to the Hudson's Bay Company establishment at The Forks when the violence erupted. Then, unable to bear the forced separation from her lover, she threw political loyalty to the winds and eloped with Grant in May, 1815. But the honeymoon was short. That summer Grant and the Metis razed Brandon House (allegedly in error) and temporarily expelled the Selkirk settlers from the banks of the Red.

John Richards MacKay managed to rebuild Brandon House and the Selkirk colonists recovered their land. In 1816, a handful of Hudson's Bay men took by surprise the Nor'Westers' Fort Gibraltar at the mouth of the Assiniboine. It was even contemplated that an attempt might be made to prevent North West Company canoes from reaching Athabaska by launching an armed schooner on Lake Manitoba. The war was fast approaching a climax.

Brandon House, burned the previous year, was a target again in 1816. Cuthbert Grant opened the campaign that spring by ambushing a Hudson's Bay brigade at the Grand Rapids of the Qu'Appelle. He stole all the pemmican-laden boats except one, which he "sent down the river to spare the colony the worst privations".[6]

By winning this booty the Canadians had cornered all the pemmican of the Qu'Appelle area; and, determined to settle the matter once and for all, they hurriedly freighted it down the Assiniboine under mounted Metis guard. "The southern party of about thirty rode behind [the Nor'Wester] Macdonell, the northern one of over forty with Grant. They rode along the tops of the valley slopes, guarding the boats which wound slowly down the river loops below".[7] As they neared the Souris mouth, Macdonell led his men to Fort la Souris and Grant sacked Brandon House.

This is the Brandon House master's version of the episode:

At ½ past noon about 48 Half Breeds, Canadians, Freemen & Indians came all riding on Horseback, with their Flag flying blue about 4 feet square & a figure of 8 horizontally in the middle, one Beating an Indian Drum, and many of them singing Indian Songs, they all rode directly to the usual crossing over the river where they all stopped about two minutes, and instead of going down the Bank & riding across the River they all turned suddenly round and rode full speed into our Yard—some of them tyed their Horses, others loose & fixed their flag at our Door, which they soon afterwards hoisted over our East Gate next the Canadian House— Cuthbert Grant then came up to me in the Yard & demanded of me to deliver to him all the Keys of our Stores Warehouses & I of course would not deliver them up—they then rushed into the House and broke open the warehouse Door first, plundered the Warehouse of every article it contained, tore up part of the Cellar floor & cut out the Parchment windows without saying for what this was done or by whose authority—Alexr. McDonell, Seraphim, Bostonais, & Allan McDonell were at their House [Fort la Souris] looking on the whole time—they broke open the store Door & Barn Door & carried away almost everything there except the Packs of Furs & some empty Kegs—they also plundered every person in the House of part of their private property & took away every horse belonging to the Company & European Servants. Those Horses that McFynn [?] J. Favill Half Breeds they had let alone; all these men were armed with a Gunsack, a pike at the end of a pole, some bows & arrows swords . . . Bostonais told that it was Mr. Robertson's fault that they had plundered our House—for taking their Fort [Gibraltar] at the Forks . . .[8]

After a liquid celebration at Fort la Souris, the procession continued from Oakland to Seven Oaks.

16

Of the countless windbreaks on the Prairies, probably none is as unfavourably known as the bluff of trees that stood near Frog Plain on the west bank of the Red about one hundred and fifty years ago. Seven Oaks was the name of this place, now in Greater Winnipeg, where on June 19 in just fifteen minutes Cuthbert Grant's little army slew the new Assiniboia Governor Robert Semple and twenty of his men.

When the Selkirk settlers saw their friends felled by grape shot, then "knifed and tomahawked . . . stripped and ripped up" like wounded buffalo in an Indian hunt, they doubtless felt justified in dubbing the incident The Massacre of Seven Oaks.

For Lord Selkirk, the Hudson's Bay Company, and the Imperial Government, this skirmish was the last straw. The bitter fur-trading rivalry had to be scotched.

North West Company control of The Forks was the immediate effect of the Seven Oaks affair. Once more the Selkirk colonists became refugees. They were packed into boats, ordered down the Red, and obliged to spend a cold winter at the head of Lake Winnipeg—once again the Nor'Westers had "cleared the two rivers". Yet, luckily for the settlers, Selkirk soon fought back. With better strategy than the Nor'Westers could have anticipated, his mercenaries overwhelmed Fort William in August; and a few months later they successfully recaptured the Hudson's Bay Company's Fort Douglas at The Forks, thus enabling the settlers to return there.

Further pressure was exerted in January, 1817. The British Prince Regent ordered all parties in "the Indian country" to stop fighting. Lord Selkirk arrived at the colony in June, with seven soldiers of the Imperial 37th regiment as a bodyguard. In addition, a royal commissioner was sent overland from the Canada's to arbitrate the dispute; and by March, 1818, Cuthbert Grant was in a Montreal jail awaiting trial for his part in the Seven Oaks incident.

It was not long before the Hudson's Bay Company was again unchallenged ruler of Rupert's Land. Eager to give the Nor'Westers some of their own medicine, Semple's

17

replacement, Governor Williams, carried through with the earlier idea of placing a gunboat patrol on Lake Winnipeg. This show of strength, coupled with the successful interception of Canadian brigades at the Grand Rapids of the Saskatchewan in the spring of 1819, proved the knock-out blow for the North West Company.

Experience had demonstrated that monopoly was essential to the prosperity of the increasingly competitive fur trade; and this was brought about by the amalgamation of the two companies under the Hudson's Bay name in 1821.[9]

REFERENCES:
1. Morton, W. L., 1957, Manitoba: A History, pp. 44-45. Toronto.
2. Morton, Arthur S., 1939, History of the Canadian West to 1870-71, p. 532. Thomas Nelson and Sons. Ltd. Also: Rich, E. E., 1959, History of the Hudson's Bay Company, 1670-1870, Vol. II, pp. 301-303. London.
3. Morton, Arthur S., op. cit., pp. 401-402.
4. Ibid., pp. 563-567.
5. Morton, W. L. and MacLeod, Margaret A., 1963, Cuthbert Grant of Grantown, p. 19. McClelland and Stewart Ltd.
6. Ibid., p. 42.
7. Ibid., p. 42.
8. Ibid., p. 43.
9. Innis, Mary Q., 1935, An Economic History of Canada, p. 118. Toronto. Also: Galbraith, John S., 1957, The Hudson's Bay Company as an Imperial Factor, 1821-1869, p. 5. Toronto. After the 1821 merger, Brandon House was one of the outposts from which the Hudson's Bay traders made sure that Indians were trading as few furs as possible to the Americans. In 1832 Brandon House was finally abandoned when Fort Ellice was established near the forks of the Assiniboine and the Qu'Appelle rivers.

Six Cents an Acre

"It is a known fact that anything will grow in this country", the master of Brandon House triumphantly recorded in 1796, after taking up "about three bushels" of fine potatoes.[1] Wheat, barley, Indian corn, turnips, pumpkins, melons, peas, beans, onions, thyme, cucumbers, calabashes and carrots were also raised there during the fur trading era.

Some seasons the harvest was poor, as this account, dated May, 1819, shows:

At Brandon House last summer the Barley was destroyed by the grasshoppers & the great & almost continued drought entirely destroyed the potatoes, turnips, &c. &c., so that there was not the least benefit derived from the labor. Since 1812 there was always good crops of everything until 1816 when the dry summers commenced the land here under cultivation was upwards of three English acres . . . but the dry weather greatly deteriorated

19

the expected produce . . . At Brandon House . . . [the soil is quite] sandy but wet or rainy seasons produce abundant crops . . . Generally the spade & hoe is used by turning over the soil in the spring when the seed is put in. At Brandon the plow is used. Manure is seldom used except for raising cucumbers, Melons or onions, The Wheat and Barley is cut down with the Sickle & the potatoes taken up sometimes with the spade sometimes with the plow and are generally secured in cellars within the house well covered with grass to secure them as well as the turnips from the frost . . . There are a number of small Lakes East of Brandon House that produce the Tisina Aquatica or Wild rice. [A] few years ago, an Indian sowed some 2 or 3 places on the South side [of the] Assiniboine which grew and multiplied. Where the water is too deep or the seasons too dry very slender crops are brought to maturity.[2]

It had taken Europeans quite a while to realize that the Prairies could be cultivated even to this limited degree. About 1720 an explorer from New France returned convinced that no grain would ripen west of Rainy Lake[3] and "the impossibility of getting men on account of their fear of dying of starvation"[4] was one of the reasons la Vérendrye had trouble reaching southern Manitoba in the 1730's. He coaxed the Indians at Lake of the Woods to cultivate corn and wild rice for his voyageurs; but "not until Cree and Assiniboin hunters were persuaded to bring in meat and fats for sale . . . [could he] advance in force out of the forests of the [Canadian] Shield . . . into the park belt and plains in 1738".[5] The same year, much of his interest in visiting the Mandan Indians in what became North Dakota "undoubtedly arose from reports that they cultivated corn and traded it with the Assiniboins for English trade goods . . ."[6]

The Hudson's Bay Company encouraged agricultural experiments to help solve the perennial problem of provisioning its posts. Indeed, the knowledge that vegetables and grain would mature at Brandon House apparently influenced the Company's decision to patronize the founding of a colony at the junction of the Red and Assiniboine rivers because in 1810 the company's employees there were ordered to supply the Selkirk settlers with seed corn, seed potatoes and horses.[7]

Selkirk's chief lieutenant, Miles Macdonell, chose the site at the end of August, 1812, accompanied by a vanguard of eighteen Irish and Scottish labourers and "Adam and Eve"—a young bull and heifer they obtained at Oxford House as the party went up the Nelson River to Lake Winnipeg. The cattle were accustomed to the rigorous climate; but Macdonell's advance party and the first group of actual settlers, who arrived two months later, discovered Manitoba was no Garden of Eden! Drought destroyed their crops the following season; and the struggling settlement verged on starvation until Peter Fidler, then master of Brandon House, sent them a carload of pemmican and seed potatoes.. The following year, Fidler again came to the rescue by shipping nearly 5,500 pounds of pemmican to The Forks so the newcomers could survive a third winter.[8]

Another noteworthy decision of the Hudson's Bay Company about this time was to co-operate with a Church of England missionary society in sending a chaplain to the Red River colony. It was this pioneer Protestant missionary in the Canadian West who conducted Oakland's first recorded Christian services in 1821. Travelling by dog sled from the Red River colony, Rev. John West reached Brandon House on Saturday, January 20 and on the Sabbath assembled the employees for both matins and evensong. On the same day he married the master of the post, John Richards MacKay, nephew of the notorious Mad Donald MacKay, and baptized his two children.[9]

"On the next morning I saw an Indian corpse staged, or put upon a few stocks about ten feet from the ground, at a short distance from the fort", the reverend gentleman said in his diary. He went on to write:

> The property of the dead, which may consist of a kettle, axe, and a few additional articles, is generally put into the case, or wrapped in the buffalo

21

skin with the body, under the idea that the deceased will want them, or that the spirit of those articles will accompany the departed spirit in travelling to another world. And whenever they visit the stage or burying-place, which they frequently do for years afterwards, they will encircle it, smoke their pipes, weep bitterly, and, in their sorrow, cut themselves with knives, or pierce themselves with the points of sharp instruments. I could not but reflect that theirs is a sorrow without hope: all is gross darkness with them as to futurity: and they wander through life without the consolatory and cheering influence of that gospel which has brought life and immortality to life.[10]

Apparently fearing lest the Hudson's Bay men fall into pagan ways, Rev. West quickly held two more services to counteract the effects of the "staging" and solemnized two more weddings and a dozen or so baptisms before continuing his expedition. "As their parents could read", he noted of those whom he had marked with the sign of the Cross, "I distributed some Bibles and Testaments with some religious tracts among them".[11]

Rev. West then went to the Hudson's Bay post in the Qu'Appelle country, but revisited Brandon House on his way back and christened several more children there. He also chatted with some men who were familiar with the habits of the Mandan Indians, and was horrified to learn that Mandan parents had been known to "lend" their young daughters to strangers "for a few beads or a little tobacco". The uncivilized habits of natives, the rugged life at the posts, and the rigour of crossing the prairies in winter gave him a sour taste of southwestern Manitoba. He called it a "heathen and moral desert" and thanked the Almighty profusely when he was again safe at the Red River settlement.

"The Indian country" may have looked grim to a man of the cloth, but industrialism was in the process of creating morally perplexing conditions in the Old Country. The Highland clearances were a symptom of the general social disruption as "dark satanic mills" disgraced parts of "green and pleasant" Britain. Several times in the first half of the nineteenth century impoverished workers rioted and threatened revolution. The terrible Irish potato famine multiplied the misery and unrest, and emigration appeared the only remedy.

A great number of Britons emigrated to North America. Not all were destitute; some were trying to keep what money they had; others sought adventure—but to most the voyage across the Atlantic promised brighter tomorrows. In the New World many prospered better than they had dared to hope. Yet the ambitious remained unsatisfied; the unlucky, discontented. To people cornered in slums or scratching a living from stony, stumpy ground east of the Great Lakes; to hired hands, debtors, and speculators; to those who tasted independence and craved more, the virgin West glistered as the rainbow's end.

Thus, the circumstances which forced the Hudson's Bay Company to encourage the development of an agricultural colony on the Red River led to serious complications. What was said of the settlement on Vancouver Island in 1838 applied to the Red River colony as well: "The interests of the Colony and Fur Trade will never harmonize, the farmer can flourish only through the protection of equal laws, the influence of free trade, the accession of responsible citizens; in short by establishing a new order of things, while the fur trade must suffer by each innovation".[12]

By 1850 the influence of independent traders, in collusion with American fur buyers, was destroying the Hudson's Bay monopoly in southern Manitoba. "The Company's efforts to restrict this allegedly illicit trade met resistance in the colony, and protests against its 'injustices' reached England, where they were used by the Company's enemies to discredit it".[13] Equally threatening as the colony grew were its contacts with the bumptious society that was feverishly building railroads and new states across the southern half of the continent. After 1844, processions of carts were regular traffic between Red River and St. Paul,

Minnesota and both Canadian and American politicians were soon jockeying to annex the Hudson's Bay empire.

The British company was unable to reverse this trend. A prominent company official who testified before a British House of Commons committee in 1857 that, "nobody would go to Rupert's Land from the United States or anywhere else for the purpose of settlement"[14] seemed simply the mouthpiece of vested interest. The very existence of the Red River colony tended to prove that agriculture could be carried on in at least part of Rupert's Land, and "this stimulated . . . search for new land resources in British North America".[15]

Professor Henry Youle Hind, a Toronto geologist commissioned by the Canadian government, was among the

Hind Expedition Drying Out at the Souris Mouth

first scientists to explore the prairies. With thirteen men, a wagon, five carts, and two canoes for the return trip, Hind started overland from Fort Garry to Fort Ellice via the lower Souris valley on June 9, 1858.

The expedition arrived at the Souris mouth fifteen days later to discover countless numbers of grasshoppers so voracious as to attack and destroy every article of clothing left for a few minutes on the grass:

Saddles, girths, leather bags, and clothing of every description were eaten without distinction. Ten minutes sufficed them, as our halfbreeds found to their cost, to destroy three pair of woolen trousers which had been carelessly thrown on the grass. The only way to protect our property was to pile it on the

waggon and carts out of reach. There were two distinct broods of grasshoppers, one with wings not yet formed, which had been hatched on the spot, the other full-grown, invaders from the prairies south of the Assiniboine. We noticed here today the first flight of these insects which afterwards were witnessed on a scale of alarming magnitude, giving rise in their passage through the air to optical phenomena of very rare and beautiful description.[16]

Yet the clouds of ravenous bugs had a silver lining!—in this case a feast:

. . . observing numbers of fish rising at grasshoppers in the Souris we stretched a gill net across the mouth of the river and succeeded in taking pickerel, goldeyes and suckers, the grey and the red. In a second attempt we caught a tartar, a huge sturgeon got entangled in the meshes of the gill net ,and before we could land him he succeeded in carrying a portion of the net along with him.[17]

The party camped at the mouth of the Souris River that night, keeping a close watch after spotting traces of the dreaded Sioux nearby. Still wary of these "tigers of the plain",[18] they followed the Souris southwest through Oakland in the morning.

Hind found Oakland and the surrounding countryside "fertile and beautiful" and the Brandon Hills "perhaps the wildest and most picturesque scenery in the area" but thought their lack of timber spoiled the vicinity for colonization purposes.[19] He was very optimistic about other districts, however, and his official report feathered the caps of Canadian politicians such as Thomas D'Arcy McGee, who prophesied in 1860:

I see in the not remote distance one great nationality bound, like the shield of Achilles, by the blue rim of Ocean. I see it quartered into many communities, each disposing of its internal affairs, but all bound together by free institutions, free intercourse, and free commerce. I see within the round of that shield the peaks of the Western Mountains and the

26

crests of the Eastern waves—the winding Assiniboine, the five-fold lakes, the St. Lawrence, the
Ottawa, the Saguenay, the St. John, and the Basin
of Minas—by all these flowing waters, in all the
valleys they fertilize, in all the cities they visit in
their courses, I see a generation of industrious, contented moral men, free in name and in fact—men
capable of maintaining in peace and in war a
Constitution worthy of such a country.[20]

By then the invention of machine-pressed cloth felt
was beginning to kill the beaver trade, and soon glossy
top hats replaced "beavers" as the most fashionable head-
gear in Western Europe. But the Hudson's Bay Company
did not surrender its land holdings without resistance.
"What!" roared the Governor of the Company when he
heard that some capitalists wanted to build a railway
from sea unto sea . . . "Take away the fertile lands where
our buffalo feed! Let in all kinds of people to squat and
settle and frighten away the fur-bearing animals they don't
kill and hunt. Impossible!"[21]

The impossible happened. The company sold most of
Rupert's Land to the new Dominion of Canada in 1869.
The following year Manitoba was organized as the fifth
province to enter Canadian Confederation; the buffalo
failed; Indians were put "on relief", and the way was paved
for opening up the West.

Cheap land that could be plowed at once "without the
tedious and exhausting labour of years required in wood-
land farming, chopping, rolling, burning, grubbing, stump-
ing and levelling"[22] was Manitoba's big drawing card in
the final quarter of the last century—especially in Ontario
where "the Manitoba fever" was more common than colds.
For just $10 one was entitled to homestead 160 acres of
prairie, provided certain improvements were made to the
land within a three-year period. Each homesteader also
could apply for a pre-emption on an additional 160 acres.

Excitement mounted with the news that Manitoba soil
would yield hard wheat which ground into magnificent
flour—velvety flour with a springy dough that rose straight

27

Propaganda Promised Instant Prosperity

up, not over the sides of the pan, and came from the oven as the whitest bread housewives had ever seen. Farmers rushed to the Manitoba frontier when it became clear the Canadian Pacific Railway would become a reality. And nobody had time for prophets of doom such as the British paper that turned up its editorial nose and sniffed:

Canada is one of the most over-rated colonies we have and eventually will have to go into liquidation. The C.P.R. (if completed) would run through country frost bound for seven or eight months of the year and end up in a province about as forbidding as any on the face of the earth. The much-touted Manitoba settlement cannot hold out for many years owing to the extreme coldness of the winters. Men and cattle were frozen to death in numbers that would frighten the intended settler if he knew and those not killed outright were often maimed for life by frostbites. In short the Dominion is a fraud and destined to burst up like any other fraud.[23]

Mind you, the ones with the emigration notion knew it wasn't going to be milk and honey—at least not at first. Catching the "Manitoba fever" was one thing; packing up and waving good-bye was another. Oakland pioneers long remembered the experience of striking out thousands of miles for a woolly wilderness.

Until the C.P.R. was completed in 1885, nearly all started from or passed through Ontario by rail, usually switching to American lines at Detroit for the long haul to St. Paul and Winnipeg. An alternate route was by steamer from Sarnia, Ontario, to Duluth. But Uncle Sam seemed determined to keep himself in cigars forever on the profits he made from the traffic to Manitoba, and the Canadian settlers lost money however they chose to travel.

"As a sample of high freight rates, I shall record a hard case which came under my observation", complained a man in Winnipeg:

One evening, when lounging around, I strayed into the Red River Transportation Co.'s office, where

29

sat a widow lady and her boy, a half grown youth. They had lately arrived from Canada. The old lady had been silly enough to pack her furniture and some household goods and ship them here via the Lakes and Duluth. The freight on the same amounted to fifty-one dollars and a half; far more (as she said) than the goods were worth. She offered them the whole stock, but they insisted on cash payment in full, otherwise the goods would be sold and she sued for the balance. She paid them all the money she possessed (twenty-seven dollars) and said she would have to wait for her other sons to come and help her out of her difficulty. And this is an American monopoly, allowed to bring British subjects on British territory. Many persons get so cheated, and consequently disgusted, that they curse the country and go home.[24]

So there wasn't necessarily tartan blood in the veins of the Ontario farmer who stuffed into his settler's carload: six horses, three cows, two pigs, three coops of hens, one dog, three land rollers, one sulky rake, one cutting box, one grain crusher, one fanning mill, two barrels and one box of pork, five hundred feet of lumber, three stone boats, one wagon rack, one pair of bellows, one anvil, one vice, one bag of tools, two complete pumps, three sets of harness, three sets of whiffletrees, one box of oats, ten bags of peas, one bag of sugar, ten boxes of sundries, four trunks, two bags of bedding, six horse blankets, one barrel of water, one gun and an axe![25]

The stock were often the worse for wear, squished into a compartment with everything but the slop pail, and shipped miles away from their quiet stables and routine life. Feed rations were kept to a minimum to leave room for other odds and ends; and the poor beasts wobbled out at the end of the line half-starved if, on the way, a blizzard had plastered the train to a standstill for any length of time. But the animals were not alone in their discomfort. Between Ontario and Winnipeg, in addition to much expense, the settlers had at least three full days of tiring travel.

A number of the early-comers to Oakland lived in longer-established parts of the province before venturing to the municipality, and for some of these the final leg of the journey to Manitoba was by steamer down the Red Lake and Red rivers from the disreputable village of Fisher's Landing, onetime northern terminus of the St. Paul and Pacific Railroad about twelve miles northwest of Crookston, Minnesota. Here is a contemporary description of the place by a Nova Scotian:

> Imagine a couple of clumps of shanties separated by a mud puddle, one clump containing fifteen huts the other about ten. At least two of these huts are designated Hotels, one on each side of the puddle. I succeeded in getting accommodation at the so-called North Western Hotel, a dirty shanty run by a villainous-looking landlord, although he appeared refined compared to the landlord of the Manitoba. Every shanty hereabouts was soon filled with Canadians . . .[26]

The same man was shocked to see business as usual there on the Sabbath:

> Sunday, but who would think it . . . The deck hands are loading the steamboat, navvies [labourers] work all day on the track, one train arrived and another departed as on a week-day rails are being torn up and laid down again. Blacksmiths are at work in their shops, the stores are all open and trade flourishing. Both saloons are in full blast, and I regret to say, some of our Canadians spent most of the day in these dens of iniquity. There is no Sabbath recognized in Fisher's Landing. God's name is only heard in blasphemy, and I find this sink of corruption even more wicked than reported.[27]

Fisher's Landing was no holiday resort. And the voyage of two days and two nights from there north to Winnipeg was no pleasure cruise. The vessels were dirty and crowded; and, since most of the way trees lining the banks obscured a view of the landscape, the scenery was monotonous—in

31

particular the exasperating forty-two-mile stretch (twelve as the crow flies) from Fisher's Landing to the Red River.

"I can scarcely convey to you an idea of the extraordinary manner in which it twists and turns itself about", marvelled the wife of Canadian Governor-General Dufferin in 1877, in a letter she was trying to pen from the upper deck of a steamboat careering along the Red Lake River:

> . . . think of a braiding-pattern, or of a zigzag path up a steep hill; or imagine sailing through hundreds of small ponds all joined together, the second being concealed by the curve of the first, and you may form an idea of it. I can only tell you that we go from one bank to another, crushing and crashing against the trees which grow down to the water-side; the branches sweep over the deck, and leave pieces behind them. I had just written this when I gave a shriek as I saw my ink bottle on the point of being swept overboard by an intrusive tree; and [Lord] Dufferin's [top] hat was knocked off his head by it. The consequence of this curious navigation is that we never really go on for more than three minutes at a time; we run against one bank, our steam is shut off, and in some mysterious manner we swing round till our bow is into the other; then we rebound; and go on a few yards till the sharp curve brings us up against the side. Our stern wheel is very often ashore, and our captain and pilot must require the patience of saints. I told you when the last branch came on board; well, I have been writing as fast as possible since, and now we are ashore on the other side; so you may easily believe that we travel 17 miles for two that we make, and were it not a lovely day, and had we not a delicious air, I don't know how bad our language might not become.[28]

Another ordeal was Canadian customs inspection at the port of West Lynne, a settlement across the river from Emerson, Manitoba. The system of bonding settlers' luggage to their point of destination wasn't in practice then. Instead, the customs officials ordered all baggage spread

32

out on shore. Sometimes, just as a large patch of prairie was littered with boxes, trunks and grips, down would come a shower. This did not worry Her Majesty's loyal inspectors, who poked around in their own sweet time. Passengers who saw antiques and irreplaceable keepsakes ruined "vowed to die in Manitoba rather than return by Red River boat!" [29]

Late in 1878 the St. Paul and Pacific put Fisher's Landing out of the immigrant business by shifting the end of its line to Pembina, Minnesota, making connections there with the C.P.R.'s new branch running north to St. Boniface, Manitoba. But the trip to Manitoba still left much to be desired—especially to women cooped up in dusty colonist cars with flocks of children. One immigrant wrote:

> The insides of the colonist cars were hardly luxurious. In fact sleeping accommodation was downright crude. Two seats of heavy wooden slats face to face provided sleeping room for four adults. Overhead was a solid wooden tray that could be pulled down at night to provide sleeping room for two. The other two slept on the slatted seats. Many an immigrant would later claim that the trade mark of these slats was imprinted on parts of his body. As for undressing, there was neither opportunity nor desire to undress. Everyone slept fully clothed. We had been glibly informed that there was no charge for sleeping room. I began to see some wry humour in this statement. We did, however, appreciate a stove at one end of the car, since it provided means of boiling water for tea . . .[30]

And—no thanks to those "heavy wooden slats"—sections of the track where the old iron horse rushed along furiously, suddenly braked, screeched, lurched, and shuddered forward to repeat the rough performance, were not very kind to homesick stomachs.

From diaries of the time, one can picture the scene as settlers rattled through the lush Niagara Peninsula headed for "The Great Lone Land". Beware of Card Sharks, Beware of Pick Pockets, the placards in the Yankee cars warn . . . Long way from home . . . Too late to turn back . . .

33

FOR the comfort and convenience of settlers going to the CANADIAN NORTH-WE

CANADIAN PACIFIC RAILWAY

PROVIDES A SPECIAL FORM OF PASSENGER EQUIPMENT, KNOWN AS

COLONIST CARS

Which are run through to MANITOBA and BRITISH COLUMBIA on the regular
Train leaving MONTREAL each week day. They are really "SLEEPING CARS," modell
the style of the first-class "PULLMAN," with upper and lower berths, closets, lavatories,
the only difference being that the seats and berths are not upholstered. Occupants may
their own bedding, or can purchase of the Company's Agents at QUEBEC, MONTRI
TORONTO, a mattress, pillow and blanket for $2.50 (10 shillings), which they can retai
end of their journey.

The accompanying cut shows the interior of a Colonist Car, with a portion of the
made up for sleeping purposes.

Holders of COLONIST or SECOND-CLASS TICKETS are allowed FREE USE OF T
CARS FROM THE BEGINNING TO THE END OF THEIR JOURNEY OVER
CANADIAN PACIFIC RAILWAY.

What if we get robbed? . . . . Lads returning to their homesteads after wintering down east standing on the steps of
the car at each station stop belting out: Good-bye, My
Lover; Remember the Red River Valley "and the girl you
left there so true" and the one about the shanty where the
hinges were of leather, the windows not of glass, and the
roof it let the howling blizzard in[31] . . . Cheer up, it will be
all right if we can just get a couple of those wonderful
quarter sections they say give 80, well perhaps 65, bushels
of wheat to the acre . . . that big brick house Jim's planning
come first fine harvest . . . With servants? . . . Maybe,
but good help is so hard to find these days! . . .

The C.P.R. Told It As It Wasn't Necessarily

What are those dark shapes up ahead, Mr. Trainman?
. . . Why them is the chimneys of Chicago, M'am, the
liveliest city in our great Reeepublic, yes surree, just a-
bustlin' like you all wooden believe! . . . sure enough it
was the amazing Chicago with its fine streets and monster
hotels and scores of teams lugging drays to and from the
harbour where tall-masted ships and fleets of steamers
lay packed against the crowded piers . . . [32]

Are we here, ma? Are we here? . . . No, Bert, now
that's a good boy . . . Try to get some sleep . . .

This morning we were rapidly crossing the somewhat wild looking State of Wisconsin . . . Low
bushes, scrub trees scattered over the broken and
barren looking land. Rocks, hills, and gulches are
the principal features to be seen . . . [33]

Aw, ma, ain't we here yet? . . . It's aren't we here
yet, but we aren't, Bert . . . So just sit still . . .

. . . but we are now fast approaching the Mississippi. The city of LaCross which seemed to be all
lumber wharves, is on the bank of this river . . .
At least a dozen steamboats were in sight, all
having two funnels and stern wheel so characteristic of Western navigation. [34]

Here we are, ma! We're here! . . . No, Bert, this is
St. Paul, where we change trains . . . Who's that, ma?
. . . Howdy, M'am! Hi, Junior! . . . Don't mind me
introwdoocing myself, Buncombe MaGab's the name, Minnesota agent You-Name-It-We'll-Promise-It Land, Loan,
and Colonization Company, almost forgot Incorpurrated
and Limutted . . . Bound for Wineepeg, M'am? Thought
so . . . Meeting your good man there? Thought so . . .
No sense to that, Manitoba's no darn good for man nor
beast, pardon the expression, M'am, iceberg in winter,
oven in summer, nothing but sand and flies, no sense,
M'am . . . Now I got just the thing, the best little farm
in North Dukkota, won't breathe a word to anyone else 'til
you get your good man to hustle right down and take a
peek, nothun to lose, fortune to make . . . Stop bothering

36

you, M'am? Hell, M'am, I mean, yes, M'am, but you'll be sorry, M'am, now I'm telling you straight . . .

> Agents offered them the best land in the world, and when, with British stupidity, they shut their ears to all temptations, obstacles were thrown in the way of their going on, and costs and charges multiplied, that the threatened impoverishment [of proceeding to Manitoba] would have become a fact . . . had they not been resolute and trusted to their own resources . . . [Even in Winnipeg] were certain touters and indefatigable sympathizers with American institutions, men who had always calculated that our North-West would drop like a ripe pear into the lap of the Republic, who had been at the bottom of our half-breed insurrection, and who are now bitterly disappointed to see their old dream never likely to become more than a dream.[35]

What's hell, ma? . . . That's where you'll go if you don't keep still . . . But, ma, aren't I going to Manitoba? . . . Bert, did you hear me tell you to keep still? . . . Yes, ma . . .

> As darkness approached we were driving through a thinly settled but finely wooded country, abounding in large lakes and lacrustine rivers.[36]

I'm sick and tired of this, ma . . . Mind your tongue or you'll buck wood all day Saturdays and no going off fishing with your father . . . Pa said in his letter there's not much wood where we're going . . . There'll be wood if I have to make it myself, now that's quite enough, young man . . .

> I was standing on the platform of the hindmost car, and looking off on the real prairie ocean, and mentally comparing the level, green, grassy sea, which extended as far as the eye could reach, unbroken by shanty, tree and hummock, to the salt ocean I had so often crossed; not a living thing was to be seen in any direction. This part of the prairie was low and wet which accounted for there being no settlers . . . After a time we passed a few mud

37

huts and scattered droves of cattle. These huts were generally not over six feet high, mere rough board shanties thatched with a mixture of the long prairie grass and mud. This part of Minnesota looked miserable indeed, a regular wet meadow, the grass did not average more than six inches high, and in some places it was too wet for anything to grow.[37]

Winnipeg! . . . Thank heavens! . . . Bert, Bert, wake up, Bert, that's a good boy . . . And mind now, Bert, tell your father we had a good trip . . .

REFERENCES:

1. Taylor, R. L., 1966, July issue of The Western Producer, p. C3. Saskatoon.
2. Stewart, David, Early Assiniboine Trading Posts of the Souris-mouth Group, 1785-1832, Transactions 5, N.S., The Historical and Scientific Society of Manitoba, Winnipeg, pp. 35-36.
3. Morton, W. L., 1957, Manitoba: A History, p. 25. Toronto.
4. Ibid., p. 27.
5. Ibid., p. 28.
6. Ibid.
   At one time the Mandans may have hauled corn through Oakland en route from their villages in North Dakota to the North West Company post at Pine Creek on the Assiniboine—judging by the following notation on Peter Pond's famous map of 1790: "Upon the branches of the Missury (Missouri) live the Maundiens (Mandans) who bring to our factory on the Assinipoil (Assiniboine) River Indian corn for sale. Our people go to them with loaded horses in twelve days." (Op. cit., Stewart, David, 1930.)
7. Rich, E. E., 1959, History of the Hudson's Bay Company, 1670-1870, p. 301, Vol. II. London.
8. MacEwan, Grant, 1962, Blazing the Old Cattle Trail, p. 8. Saskatoon. Also: Morton, W. L., op. cit., p. 46. Toronto.
9. West, John, 1824, The Substance of a Journal During a Residence at the Red River Colony, British North America, p. 30. London.
10. Ibid., p. 33.
11. Ibid., p. 34.
12. Galbraith, John S., 1957, The Hudson's Bay Company as an Imperial Factor, 1821-1869, p. 12. Toronto.
13. Ibid., p. 311.
14. MacEwan, Grant, 1952, Between the Red and the Rockies, p. 28. Toronto.
15. Galbraith, John S., 1957, The Hudson's Bay Company, p. 311. Toronto.
16. Hind, Henry Y., 1859, Report on the Assiniboine and Saskatchewan Exploring Expedition, p. 42. Toronto.
17. Ibid.

18. Cowie, Isaac, 1913, The Company of Adventurers: A Narrative of Seven Years in the Service of the Hudson's Bay Company During 1867-1874 on the Great Buffalo Plains, p. 170. Toronto.

19. Hind, op. cit., p. 31.

20. McGee, Thomas D., 1937, 1825-D'Arcy McGee-1925, (ed. Hon. Chas. Murphy), p. x. Toronto.

21. Innis, Mary Q., 1935, An Economic History of Canada, p. 218. Toronto.

22. Grant, Rev. George M., 1925, Ocean to Ocean, pp. 103-104. Toronto.

23. Kenton Women's Institute, 1956, Cradle to Combine, p. 3. Kenton, Manitoba.

24. Barnes, H. H., 1879, Journal of a Trip to Manitoba and Back, June and July, 1878, p. 13. Halifax.

25. Brandon Daily Sun, April 16, 1884.

26. Barnes, op. cit., p. 6.

27. Ibid., p. 7.

28. Dufferin, Marchioness of, 1891, My Canadian Journal, 1872-1878, p. 317. London.

29. The Carberry Plains, 1959, p. 5.

30. Shepherd, George, 1965, West of Yesterday, p. 15. Saskatoon.

31. Lowes, Ellen (McFadden), manuscript of her memoirs (1882-1900), pp. 5-6, in Public Archives of Manitoba, Winnipeg.

32. Butler, Col. W. F., 1883, The Great Lone Land, p. 48. London.

33. Barnes, op. cit., p. 4.

34. Ibid.

35. Grant, op. cit., p. 97.

36. Barnes, op. cit., p. 5.

37. Ibid., pp. 5-6.

About Coming West

Do not come west with a family unless you have enough money to make a fair start.

Do not borrow money to come west. The majority of those we have met in their western homes, who have failed, have been those who came on borrowed money, or without enough funds to ensure a send-off.

After reading this article, select such regions as you think you will like best. People generally prefer to keep in the latitude they have lived in.

Come in the spring and get acclimatized.

Bring as little baggage and as few heirlooms as possible. They cost money for freight; and, in addition, are very likely to be an encumbrance in a new home.

If you are able to do so, you had better first come out and explore the country before bringing your family with you.

Do not attempt to explore too much. We have met people beyond the Mississippi River, who had visited nearly all the land grants; and the more they had travelled the more unsettled they were as to where to locate.

Decide upon your climate and locality and then select your land. If you wait too long you are apt to become very much unsettled.

Do not come west not expecting to be homesick for your forests and streams, which present such a contrast to the monotony of endless prairies. It may be very lonely at first, but you will soon plant your own trees, have pleasant surroundings and near neighbours.

Do not come expecting to become rich immediately. Several years of good crops may be required to place you in easy circumstance.

If you are a clerk on small salary in the city and have a few hundred dollars ahead, give up your clerkship and strike western lands. There is no very great experience required in cultivating these prairies.

If you have abundance of money, settle in the lands in the near west. If your funds are comparatively limited, go still farther, where as good lands can be purchased at lower figures.

Brandon Daily Sun
March 23, 1882.

A Fine How~do~you~do!

Had they known that a bag of earth from the valley of the River Jordan was laid in the cornerstone of a Winnipeg building in 1883, the majority of the Oakland settlers might have chuckled. To them Winnipeg was rather a Broken-Promised Land.

Not that they expected the most respectable city in the world. Less than a quarter-century before: "Only in the great houses of St. Andrew's and the prim cottages of Kildonan, around the cathedrals and in the offices of Fort Garry, was it possible to escape the slovenly barbarism of the encamped cart brigade, the drunken revels of the tripmen back from York, the 'tipis' of the visiting Indian encampments, the pungent presence of 'some old smoke-eyed Bungay' wrapped in his blanket and smoking his pipe. The churches, the schools, the society of clergy and Company officers, the considerable resources of the Red River library . . . founded in 1847 . . . the influence of the historian, Alexander Ross, and of the scientist, Donald Gunn, correspondent of the Smithsonian Institution, were strong foundations of civilization. But around them washed the dull waves of an essentially primitive life, an economy founded on the hunt and the trap line, a society based on the union of the nomad and the trader".[1]

Neither would they have been surprised if every second building was a saloon, because in 1876 Winnipeg and Barrie, Ontario, were termed the "two most evil places in Canada", and both were prayed for at the Young Men's Christian Association convention of that year.[2] (Though "if any mortal had good cause to frame an excuse for visiting those dens of iniquity, the stranger in Winnipeg is that mortal. He cannot drink the water of the wells, if he does diarrhoea is the sure consequence, whilst the River water is sickening to his taste. To allay the thirst he strolls into a saloon and calls for a glass of mild ale . . .")[3]

On the other hand, no one denied that Winnipeg's progress was incredible. "All the ladies were well dressed and the dancing as at Ottawa or London", wrote Lady Dufferin in 1877 after attending a ball at Government House. "Six years ago, at a ball here, ladies would have come in moccasins and danced nothing but the Red River Jig . . . the change shows how rapidly the place grows, and how quickly outside ideas make their way in".[4]

By 1879 Winnipeg could boast a university and a historical and scientific society. The steam-powered Winnipeg Free Press had installed a new-fangled contraption called a telephone. And heaven knows what will happen next, people said, when Manitoba prospered in the early 1880's "with a recklessness that only the wildest 'booms' in the States could parallel".[5]

As investors hopped on the bandwagon, "a clatter of hammers and saws, rounds of drinks and rolls of money"[6] whipped the frowsy fur centre into a solid-looking community with many brick buildings three and four storeys high; teams of splendid horses and elegant carriages began replacing rude ox carts on the broad streets; busy river boats churned the muddy Red into a creamy foam; and when land values began to soar in the spring of 1881:

. . . Winnipeg lived in a frenzy of speculation. Lots on Main Street were exchanged for higher prices than those commanded on Michigan Avenue in Chicago. Auctioneers chanted day in, day out, and far into the dusk on every street corner. The advertisements screamed out the fleeting opportunities to invest in the limitless future of the boundless West. All were drawn into the whirl—tradesmen, workmen, lawyers, ministers—buying lots on margin, on options, and on agreements of sale in mushroom subdivisions and bubble town sites. Syndicates, the latest financial device of the day, were formed to provide the easy credit which buoyed up the boom. Canada had never seen anything like it, nor was it ever to see quite such a delirium again.[7]

To quote a gentleman heading to the present Souris, Manitoba, from Millbrook, Ontario, in April of that year:

Winnipeg is a very nice place, and the liveliest town for business I have ever been in. The streets are perfectly dry now and the whole place in the most thriving order . . . I feel quite at home since arriving here. Almost everyone I meet is from Ontario and they all seem so glad to see us. People I have never seen before will say, "Well, well, you're from Ontario, how are all the folks down there?" I do not feel far from home at all, and everyone seems jolly and happy, and so busy. Mr. Benson, a man from Peterboro, who is now doing business here, says that there is more business done here in one week than there is back home in two weeks.[8]

The problem was that, with so much money pouring in, honest dollars tended to be hard to find, and many found Winnipeg little more than a glorified swindle. "I believe there is a great deal of fraud about Winnipeg", revealed an observer in 1879.

Ring speculators seem to have control of the city and even of the Dominion lands. I dare say this last statement may be disputed, but any one who feels

46

inclined to do so should try to go through the mill themselves. Should they undertake this, probably they would see many an immigrant enter the Dominion Lands office, asking for and receiving a list of unoccupied sections, half sections, or quarter sections . . . as the case may be . . . the emigrant takes the list furnished him of unoccupied sections and goes out to examine them. Of course, if any of these consist of swamp or scrub bushes (generally poor land besides being hard to plough) or where water cannot be found, he will pass them by and search until he finds a good high rolling prairie section, where water is to be had. Such a farm he concludes will suit him, then after, perhaps, three or four weeks of the hardest kind of tramping, if fine, under a broiling sun; if it rains, soaked to the skin, he again enters the Land office with his mind fully made up. Seeing the poor fellow is a good judge of land, they question him as to the quality of the soil of the different sections he has visited and afterwards inform him that his particular choice has been taken up during his absence. How is it these speculators never own poor land, and how is it impossible for an emigrant to get a good farm unless he buys of them? My humble opinion is, that whenever a poor emigrant finds a good spot of land and describes it as such at the Land office, he will always find it taken and that by the same parties who question him, having made up their minds to do so while he is talking. Soon after, I doubt not, it will appear in some lawyer's or land agent's office window marked at a price high enough to realize a profit of three or four hundred per cent.[9]

Swindlers weren't only in the Land office; the city was crawling with them. Why, some ventured to say they even controlled the mud on the Winnipeg streets!

In short, Winnipeg posed just another obstacle in the path of the pioneers. After "boomsters" and "gumbo", the prospect of obtaining title to a good parcel of prairie looked increasingly inviting. Or was it all merely a crooked promotion stunt? Hoping against hope that this was not so, they proceeded west on Portage Avenue to conquer the "sea of grass . . . dyked at intervals by the dark lines of trees along the water courses and islanded by the 'îlots de bois', the 'bluffs' of oak and wild plum . . ."[10]

Those who jogged and jolted the 150 miles to Oakland by ox-cart or wagon usually waded through a good deal more mud, however. Hugging the north bank of the Assiniboine to Portage la Prairie, the trail had until recently been part of the Hudson's Bay Company's important route to what is now Edmonton, and was, therefore, deeply rutted in spots from heavy Red River cart traffic. The party of settlers that escaped being mired was extremely fortunate.

Predominantly gentle folk must also have had rather uneasy thoughts, realizing that it would be a long time before the surroundings could be called civilized. True, the shrill cacophony of creaking wheels, which broadcast the approach of gangs of overland freighters, had virtually faded into oblivion; respect for due process of law was being insisted upon by the newly organized North West Mounted Police; and Headingley, Manitoba, already had a pentitentiary. But strong reminders of the era when fur was king could still be seen in southern Manitoba. A case in point was the Hudson's Bay Company store at Portage la Prairie, which still was doing a fair fur trade on the site the explorer La Vérendrye had chosen for the same purpose back before the conquest of New France.

But in other respects Portage lived in the future. Whereas other early Manitoba settlement was along river fronts, owing to concern about water and wood supplies;[11] the later-bonanza farms of Kenneth McKenzie and his son, Adam, near Portage, were beacons of faith in the agricultural possibilities of the open spaces. After the success of the Mennonite colony south and west of Winnipeg in 1875 had broken the spell of apprehension about "bald prairie",[12] Portage businessmen profited from their position on the frontier. Portage la Prairie residents of the day even dreamed of becoming more important than Winnipeggers —especially when they heard the news about the C.P.R.!

The winner of the 1878 federal election in Portage was given strict instructions by his constituents to favour the faction that would guarantee the community a railroad. An alliance with the administration of Sir John A. Macdonald, Canada's first prime minister, served the purpose. And back home, the glad tidings were received deliriously:

> At the foot of Main Street, and in front of the Portage Hotel, was a huge bonfire of boxes, barrels, crates and every conceivable material of this nature, while dancing around it, in joyous glee, catching each other's coattails, pulling off one another's hats, and throwing them in the fire . . . [Then the Hudson's Bay Company storekeeper] sent an omnibus, with an invitation to the revellers to come and sample the cellar, which was at once accepted . . . music and dancing, toasting and singing, followed in quick succession till the dawn of the following a.m.[13]

The way from Winnipeg diverged at Portage. Two branches bent in the general direction of the present Minnedosa, Man. A third guided early landseekers southwest towards the heart of a

> park-like country . . . studded with young oaks; vast expanses beyond, extending on the north to the Riding Mountains, and on the south to the Tortoise (Turtle) Mountain on the boundary (49th parallel); a beautiful country extending hundreds of square miles without a settler, though there is less bad land in the whole of it than there is in the peninsula of Halifax, or within five or ten miles of any of our Eastern cities.[14]

The effect of the picture of opportunity was enhanced as this so-called Yellow Quill Trail neared the mouth of the Souris River.

Since the Oakland pioneers apparently left no detailed descriptions of the experience, their descendants can only suppose how it felt to coax a "prairie schooner" through the sandy hills and stretches of what has become the Carberry district. Meals of fried flour and water had done little to soothe tired muscles—much less to nurture nerves tingling from the coyote cries that had made so alarming the previous night under the stars. Quite conceivably a couple of the white-toothed, lop-eared, large-jointed cowards still pseudo-threatened from a safe, distant slope. Now slinking along in devious "loop-like curves", now feigning a limp, sometimes taking little leaps or standing motionless, these "vagabond outcasts" of the animal world made weird and worrisome escorts.[15]

Insects provided serious harassment; and "smudges had to be lit at night to prevent the cows and oxen from stampeding into the bluffs to brush them off".[16] Indeed, here is an exaggeration with some basis, by an emigrant from the Old Country:

> There is nothing in the least incidental or casual about the [Manitoba mosquito's] method of attack. He alights on your forehead, or neck, or nose —the tenderest and most inviting spot—a thin, leggy, anaemic-looking gnat. He proceeds to unroll his proboscis, like the hose of a water-cart, and makes an incision, swift and deep, like the dentist's preliminaries to extracting a tooth without pain, and equally painful. Withdrawing his needle, wiping it carefully, and putting it away in his instrument case, he then screws the nozzle of his nose into your flesh, and proceeds to pump blood. If suffered to carry out his design to the end, he swells and swells to the utmost limit of the expansion of his skin, and finally withdraws and rolls up his nose and flies off with a wobbly and drunken flight, to sleep off his debauch among his depraved companions.[17]

Also stories were recorded of a cow having been choked to death by a ball of mosquitoes; and of a horse's mane "standing on end with the crowd of flies in the hair, one on top of the other, all struggling for blood".[18]

The queerly contoured, seemingly God-forsaken terrain with stunted firs did not precisely ooze charm either. Yet imagine the same scene bathed in the multicoloured majesty of a Western thunderstorm. Would not even these

50

barren dunes proclaim the compelling grandeur of the "most magnificent bit of virgin soil that remains unsubdued on the face of the earth",[19] if every

form of beauty were combined in the sky . . . to the south it was such blue as Titian loved to paint: blue, that those who have seen only dull English skies say is nowhere to be seen but on canvas or in heaven: and the blue was bordered to the west with vast billowy mountains of the softest, fleeciest white. Next to these, and right ahead of us, and overhead, was a swollen black cloud, along the under surface of which greyer masses were eddying at a terrific rate. Extending from this, and all around the north and east, the expanse was a dun-coloured mass livid with lightning, and there, to the right, and behind us, torrents of rain were pouring, and nearing us every moment. The atmosphere was charged with electricity on both sides; lightning rushed towards the earth in straight and zig zag currents, and the thunder varied from the sharp rattle of musketry to the roar of artillery; still there was no rain and but little wind . . . but there was to be no escape. With the suddenness of a tornado the wind struck us—at first without rain, but so fierce that the horses were forced again and again off the track. And now, with the wind came rain—thick and furious; and then hail—hail mixed with angular lumps of ice from half an inch to an inch across, a blow on the head from one of which was stunning . . . It was a picture for Rosa Bonheur; the storm driving over the vast treeless prairie, and the men and horses yielding to or fighting against it. [But in] half an hour . . . the fury of the storm was past, and in less than an hour the sun burst forth again, scattering the clouds, till not a blot was left in the sky, save fragments of mist to the south and east.[20]

Emerging from the Sand Hills, the Yellow Quill Trail presented a gentler rolling, more characteristically prairie panorama.

51

Here were scattered clumps of scrub oak and quivering white poplar (the hard, ashless aspen that Plains Indians called "women's tongues", the leaves being never still); possibly a few black poplar, too, the gilead used for balm, or plumes of cotton grass guarding yellow star grass and sedges in the marshy hollows.

There thickets of wild plum, cherry, high bush cranberry, gooseberry, service berry and white thorn bushes tended to tangle with raspberry rakes, vetches, horse-tails, hedge bind weed, wild balsam, apples, grapes, and virginia creepers.

And most everywhere meadows "smooth as a gentleman's lawn" caught the eye—truly a hymn to spring when "thousands of beautiful crocuses showed their purple flowers in every direction". In the drying winds of early summer the meadows loomed broad and billowing, and flecked with flowering yellows, purply blues, whites, and pinks—an unforgettable weave of pasture greens, sunshine daisies, twilight mauve members of the pea family, snowy-petalled patches of wild strawberries, and the auroral freshness of rambling roses.

The puzzle of where to settle continued until the welcome hues of the Brandon Hills appeared on the skyline —a "dark blue shoulder" that rose from the plains, pledging water, wood, and shelter from the stormy blasts for years to come.

REFERENCES:
1. Morton, W. L., 1957, Manitoba: A History, p. 90. Toronto.
2. Ibid., p. 171.
3. Barnes, H. H., 1879, Journal of a Trip to Manitoba and Back, p. 16. Halifax.
4. Marchioness of Dufferin and Ava, 1891, My Canadian Journal, pp. 322-333. London.
5. Hansen, M. L. and J. B. Brebner, 1960, The Mingling of the Canadian and American Peoples, Vol. 1, p. 16. Toronto.
6. Leacock, S. B., 1942, My Remarkable Uncle and Other Sketches, p. 5. New York.
7. Morton, W. L., op. cit., p. 200.
8. McMorran, G. A., 1956, The Souris Plains, p. 22. Souris, Manitoba.

9. Barnes, H. H., op. cit., p. 13.
10. Morton, W. L., op. cit., p. 31.
11. Ibid., p. 158.
12. MacKintosh, W. A., 1934, Prairie Settlement, The Geographical Setting, Vol. 1, The Canadian Frontiers of Settlement, pp. 58-59. Toronto.
13. Hill, R. B., 1890, Manitoba: History of Its Early Settlement, Development and Resources, pp. 398-399. Toronto.
14. Grant, Rev. George M., 1925, Ocean to Ocean, p. 8. Toronto.
15. Ferguson, E., 1910, Janey Canuck in the West, p. 37. London.
16. Swainson, J. L., n.d., Our Ancestors Arrive in Manitoba, Winnipeg.
17. Gill, F. A. W., 1912, A Manitoba Chore Boy, p. 86. London.
18. Marchioness of Dufferin and Ava, op. cit., pp. 338-339.
19. Sutherland, A., 1881, A Summer in Prairie-Land. Toronto.
20. Grant, op. cit., pp. 92-93.

Glorious Manitoba

This little spot so fresh and fair,
Where softly blows the balmy air,
No country can with it compare,
      Glorious Manitoba.

On fairer fields the sun ne'er shone;
On better land wheat ne'er was grown;
None but a selfish man would own
      He hated Manitoba.

Our winters are so soft and mild,
They scarce would freeze a little child;
And yet they say we're surely wild
      To live in Manitoba.

Here no howling blizzard blows,
Surely they who live here knows;
Besides it hardly ever blows
          In glorious Manitoba.

The crops are always put in soon,
And quickly they come through the loom;
It never rains except in June,
          In glorious Manitoba.

The sun shines down with steady beam
Upon a fair and pleasant scene,
While storms are few and far between
          In glorious Manitoba.

Our gardens they are trim and neat,
And grow us all we want to eat;
We strangers are to frozen wheat
          In glorious Manitoba.

Now, All ye who toil and slave
Don't believe what people rave;
My advice is—Cross the wave
And come to Manitoba.

                    Adam Christie
                    aged 14 or 15
          Carrolton, Man. 1884.

Bald Prairie Gets a Trim

The years 1875 to 1882 in Manitoba were marked by excessive rainfall that water-logged low lying areas. Combined with a "land lock" created by the fact that rather extensive tracts of the "Postage Stamp" province were either reserved for group settlement or in the hands of speculators, the exceptionally high precipitation encouraged prospective settlers to "push up into the highland beyond".

Population spread to the Big (Carberry) Plain in 1877, and about the same time a colony to be christened Rapid City was planted in a picturesque valley of the Rapid (Minnedosa) River. Among the pioneer settlers of the Brandon area were three farmers named Lambert, who are said to have travelled by ox-cart in 1877 from Winnipeg to near where the Minnedosa River empties into the Assiniboine. The McVicar and Mair families closer to the Souris River mouth also were early-comers, as were members of the Rev. George Roddick party from Pictou County, Nova

Scotia. The Roddick party had been bound for the Presbyterian mission at Prince Albert, Saskatchewan, before settling north of the eastern end of the Brandon Hills in 1879. The following year, Colonel R. Z. Rogers of Cobourg, Ontario, began to develop Millford, a townsite just east of Oakland at the junction of Oak Creek and the Souris River.

The series of wet seasons facilitated the use of steamboats on the meandering Assiniboine. At first Rapid City had been supplied by Red River cart from Portage. But, in 1878, goods were successfully shipped to the rapids not far downstream from the present Brandon (briefly Rapid City Landing, later Currie's Landing) and from there transferred overland to Rapid City. Subsequently this service was extended to Fort Ellice (occasionally even to Fort Pelly)—the water table being so high some springs that, had the river been "less crooked, and its water not thus backed up, no boat could ascend the stream".[1] As early as 1880, a small fleet of these awkward vessels were carrying "hundreds of tons of freight";[2] and this, in turn, speeded up the influx of immigrants.

It appears impossible to know definitely who had the distinction of being Oakland's first settler. The year was almost certainly 1879, however, and one of the originals was young Augustus (Gus) Cory, the sixteen-year-old son of Richard (Dicky) Cory, an ex-Devonshire policeman who had crossed the Atlantic to Port Hope, Ontario, in 1870. A memoir Gus wrote about forty years later, after retiring from a railroad career, relates how he happened to face famine in the "old link pin and hand brake days".[3]

Scouting for land on behalf of friends in the Port Hope area, Gus and his father reached St. Boniface by train in April, 1879. They stayed at the Windsor House a couple of weeks and then took the Winnipeg and Western Transport Company steamboat "Alpha" to Portage. A fortnight later they travelled with a yoke of oxen, two Red River carts and a plow to High Bluff, where they sowed a crop of oats. In June, Thomas Elliott, one of four brothers who figured prominently in the laying of Oakland's foundations, and Orlin S. Elliott (reputedly no relation), arrived at High Bluff, as well as Francis (Frank) and Richard (Dick) Kinley, two sons of a Manchester weaver who became a school teacher at West Cape, Prince Edward Island. Together these six men started west "to get land for others".[4]

The party was obliged to mark time at Rat Creek for nearly a week, rain having quagmired the trail. At Mc-Vicar's' Landing, near the present site of Brandon, there was a delay for the construction of a makeshift ferry in the manner of the day (a wagon box caulked with rags and soap, pulled across the river by means of a rope that Gus had swum over to fasten on the opposite bank).

Their route then angled to the Brandon Hills where they apparently camped beside the Little Souris River in the neighborhood of the Roddick settlement. They worked for the Roddicks until they found promising land for themselves about eight miles south and a little east alongside the stream which Dicky Cory named Black Creek.[5] The story is told that when they came upon the stream late one evening, it looked inky and foreboding. "Hustle and we'll call it Hink River!" exclaimed Dicky, pronouncing an "H" before the "I" as many Englishmen do to this day. But the waters looked shallower and more pleasant in the morning, so he changed his mind: "Hustle and we'll call it Black Creek."[6]

At the Little Souris River, Gus, being the youngest, had done the cooking in a "mud oven" and was, therefore, a "good cook" by the time the group moved to Black Creek. Once when he was alone in camp "500 Indians" paid him a surprise visit, and "how they laughed" as he felt for an old revolver which was stuck in his pocket. The Indians "bought him out" of "sough belly (dough)".[7]

That fall, after staking out homesteads and pre-emptions, and cutting a winter's supply of hay, the group returned to High Bluff to harvest the oats, which yielded 95 bushels to the acre.

The Corys, Dicky, Gus and Gus's older brother Richard (Dick), plus Orlin Elliott, then returned to Black Creek only to find the country blackened by prairie fires; "our hay, good clothes, machinery and tools all gone despite the fire guard they had ploughed". This blow taken in stride, the four set to work building a temporary log and

60

sod shanty farther south on the lightly wooded bank of the Souris. Gus did the hauling, the others felled and hewed logs, and they were careful not to stay out after dark on account of packs of "hungry timber wolves".

On March 1, 1880, Richard Cory, Sr., and Orlin Elliott —leaving the lads on their own—travelled to Portage to purchase more provisions because "the cupboard was bare", with the exception of flour and tea. For young Dick and Gus, left in the lonely shelter, the end of their first long Prairie winter became a nightmare. They played checkers day and night until the game lost its savour, "then we played some more". Bannock and tea also became tasteless; throughout the ordeal they were able to vary the diet only with one snared rabbit. Once Gus chased a deer with an axe. His chances seemed good, because the surface of the snow could hold a man but not a deer. Alas, as he was manoeuvring to club the fresh meat, Gus, too, broke through the crust, losing the prey. He wept.

". . . days and weeks lengthened into months." The oxen died of starvation and doubtless the human pair pondered a similar fate as they scanned the acres of snow hoping for the speck on the horizon that would mean help was on its way.

Gus Cory's account states that it was not until one dawn in May, 1880, that they were awakened to the singing and shouting of Thomas Elliott's three brothers, James, Rev. Joshua and Jabez; Sam Powers and his sons, George and Lafontaine; the brothers Thomas and Amos Smith; the step-brothers William Noble and Ingram Robinson; John Barkwell and William Payne—all from the vicinity of Port Hope. Also there was Uncle Thomas and Aunt Lucy Cory with their children, from the Seaforth, Ontario, district; Albert E. Rome from Clinton, Ontario; John and Neil M. Gray, and one Andrew Edsoll, a bank clerk said to have been toting a suitcase full of brandy. Edsoll had been sent to the great Northwest by his mother to mend his dissipated ways, and was probably one of the earliest remittance-men.

In a later memoir of R. (Fred) Cory,[8] the eldest son of Thomas Cory, the story is somewhat different as to the sequence of arrivals and the people involved. Fred Cory,

Souris River, 1880's

A high plateau
  And down below;
The Souris River passes near
  Old Gregory Mill, the pioneer
Of flour from yon "golden fields"
  Rich prairie lands for future yields.
Impressive spot, where passer by,
  Would pause while beauty fills the eye;
As if Dame Nature in retreat,
  Threw space and beauty at his feet.
Far to the east the waters gleam—
  The Souris and her silver stream.
To right, the high-capped Tiger Hills,
  Where morning sun her glory spills.
On left, a sheltered cabin spot,
  The Cory habitation lot—

When Gus and Dick, that winter through
    Hunger and chill, in Manitoba knew.
The Souris now in lower bed,
    Curves with the deeper bank ahead,
Circling wide Twin Dales of Oak,
    It follows close the sculptor's stroke;
The deep carved bank, the artistry
    Of Berg and Rock, on Agassiz.
Canadians we, with beauty strewn;
    In our by-ways, Historic Ruin;
Would do so well to give attention
    To Treasure spots, we scarcely mention.

James J. Brander
Nesbitt, Man.

who was 14 years old in 1880, makes no reference in his detailed account to the rescue of his starving cousins. He also makes no mention of the Smiths, the Grays, Barkwell, Payne, Robinson, Noble, the Powers or Edsoll. Those he does mention are Frank and Dick Kinley and their families, Joseph and Samuel Townsend, Orlin S. Elliott, James Brander and son John, and W. S. Henderson and his sons Nelson and John—all of whom, like himself, travelled by land.

Fred's memoir says he drove the family goods overland, while his parents, his brothers William and Milton, his sister Selina and Mr. and Mrs. Jabez Elliott made the journey by boat.

The sequence of events related by Fred Cory indicates his family and the total party of twenty-two persons arrived at what became known as the Elliott Settlement in late May, 1880. This party was led by Rev. Joshua Elliott who met the group in Winnipeg while purchasing supplies for a return to the settlement. Was it he who rescued the starving Cory boys some time earlier in the spring?

Two of Dick Kinley's grandchildren, C. R. McFadden and his sister, Mrs. Jemima Webster—both of Winnipeg—recall a somewhat different version of the events which led to the founding of the settlement at Black Creek. Their verbal account to the author confirms the major events in the Gus Cory memoir as far as March, 1880, when Richard Cory Sr. and Orlin S. Elliott headed back to Portage for supplies, leaving the two Cory lads behind in the shanty. Mr. McFadden and Mrs. Webster believe that their grandfather, on his way to Black Creek with a sleigh-load of supplies, met Cory and Elliott in the vicinity of present-day Carberry. Kinley proceeded to the shanty, where he found the Cory lads "like two starved Indians". Presumably Kinley gave them supplies before returning to Portage.

Bearing the above three accounts in mind, it seems plausible that the Cory lads underwent more than one period of starvation. One relief by Kinley in March may have been followed by another in early May.

On the arrival of the large Elliott-led party in May, 1880, Gus Cory recalled that he cooked breakfast, Rev.

64

Richard Cory, Sr.

R. (Fred) Cory

John Smith and Children

Mr. and Mrs. Richard Kinley

William Fleming

William Bertram

Joshua Elliott offered up thanksgiving and read from the divine scriptures, and the Smith brothers fell asleep on their knees, having stood sentinal all night against wolves.[9]

The Elliott settlement flourished so that two and a quarter years later a special correspondent of the Manitoba Daily Free Press, who was completing a tour of southwestern Manitoba, was inspired to write:

> The Elliott family, who are the pioneers of this, the best stretch of land we had yet seen, deserve the greatest confidence and regard of the settlement they have worked so hard to establish. When we drove past their splendid fields of grain, and past their comfortable farm homes, and saw what improvements had been made . . . we could only compare them to the happy Acadians so graphically described by Longfellow in Evangeline.[10]

Elsewhere in Oakland, other settlers survived the "terrible" winter of 1879-80, in which "frost cracked trees so they split like a pistol shot and the northern lights pink and gold, and green waved and fluttered in the sky like curtains hanging on a clothesline on a windy day".[11]

William Bertram—an Edinburgh bank clerk advised to emigrate for reasons of health—and his cousin John Mitchell arrived in the municipality in November, 1879. They survived the winter in a shack in a hollow at the eastern end of the Brandon Hills on property that Bertram later homesteaded and called How Park after his parents' farm overseas.[12]

Two others who may have settled in Oakland that winter were John McKenzie and Hugh Rutledge, both from Strathroy, Ontario. They set up adjoining homesteads on Section 14, Township 7, Range 17 (14.7.17) in what was then the Millford district. (The land survey system of southern Manitoba is outlined in the first item of the appendix.)

One of the first people to sink roots in what became the Carrolton, (later Carroll) district, William Fleming, came to the prairies in 1879. Although he did not settle there until 1881, his land-prospecting trip from the Red River

Valley to the Souris River west of the Turtle Mountains in November, 1880, shows how relatively uninhabited southwestern Manitoba was then, and gives further insight into the stamina of those who often risked life and limb making its acquaintance.

On the first leg of his trip, Fleming journeyed with a family who had chosen to homestead near where Boissevain, Manitoba, is now. There was "little or no snow", but the many creeks and rivers that had to be crossed from Winnipeg to Nelsonville (close to today's Morden, Manitoba), Calf Mountain (in the present district of Manitou, Manitoba), Badger Creek (Crystal City, Manitoba), and so on, were coated with a sheet of ice that would not hold the oxen, and played havoc with their legs when they broke through. On one occasion, Fleming took off his boots and socks and broke the ice for the oxen, their legs being so sore that he could not bear to see them suffer more cuts.[13]

Using the Boissevain homestead as a base, he made an extensive exploration of the surrounding countryside on foot. One such hike was to the future site of Melita, Manitoba, at least forty miles away, and in the whole distance "only two evidences of civilization were seen. One a settler's tent in a ravine near where Deloraine is now and the other was a haystack near the (Souris) river to the west. Into the haystack he crept to spend the cold November night".

Towards the end of November, he decided to walk to Winnipeg, and was relieved to reach a dwelling in Lang's Valley (Langvale) before the first nightfall. In all his ramblings on the prairie, Fleming later said, he was "never so glad to strike a settler" as he had dreaded "spending the night on the prairie without shelter". The fear was not unfounded—a raging blizzard forced him to stop over a second night.

When the storm was over he crossed east of Lang's Valley into a section of the Tiger Hills. This walk he described as "a long, lonesome trip" before taking the Millford ferry and continuing to the mouth of the Souris, where he spent the night at the ferryman's home. The next morn-

ing they tried to cross the Assiniboine but the ferry got caught in the ice floes and the cable was in danger of breaking. After a couple of hours they had to return to the south bank. Another attempt was made late in the afternoon, when two men appeared from the Elliott settlement en route to Portage with a team and wagon. This time they succeeded in crossing to the north bank, and Fleming accompanied them the same evening to a stopping house about twenty miles away.

William Fleming made another expedition in 1881— this time accompanied by his younger brother, Robert J. Fleming, and their cousin, James H. Fleming, who the same year commenced farming along the western boundary of Oakland (24.7.20 and W 30.7.19). James Wiggins, who in 1879 erected the first shack and turned the first furrows in the Plum Creek (Souris, Manitoba) district, and his two cousins surnamed Irwin also were members of the six-man party. (One cousin, George Irwin, subsequently settled in Oakland, and official land records date his entry for NE 32.8.19 as January, 1882.)

As did most early settlers, the members of this 1881 expedition to western Oakland suffered hardships. Sleeping in a tent with deep snow surrounding them was common, but the lack of established trails in this area made the going particularly tough. Snow blindness struck the party. Even the oxen laboured along with their eyes shut completely. Two or three yards of green gauze purchased by William Fleming in Portage served as eye coverings for the animals. Thereafter, it was common to hear people met along the way exclaim "look at the veils of the oxen".[14]

Other parties were surveying Oakland more technically in 1879 and 1880—Ministry of the Interior employees, equipped with crews of Gunter's chain men, picket men, mound men, axe men, cooks, and teamsters to handle horses and carts. The road allowances on the eastern and most of the northern boundaries of the municipality had been established by the end of October, 1879, so the earliest settlers (some of whom had surveying experience) were able to figure out fairly well where the section lines would eventually be located. Because it was impossible to buy or otherwise take up land until its measurements had been registered in Ottawa, the "squatters" anxiously awaited the section surveyors who arrived September, 1880, and completed their field work in October of that year. It was several months, however, before this section survey was registered.

The first homesteads entered for in Oakland were those of William Bertram, Alfred Birch, Christopher Cook, Robert Dobson, George Findlater, Levi Fisher, James Flannery, George G. Harley, William Hill, John Leslie, Lindsay Marmont, James McKay, Abel Miller, Samuel Rounthwaite, Jacob Sherk, David W. Shields, Charles Stewart and William Taylor—all in Township 8.18 in May, 1881. These homesteaders formed the basis of what became the Rounthwaite community.

But settlement of Oakland did not proceed as fast as the sinking of a network of Roman-numeralled survey posts largely owing to the incompletion of the main line of the Canadian Pacific Railway to the Brandon area. For instance virtually no sod was broken in townships 7.19 and 8.19 until the tracks reached Brandon late in 1881. It appears that only a few settlers besides those connected with the Elliott settlement and the Rounthwaite community wished to gamble on making a fresh start in Oakland before this date.

But what was Brandon? In May, 1881, it was not much more than a "paper townsite". Four months later it boasted a railway depot, a riverboat landing, a post office, an express office, a lawyer's office, an engineer's office, a planing mill, a saw mill, two hardware stores, three temporary churches, about two dozen general stores, about twenty real estate offices—as well as makeshift hotels, boarding houses, and livery and feed stables, and a regular flap of tents. Truly, it had become a "Wonder City" at the end of the steel railroad. The first train entered Brandon that October.

The first edition of The Brandon Sun, January 19, 1882, listed the building count at 200 worth $200,000, and estimated the population at 800 to 5,000 persons including transients. On a single day, one grocer's assistant sold twenty wedge tents at $18 apiece,[15] and a hardware store sold 750 cook stoves at $40 each in this 1882 season.

Boomsters and land speculators wasted no time in moving in for financial kills. According to "Truth", writing in the Manitoba Daily Free Press of April 22, 1881:

> A host of surveyors are searching for a suitable crossing place [of the Assiniboine for the railroad] in the neighbourhood of Grand Valley [forerunner of Brandon] and Brandon Hills. There are plenty of land grabbers and speculators.

A Church of England missionary posted there in January, 1882, recalled that "nothing but lots" was "thought of or talked about day in and day out. I was perhaps an almost solitary exception, not because I was a parson, but because my pocket was empty".[16] And the pastoral address of the Manitoba and North West Conference of the Canadian Methodist Church of that year proclaimed:

> The spirit of reckless speculation has kindled the fires of an unrestrained avarice, which devours and destroys the spirit of simple piety and ushers in utter shipwreck of faith and good conscience.[17]

This lottery spirit was infectious. The Brandon area buzzed with once-in-a-lifetime opportunities.

One of many such abortive schemes that might have affected Oakland had it materialized was the attempt of Colonel Rogers, the founder of Millford, Manitoba, "and others", to procure a provincial charter to build and operate a railroad from "some point" near Rapid City to "some point" near the present Roblin, Manitoba—"other branches running therefrom in any direction in the province or to connect with the States", and specifically a branch line southeast to the Millford district (as announced in the Manitoba Gazette of November 19, 1881). Another was the proposed incorporation of "The Assiniboine and Pembina River Railway Company" having power to grade a line from Brandon "through Souris Mouth and Millrace City to Pembina River Crossing of the South Western Railway".[18]

Oakland pioneer Charles Stewart's plans to develop a townsite on the west side of the ravine on his homestead (NW 36.8.18) in what became the East Brandon school district also fizzled. "We here were surprised by the glowing description of the town East Brandon over the signature of Sigma in the last issue", a letter signed "Brandon Hills" complained to The Brandon Sun of March 2, 1882:

A town is quite as likely to spring up on the highest peak of the Brandon Hills as the site specified and hopefully the public won't be deceived by any such bogus affairs—investors may become disgusted with 'paper towns' and look upon our great country as a gigantic fraud and invest their money elsewhere.

Sigma's (Stewart's) reply registered his "considerable pain and surprise" at the verbal attack. The townsite being considered was not a "bogus affair" and he and his neighbours had "long been of the opinion that a town was much needed in this locality which is situate on the main road between Brandon and Millford"—fifteen miles equidistant from each place. The Millford-Brandon branch line would pass in the vicinity of his land. "No more convenient spot could be found for a railway station," Stewart added. Whereupon "Veritas'" from Brandon Hills scornfully retorted:

The prospect of a Birmingham or Manchester rising on every man's quarter-section appears to me remote. But does not Stewart inform us that East Brandon lies midway between Brandon and Millford, and that a town is needed there? There now, is not that a sufficient reason that East Brandon is to be the 'Queen City' of the West?[19]

Other implied references to the proposal are a remark in the March 19 Brandon Sun to the effect that a party wished to buy part of NE 36.8.18 and to commence brickmaking as soon as the snow was off the ground; and the fact that the initial East Brandon school board both adopted the name of the intended town and accepted trustee Stewart's offer of a free half-acre on the site under discussion.

Some eight years later, the village of Rounthwaite grew up about a railway station less than three miles south of Stewart's futile dream property.

A contemporary investment that came relatively close to maturing, on the other hand, was the Toronto, Manitoba and North West Land Co.'s townsite on W 16.7.17 and E 17.7.17—better known as "Old" Souris City. Unfortunately the circumstances which led a group of Toronto businessmen to begin developing this square mile of Souris River flats about three miles west of modern Wawanesa are almost a complete mystery; and to date a search for the operating records of "The Toronto Company" has been to no avail.

About all that remains of Souris City are a few nearly filled-in cellars and the odd ink pot on a grain field belonging to former Oakland councillor, Noel J. Fisher, somé signs of old trails used more than eighty years ago, and the remains of bridge abutments. Nevertheless, sufficient information has been gathered to catch at least a glimpse of the first village in Oakland municipality's all-but-forgotten past.

An early resident of the eastern part of the Elliott settlement was one William Scott, a Toronto contractor who arrived there sometime after October, 1880. (This may have been the same William Scott who unsuccessfully opposed J. W. Sifton in the Brandon area's first provincial election in November, 1881.) By the fall of 1881, Scott owned W 16.7.17 and had agreed to buy 9.7.17 and E 17.7.17 from the C.P.R. His son, William J. Scott, also a contractor, owned E 16.7.17 and had made arrangements with the C.P.R. for E 15.7.17 and SE 21.7.17.

A surveyed townsite plan of the proposed Souris City (W 16.7.17 and E 17.7.17) subsequently was prepared by J. W. Vaughan of the Winnipeg firm of Vaughan and Dennis.[20] The plan was registered November 14, 1881.

About three weeks later, the Scotts sold all their land, including the townsite, to a company called the Manitoba and Nor'West Land Co. Ltd., of which William Scott was himself one of the promoters. This company became the

Toronto, Manitoba and North West Land (joint stock) Co. Ltd. in March, 1882. The townsite was abandoned in the late 1880's when an anticipated railroad line did not cross the Souris at that point.

There is no doubt that the promoters of Souris City hoped to make it a roaring success. The Sun reported on March 16, 1882, that one day that week seventeen teams had been in Brandon loading building materials for the townsite. These must have been put to use quickly, because by the summer the village consisted of a gristmill and a twenty horse power sawmill (both from London, Ontario), two stores, a hotel, five private houses, a blacksmith shop, and several tents, and a school house and a Methodist parsonage were in the course of erection.[21]

To have made such progress there could not have been very many days like that near the end of February when the "Souris City boom was totally eclipsed . . . by the marriage of Orlin S. Elliott, the pioneer settler of the Souris Valley, to Miss L. J. Henderson, only daughter of Wm. L. Henderson, Esq. . . ."[22]

The Manitoba Daily Free Press correspondent whose glowing August, 1882, description of the Elliott settlement appears earlier in the chapter was also much impressed by Souris City's "considerable start towards a metropolis":

> From Langvale the trail runs over the Tiger Hills to the crossing of the Souris at Souris City, which we found to have made a considerable start towards a metropolis. Mr. Scott, the energetic founder of the town, is one of the solid men of this section of the country and his liberal policy of granting free sites to all who wish to build in Souris City is sure to bring a good class of settler to this already rich and well settled district.[23]

Commenting on the shipment of the two mills to Souris City in 1882, the London (Ontario) Advertiser said that the Toronto, Manitoba and North West Land Company was "composed entirely of Toronto capitalists, and from the energetic way in which they are pushing matters, bids fair to become an important factor in the settlement of the great Northwest".[24]

Quite apart from any power or glory that William Scott and "The Toronto Company" may have gained by the establishment of Souris City, it was naturally of great benefit to the settlers in the surrounding countryside. No longer, for instance, was it necessary for settlers in the southeast part of Oakland to travel the see-saw, switchback trail to Millford for "a grist" because the service could be obtained at Souris City. The grist mill was located down on the bank beside the river on the east side of the flats, and was said to have been steam-powered.

Another stand-by was the smithy. Before Souris City was founded, Dick Kinley apparently did the blacksmithing for the Elliott settlement on his farm, using a small outfit which Thomas Elliott had brought from Ontario on his second trip west in 1880. Afterwards Kinley set up shop in Souris City "until he was able to sell to a new arrival, Harry Goodman. He in turn sold out to a young man named Haighs who continued the shop until the village commenced to disintegrate".[26]

There were general stores, too. Jabez Elliott, who had previously operated a small store on his homestead (in a tent, until his first home was built), later opened a similar business at Souris City. There was also the "Elworthy store", clerked for some time by certain Messrs. Ballantyne and McTaggart, and the "Red Front store" owned by Thomas Harrison.[27] By June, 1884, Souris City was down to one store, according to this advertisement:

> The subscriber offers for sale or exchange for farm property a well-founded store, one and a half storeys high, with cellar in Souris City; excellent opportunity as no store in place at present. Apply Jabez Elliott.[28]

It seems that Elliott managed to rent or sell the store to David Ricker, who was afterwards a pioneer merchant in Wawanesa.

Another entrepreneur was Ontario farmer John Harris, who lived at Souris City for a time before moving to land

M _King_

Bot. of **Thos. Harrison**

GENERAL DEALER IN

DRY-GOODS, GROCERIES, PROVISIONS

BOOTS & SHOES, HARDWARE, STOVES, TINWARE,

Agricultural IMPLEMENTS, LUMBER, Lath, Shingles

AND EVERYTHING A SETTLER REQUIRES.

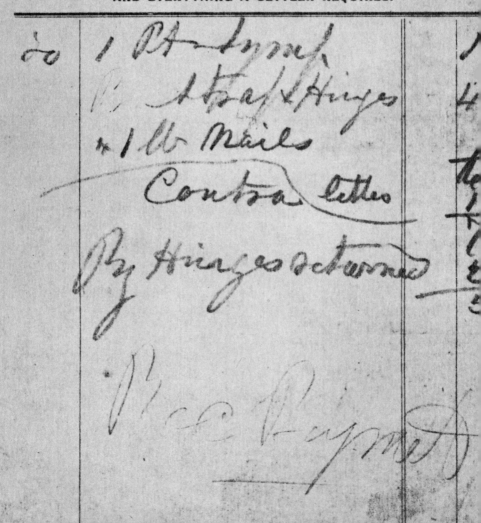

south of Oakland in Riverside municipality. To help support his large family, Harris fashioned axe and hammer handles. One of the places he travelled to peddle his wares was Millford.[29]

Mail service also drew settlers to Souris City—though there must have been confusion over the address. Whereas the village in Oakland was always called Souris City, the first post office opened there was officially "Sourisbourg". (This was possibly to distinguish it from a townsite of the same name on the Souris River south of present-day Melita, which was abandoned the year "The Toronto Company" began operations.) On October 1, 1883, the postal address was changed to "Wawonaissa"—meaning whippoorwill— a name probably taken from Longfellow's "Hiawatha", since whippoorwills were commonly heard in the district in those days. On May 1, 1884, letters to Souris City were once more to be directed to "Sourisbourg"; and not until September, 1884, was the address finally Souris City post office —a name retained until it was closed in 1890.[30]

As far as mail delivery was concerned, by 1883 Souris City was on a semi-weekly "stage" route from Brandon to Rounthwaite, Wawonaissa, Millford, Two Rivers and Brandon. There was, in turn, service twice a week from Souris City to such points as Langvale, Alcester, Rayfield, Fairburn, Ninga, Killarney and Rowland—then making a rough figure-eight back to Souris City through Alcester and Langvale.[31]

Bricks were available at Souris City. The brick yard was situated high on the hill past the northern surveyed limit of the village, and was either managed by or the property of "Messrs. Freek and Coupland".[32] The bricks were used for wells in the neighbourhood, it is recalled, but apparently not for buildings.

A fatal accident was associated with the brick yard. One Sunday morning a young Englishman named Aborn, who was employed there, drowned while bathing in the river. Funeral arrangements were made by his younger brother and a few of the leading men in the village, including Dick Kinley, a skilled carpenter, who made and

81

trimmed a coffin. "The whole village turned out for the funeral".[33]

This was the first recorded death at Souris City.[34] Were Aborn's final resting place known, light might be shed on the current debate as to whether or not a public burial ground was located at the southwest corner of SE 17.7.17, where the grave of Souris City district pioneer Stewart Robertson is marked by a tombstone. Rumours of several rough boxes having been exposed by the erosion of an embankment near this spot—suggesting that a number of bodies are or were once placed there—cannot be substantiated. In any case, it seems that only settlers south of the river buried their dead there. James Henderson, head of the "Scotch Henderson" family from the Aberdeen area in Scotland, who died soon after emigrating in 1887, was laid to rest north of the river in the Amos Smith private burial ground.

Among other known deaths at Souris City were those of Dick Kinley's aged mother and the respected Methodist minister Rev. Isaac Newton Robinson—both in the typhoid epidemic of 1887—and Mr. and Mrs. Jabez Elliott's four-year-old son the following year, also of typhoid.[35]

Another tragedy was the death of the village's second school teacher, an Englishman named Edmund Batty. Batty drove out into the country on October 10, 1884, to help another man fire-guard a stack of hay. Hoping to bag a plump prairie chicken, he had taken along a gun. He was lifting the gun over the wagon seat when the cocked trigger accidentally caught, firing a "terrible wound" into his upper left arm. Batty's companion did what he could to bind the wound and, after catching the horses which had bolted at the noise of the shot and the injured man's screams, conveyed the victim to Souris City as quickly as possible. Dr. McDairmid was summoned from Brandon, but arrived too late to save the patient who had lost a great deal of blood. He died the next day, leaving to mourn a wife and five youngsters, the eldest only eight. It is understood the community raised a subscription to assist Batty's widow, who returned to the Old Country shortly thereafter.[36]

The teacher's misfortune did not long interrupt the

course of formal education at Souris City. The schooling, which had begun in the summer of 1882 with David H. Lent wielding the rod, was continued under the tutelage of Misses Jenny and Mary Nichol, and a Miss McKay.[37]

It should be noted that the Misses Nichol were daughters of the "lively and energetic" Thomas Nichol, who replaced William Scott as resident overseer of the townsite in 1884. The Nichols, with their brood of attractive girls, became a popular "institution" in Souris City. Hence, "Civatas" reported from Souris City on January 2, 1886, that "nothing unusual happened" New Year's' evening when forty of the "youth and beauty of the neighbourhood" gathered at the Nichols'; satisfied the inner man at midnight, and tripped the light fantastic until the wee sma' hours.

The school doubled as a place of worship—a common practice in the pioneer days. "We would take the wagon Sunday morning, gather up the neighbours and drive to church. Oh! We used to have such a good time, all together", Mrs. Thomas Banting (later of the Methven district) recalled in her eighty-eighth year. Although both Presbyterians and Methodists regularly converted the classroom to a "house of many mansions", it appears that the Methodists in the village were organized earlier—the pioneer being Rev. Thomas Wellington Hall, who, it is recorded, presided at the inaugural meeting of the "Quarterly Board of Grand Valley Mission" in the Souris City residence of Thomas Harrison on May 9, 1881.[38]

Rev. Hall was then living at Millford, and it was he who nursed the eldest Mooney girl of that district through a serious illness in March, 1881. The nearest doctor was eighty miles away at Portage and, when Lizzie had an illness that could not be cured with "turpentine and goose oil and mustard footbaths", Mrs. Mooney is said to have cried out to her husband in anguish: "My little girl is dying for want of a doctor in this cursed place—that never should have been taken from the Indians . . . We shouldn't have come, John, so far — so cruelly far — What's money? — What's land? What comfort can we have when we remember this — dying for want of a skilled hand — the best child I ever had." Then, as if answering a prayer, came someone "as welcome as an angel of God . . . I heard you had a sick girl", he said, "and I have some medicine in my bag. I am the Methodist minister who has just come to Millford. My name is Hall — Thomas Hall."[39]

Once at a revival meeting in Souris City, the same Rev. Hall read a passage from the Book of Revelations which induced a "patient and kind" mother of eight, who was present, to confess a "mishap in her childhood" on the Isle of Skye 30 years before. With that, the woman's husband, a "coarse, cursing, rough fellow'", kicked her out of the house "without a dollar" and she slunk away in disgrace to work in a Brandon hotel.[40]

By 1883 the "sister towns" of Souris City and Millford were linked in a Methodist circuit under Rev. G. K. Adams, a new incumbent who was evidently both conscientious and well-liked. The parsonage was then at Souris City. At one stage in his ministry, Methodist services were being conducted at Souris City "every night", prompting "a number" to lead a "new life".

Rev. Adams' popularity is further suggested by a Brandon Sun report after a surprise presentation to him of a suit of clothes November 7, 1884, at the John Henderson homestead (W 2.7.17). The humour was not only that the cleric's measurements were obtained "on the sly" by one of his colleagues, but that he had been obliging enough to announce his own "social", as it turned out to be, from the pulpit; he had also promised to be on hand, forgetting, he later recalled, to ask what the occasion was. Another feature of the affair (which included an evening of music, both vocal and instrumental, and readings and recitations) was that the young ladies outnumbered the men so overwhelmingly that "one could hardly believe this was Manitoba". The newspaper continued:

> We know of one young gentleman whose nervous system was so shattered at the quantity of sweetness wasted in the desert air that it will be a miracle if he recovers his equanimity sufficiently to preach on the Sabbath![41]

84

Whether or not the flabbergasted "young gentleman" mentioned above was the guest of honour is not specified. Perhaps it was the Souris City Presbyterian, Rev. M. Hoskins, who had disrupted the "usually quiet settlement of Chesley" earlier that year by marrying William H. Cory and Miss A. Townsend "in a manner that almost makes the most timid bachelor pick up courage to think he, too, could stand the ordeal".[42]

For a Presbyterian minister to have been in attendance at Rev. Adams' presentation would not have been improbable. It seems that Methodists and Presbyterians often co-operated in those days. A good example was a largely attended Chesley picnic on June 26, 1885, at which a collection was taken for local preachers of both denominations. Otherwise it was apparently a good excuse for a get-together. Among the highlights of the programme were a solo by John Barkwell, his duet with Thomas Nichol, R. B. Fawcett's recitation of "The Ocean" and a baseball match between Sourisbourg school district and the Brandon West team. (The visitors received the "usual cheers" despite their thirty-two run "edge" after seven innings of play.)[43]

At the settlement in Township 8.18, meanwhile, the Church of England had been established. The first records indicate that Rev. L. N. Martin, representing the church's Brandon mission which then included the settlement in Township 8.18 as well as Millford, began his preaching in January, 1882.[44] The present St. John's Anglican Church at Rounthwaite—the first church built in Oakland—was begun late in February of that year by Rev. J. Boydell of Brandon;[45] and apparently was finished by Rev. John F. Rounthwaite, a man of exceptional character and ability who emigrated to Oakland from England in 1882.

Rev. Rounthwaite's sister Elizabeth, a religious woman who almost entered the Church of England sisterhood, had visited their brother, Samuel Rounthwaite, in Oakland, and returned home with impressive tales of how badly churches and schools were needed in the Canadian West. Rev. Rounthwaite was determined to answer this call, even at the expense of an early grave. He purchased S 13.8.18, which he strove to farm in the evening. During

85

the daytime he devoted himself to such strenuous matters as supervising the church building program at Rounthwaite, administering to congregations both there and at Millford, and inspecting schools in the country immediately south of Brandon — a crowded schedule that proved too much. On Christmas Eve, 1883, he died suddenly at the age of 44, leaving a widow and nine young children.

The Brandon's Sun tribute glowingly sums up the immense esteem held for this energetic man:

His loss to the settlement is an irreparable one. Quiet and unassuming in disposition he was nevertheless ever forward in good works, his time, his means and his energies being freely given in promoting any public benefit. He was a ripe scholar, a cultivated gentleman, and a good man. His death is sincerely deplored by the [Brandon] community who extend to the members of the family their sincerest sympathies—[46]

Until Brandon boomed, the only post office in Oakland was located on Samuel Rounthwaite's homestead (SW 14.8.18) and settlers collected mail there from as far away as Township 5.18.[47] (His niece recollects that the Dominion Government asked Rounthwaite, fresh out from King's County, Ireland, to supply an Indian name for the post office and that, when Rounthwaite replied that he did not know any Indian names, the authorities informed him of their decision that Rounthwaite was "Indian enough"!)[48]

But several "post settlements" soon appeared on the horizon when a number of the hundreds then pouring into Brandon chose land in Oakland. By April, 1884, in addition to the service provided at Rounthwaite and Souris City, stamps were being cancelled at Carrolton (19.7.19) by Alfred H. Carroll, at Hayfield (22.8.19) by Leslie Bobier, and at Stratherne (16.8.17) by George Stewart. That summer Hazelwold post office did business on 34.8.19. (If not initially, James H. Cleveland was later in charge.) Completing the list of Oakland's post offices in the 1880's was Minnewawa (24.7.18), which was operated by John Young.

86

Another place settlers congregated was NE 4.7.18, where Charles Kent ran a small store on the track leading south to the grist mill erected by John Gregory on the Souris River in 1884. It would seem that a townsite was once planned there as well, according to a local news item of June, 1884, that stated: "This infant city [of 'Whitehead'] has not shuffled off this mortal coil, but promises to be a fine place if only the railroad would come anywhere near".[49]

Moreover, the demand for local improvements grew, as the population of the municipality increased. Oakland was part of the unorganized Northwest Territories, prior to the western Manitoba boundary extension of 1881. Co-incident with receiving provincial status, southwestern Manitoba was divided into counties "for county purposes and for convenience for [electoral] registration and the holding of county court". The counties were, in turn, sub-divided into municipalities. Thus the original Brandon municipality was composed of the present rural munici-palities of Oakland, Glenwood, Whitehead, Cornwallis, Elton and Daly; and this large municipality was part of the even larger County of Brandon, which included town-ships 7 to 12, ranges 16 to 22. Brandon was, therefore, the seat of a six-ward municipality, before it was incorporated as a city in May, 1882.

The first council of the old Brandon municipality met in January, 1882. Thomas Harrison, of Souris City, was the representative of Ward I (which became Oakland). The warden, the equivalent of reeve, was Rev. George Roddick, of the Brandon Hills.

Although Oakland was not a municipality in its own right until the redefinition of boundaries of 1883, the rate-payers of Brandon municipal Ward I watched the progress of local government with great interest.

Among the official acts of this old-style council (seem-ingly in response to the petition of Edwin A. Lockhart (NE 22.8.18) and eighteen others) was the passage of a herd law, whereby all unsupervised animals might be "de-tained for their damages regardless of fences" from May

15 to October 15; and that from October 15 to January 1, all stacks of grain or hay were to be protected by fences.[50]

Notwithstanding the fact that townships 7 and 8, ranges 17 to 19 (i.e. Oakland) constituted only one-sixth of the old Brandon municipality, some forty-three per cent of the municipality's 1882 public works allotment was spent in Ward I—largely owing to the important trails to the new city from the "South Brandon country". Two of these expenditures were those of $9,000 on a bridge at Souris City and of $900 on a bridge across the Black Creek (28/29.7.17).[51]

This did not satisfy NW 32.8.17 ratepayer William Newcombe, who was "livid" when Councillor Harrison vetoed a plan to bridge the "crossing of Spring Creek and the east end of the Mountain", against the wishes of a

large number of meetings held in settlements to the east of the crossing, and deputations appointed to wait on the council and explain the utter impracticability of the road as it is presently located and its uselessness to the settlers on account of the swamp between Spring Creek and the aforementioned crossing of the Little Souris.

Warden Roddick, who also "knows the [swampy] ground thoroughly", and Harrison "had better explain in print, or we'll form harsh conclusions", the ratepayer insisted. "This settlement which aided so materially in placing Mr. Roddick in his present position, anxiously await his explanation of his course in this matter."[52]

Another ratepayer pointed out that Brandon municipality contained "some of the finest tracts of agricultural lands in the province" and that autumn (1882) would have "large quantities of grain for market". But regrettably, at the speed the council was moving, it would take five years to get the required bridges built, let alone the grading of the roads, he predicted. The writer also maintained that the grant of $5,000 for roads and bridges in each ward (passed February 28, 1882) was "totally inadequate". He praised Oakland Councillor Harrison's unsuccessful motion of a bylaw to issue debentures to finance

88

these necessities—"the true principle under the circumstances . . . but presumably beyond [the rest of] the Council's limited comprehension". In conclusion, he questioned what he stated he thought was the majority of the councillors' philosophy—that it was best to make "the poor struggling pioneer pay for the improvements, which will benefit those who settle in the country for years to come".[53]

Spending now and paying later had embarrassing results for the "poor, struggling pioneers" who sat on the first East Brandon school board, which was formed by this same Brandon municipal council in 1882.[54] Since there were approximately forty-two school-age children in the East Brandon district, their parents were eager to get a school erected there as soon as possible after a site had been chosen at a ratepayers' meeting of May 16. The trustees were consequently given local authority on June 16 to borrow $2,500 for construction costs and initial operating expenses. Councillor Harrison offered to do what he could to help negotiate the loan (he advertised for tenders about September 6), and by September 8 the lieutenant-governor had formally given his assent to the borrowing proposal. However, Harrison's poor health that summer delayed proceedings. Meanwhile the trustees were obliged to borrow some $1,200 from the Merchants' Bank in Brandon in order to pay the contractor, purchase supplies, and hire a teacher.

The pressure was temporarily relieved towards the end of November when the board accepted the offer of Messrs. Burnett and Johnson, of Millford and Brandon, to float debentures for the $2,500 at nine per cent par for ten years (interest $112.50 semi-annually). In addition, Hugh Blain was engaged to commence teaching on November 17 at a salary of $50 a month.

In May, 1883, Miss Fannie Parrott replaced Mr. Blain as teacher (at $43 a month), and on June 15 the trustees "examined the school children, who passed a very satisfactory examination".

Encouraging, too, were the results of a "public examination" of the pupils on June 29. Present, besides the pupils, were William Bertram, chairman of the school board, and Mrs. Bertram, Dave Shields, Sr., one of the trustees, C. Shields, Miss Doherty, Mr. Stady, Mr. Scott and Rev. Davidson, a Presbyterian minister who two days later conducted the first church service held in the school house. (Charles Stewart, the third trustee, and Rev. J. Boydell of Brandon both wrote letters of regret that they were unable to attend the function.)

On behalf of the visitors, Rev. Davidson expressed satisfaction at the "very efficient manner" in which the children had gone through their examination. He also congratulated the trustees on having secured the services of "so excellent" a teacher as Miss Parrott and the neighbourhood upon possessing "so commodious and beautiful a school house as that in which they were assembled". Mr. Stady then moved a vote of thanks to Miss Parrott "for the kindness with which she treated the children under her charge and for the painstaking manner in which she performed her duties". This was carried unanimously. (Miss Parrott left on October 31, after refusing to teach on holidays.)

Yet the financial difficulties remained basically unsolved. It seems the newly formed Oakland council tabled an East Brandon request for a $300 advance on the district's 1884 school taxes and, although the Merchants' Bank manager approved a cautious loan of $55 about that time, $200 of the money borrowed from the same institution the previous year was still outstanding, though longsince due. Furthermore, a ratepayers' resolution of February 4, 1883, begging the provincial government to increase the annual education grant to school districts from $100 to "say, $500 or $600" had fallen on unreceptive ears.

The school was closed for lack of funds on April 28, and a month later Bertram and Stewart stood trial for three days in the County Court at Brandon as defendants in the suit Merchants' Bank v. Bertram, Stewart, and Shields, after action had been taken to recover the $200 owing on the overdue note. The defence rested its case on the plea that the note had already been honoured by the payment of a cheque to the plaintiffs, but the judge decided in favour

Oakland   Councillors

Reeve Hector

is premier of our local cabinet. Mr. Hector is the oldest member of our council, and fills the chief magistrate chair with dignity and 200 pounds of solid flesh. He is a fluent debater — when talking to a friend — a jolly good fellow, and always stands by the boys. He votes with the majority and is willing to do just what the people say. "You can't ask no fairer".

Mr. George Stewart

is finance minister, and makes a specialty of the municipal budget. He is thoroughly at home on this subject, and, next to discussing finances, he likes to talk to Sunday school children. Mr. Stewart is up on bridges and culverts, and is a valuable man in the council.

Mr. James Brander

is a prominent member of the council and is a good extempore speaker on all subjects and always stays for the benediction. Mr. Brander is regarded as watch dog of the treasurer.

Mr. James Elliott

is a business man from the word go. He is minister of marine and has charge of the scows and dredges that navigate "Black Creek" when it is passable. We understand that he intends making the fishing and dock privileges along the banks of this sparkling stream a source of revenue, and will devote the proceeds towards building a house of refuge for the families of those who have been lost in attempting to cross Black Creek bridge. He sings tenor and never takes anything stronger than creek water.

Mr. William Stinson

is a farmer by occupation, and fills the office of public works. Mr. Stinson is one of the shrewd members of the cabinet and favours a progressive policy. He takes up the collection in Trinity church, smokes cheap tobacco and generally retires about 9 p.m.

Mr. Samuel Rounthwaite

is a new member of the cabinet, and was born while very young in merry England. By force of natural talents he has risen to fill the proud position he occupies to-day, therefore he is a good judge of roast beef. Mr. Rounthwaite is of sanguine temperament, and never, hardly ever, complains, even when business cares and dyspepsia annoy him.

Mr. H. C. Graham

is a man of facts and figures every time, and is a great debater, and his speeches are noted for the forcible and picturesque language. Finance is a specialty, and he can tear any public statement of expenditure, etc. to pieces, with great fluency and emphasis. He has several times been requested to run for reeve, but has invariably declined the honour.

Mr. W. S. Moody

is secretary-treasurer, and fills that office to perfection. He is inclined to be extravagant and hardly a year passes without his spending a quarter.

The Brandon Sun
July 22, 1886.

The Old Brown Schoolhouse

In memory's hall stands the picture
  And years of sad care are between;
It hangs with a beautiful gilding,
  And well do I love it I ween.
It stood on a bleak country corner,
  But boyhood's young heart made it
    warm;
It glowed in the sunshine of summer,
  'Twas cheerful in winter and storm.

The teacher, O well I remember,
  My heart has long kept him a place;
Perhaps by the world he's forgotten,
  His memory no touch can efface.

He met us with smiles on the
    threshold,
  And in that rude temple of art,
He left with the skill of a workman,
  His touch in the mind and the
    heart . . .

We sat on the old-fashioned benches,
  Beguiled with our pencil and slate;
We thought of the opening future,
  And dreamed of our manhood's
    estate.
I cast a fond glance o'er the meadow,
  The hills just behind it I see,
Away in the charm of the distance,
  Old school-house; a blessing on
    thee.

                The Brandon Sun
                March 9, 1882.

of the bank. A month's grace was given to the trustees to scrape up the wherewithal.

The judgment doubtless set East Brandon tongues wagging. As for the trustees, they mitigated their defeat by indemnifying themselves for their time and trouble in going to court. Bertram was reimbursed at the rate of $4 a day for driving his team and wagon to the trial. Having been merely a passenger, Stewart received half that amount.

When Ward I of the old Brandon municipal council became the rural municipality of Oakland in 1883,[55] public works, the supervision of school boards, the adoption of herd laws, and the appointment of assessors, poundkeepers, pathmasters, fire wardens, and constables were among the topics of legislation passed at the monthly council meeting. But all of Oakland's municipal records prior to about 1913 (with the exception of the assessment rolls) have been destroyed—perhaps in a fire that year in Frank Capel's store at Carroll. Thus virtually the sole source for studying the early history of the municipality is an incomplete and often nearly illegible series of news items in the files of The Brandon Sun. There one reads that in the 1880's the council usually rented relatively central Chesley School for its meetings, although on occasion they were held at Souris City, Paisley School, and Foster's school house.

Some early examples of the council's deliberations were:

(a)—that the pathmaster of the district be notified to repair Barkwell's bridge and have the snow removed from the approach to Black Creek bridge (April, 1884);

(b)—that the Finance Committee recommended the purchase of six road scrapers for municipal use; and that $50 reward be offered for the arrest and conviction of horse stealers, with one hundred printed notices to this effect to be posted throughout the municipality (May, 1884);

(c)—that W. H. Gammon and four others be granted a petition to do their statute labour on the trail running through the Brandon Hills; and that notices be posted at Rounthwaite and Stratherne post offices as well as on the

95

Spring Creek bridge advising that the Reeve and Clerk would be at the bridge at one-thirty o'clock in the afternoon of June 20 to let contracts by auction to the lowest bidder for what improvements may be necessary for the safe and proper crossing provided the approaches to the same are made by statute labour (May, 1885);

(d)—that owing to the number of schools with competent teachers already supported by this municipality, the council cannot entertain the idea of contributing any financial assistance to Brandon Collegiate Institute (October, 1885);

(e)—that the assessor's salary for 1886 be set at $60, that amount to cover all extras (January, 1886);

(f)—that the reverend gentlemen J. W. Sutherland and G. K. Adams each be supplied with a book for the registration of births, marriages, and deaths (April, 1886);

(g)—that the municipality be divided into road divisions (April, 1887);

(h)—that E. A. Lockhart be paid $150 as compensation for two horses destroyed by the District Veterinarian on account of glanders; and that the Reeve be authorized to fill R. Lammie's request for tree seeds at the lowest rate (August, 1887).

Preserved by local legend is part of the story of the Souris City bridge—which presented a recurring municipal problem during most of the decade. The bridge was located near the so-called "West Crossing" of the Souris River at Souris City, which in 1882 was apparently a 320-foot structure built with about $9,000 of public funds.[56] It is said that a leading representative of the provincial government was to have dedicated the bridge one early spring day. The dignitary and some thirsty villagers enjoyed a good time on the eve of the scheduled ceremony. The following morning, to their dismay, they discovered that an ice-packed freshet had made off with a portion of the paragon of civic pride.

However and whenever it happened, records show that the bridge was, in fact, washed out at least once. In April,

1884, the Oakland Board of Works Committee recommended that "The Toronto Company" be permitted to replace the bridge "subject to the supervision of the Council in consideration of getting back the value of statute labour for 1882 when that sum comes into the hands of the Council". The council also offered the Company twelve days statute labour from the surrounding district. In the meantime, while the bridge was out, the Board of Works suggested that the Company might operate a ferry at Souris City between the hours of six o'clock in the morning and eight o'clock in the evening at the rate of twenty-five cents per team, and ten cents for pedestrian passengers (return free of charge the same day).[57]

The troublesome bridge was refurbished though it is not known by whom. The centre spans were removable, to avoid further calamities at spring break-up—an arrangement which did not entirely please the Oakland council because of the increased maintenance required. At the April, 1885, meeting, therefore, the council stressed that it did not consider itself "bound either to maintain or replace such a bridge" and that, in future, they expected financial assistance from rural municipalities south of the river which benefited from the existence of the bridge more than Oakland. There is no indication that the other municipalities concurred with Oakland's views on the situation. In any case, Oakland ratepayers continued to pay an annual Souris City bridge bill until 1889. Evidently in that year the bridge was dismantled and some of the materials were used for a culvert-building programme in the municipality.

Indications are that Oakland's municipal election of January, 1884, was a bitter struggle. Robert Dobson of Rounthwaite emerged the winner of a three-man race for the reeveship. Stewart Robertson collected thirty votes to Joseph Wells' fourteen in Ward 1, and Messrs. W. O. Fowler, A. H. Carroll, James Hector, and Donald Cameron were acclaimed in wards 2, 3, 4, and 6, respectively. But in Ward 5, where Edwin Lockhart squeezed past Samuel Rounthwaite by twenty-one votes to twenty, the contest continued long after the event.

Rounthwaite started the political football rolling by declaring in a letter to The Brandon Sun[58] that the milk had been soured, rather than spilt. He maintained that two votes had been illegally cast from one half of 12.8.18— one by an elector who swore he owned the land, and one by another elector who swore he occupied it.

An observer from Brandon Hills, who signed himself "VIVE, VALE", countered that Rounthwaite's charge was "most untrue and an insinuation on the character of the returning officer".[59]

Casting further aspersions on Rounthwaite's motives, "VIVE, VALE" asserted that the defeated candidate, "with his usual egotistical bluster", felt his loss so keenly because he had proclaimed "to all and sundry the certainty of his election for weeks before the nomination. He has been tried at last in a small way and found wanting, after years of scheming for public recognition". After all, he added, Rounthwaite was "the same individual who at the first [provincial] election actually voted for Sifton [J. W. Sifton, Grit], and at the last election promised his vote to both Woodworth [Joseph E. Woodworth, Tory] and Sifton and canvassed for the former and voted for neither. His treachery was probably unknown, as he was elevated by the powers that be to a J.P. (justice of the peace)".[60]

The victorious Edwin Lockhart also submitted his views to the Sun's readers stating that Rounthwaite had stretched the truth to an intolerable point, and that he, Lockhart, had a pudding of proof to verify his integrity.

With that "PRO BONO PUBLICO", an unknown contributor from the Rounthwaite district, spoke up in Rounthwaite's defence. Rounthwaite had not been "scheming for years for public recognition", nor had it been his intention to vilify Lockhart. On the other hand, there was no doubt that Lockhart had received two votes on the half section of 12.8.18 in question, this writer stated. In addition, he claimed that one illegal vote had been cast on 22.8.18; and that a brother of Lockhart had sidled into the municipality on election day to lend a helping vote, though it was "well known that he had no property in the township, having sold his homestead months ago".[61]

Finally the editor of the newspaper felt it his duty to referee the "chewing match". "The matter is much too trivial for the space it has already occupied," he pronounced on January 23, 1884, in an editorial entitled "The Oakland Tempest". If Lockhart worked harder and "got out all his support", he deserved to win the election. Concluded the editor:

> There has been a manifestation of feeling over the the matter wholly unworthy [of] those connected with it, and the most seemly thing they can do now is not only to let it drop, but to haste as fast as they can to forget all about it.[62]

REFERENCES:
1. Macoun, J., 1882, Manitoba and the Great North West, p. 65. Guelph.
2. Macoun, J., op. cit., p. 47. Macoun states in the same volume that the Souris once was considered "navigable south to the American border" (p. 470), but the author was unable to find any documentary evidence that this river ever was used by steamboats.
3. Unpublished memoir, n.d. Copy in possession of Mrs. N. Rogers, Morden, Manitoba.
4. Ibid.
5. Ibid.
6. Personal communication with Mrs. Jemima Webster, Winnipeg.
7. Cory, A., op. cit.
8. Unpublished memoir "as told to his daughter" in 1950. Copy in possession of Miss Ruby Cory, Wawanesa.
9. Cory, A., op. cit.
10. Barnes, C.J., 1946, Seventy Years in Southwestern Manitoba, p. 11. Medora, Manitoba.
11. McClung, N., 1964, Clearing in the West, p. 47. Toronto.
12. Personal communication with Mrs. J. L. Grossart, a daughter of Wm. Bertram.
13. Article in the Souris Plaindealer, April, 1926. McMorran, G. A., 1956, The Souris Plains, p. 19. Souris.
14. Ibid.
15. Kavanagh, M., 1966, The Assiniboine Basin (reprinted edition), p. 158. Old Woking, Surrey.
16. Trotter, B., 1925, A Horseman in the West, p. 221. Toronto.
17. Methodist Church Reports, 1882. Toronto.
18. Manitoba Gazette, January 21, 1882.
19. The Brandon Sun, March 16, 1882.
20. Documents 1508 and 1815 Brandon Land Titles Office. The ten original shareholders of the joint stock-company all were Torontonians: James Baines, of W.

& C. Baines, stock brokers and land agents; Arthur Radcliffe Boswell, attorney; Thomas Davies, of Thos. Davies & Co., "ale and lager beer, brewers, maltsters and bottlers"; George B. Gordon, attorney; Andrew Heron, land agent; Wm. H. Knowlton, merchant; Abraham W. Lander, attorney; Alexander Manning, contractor, later mayor of Toronto; John Small and Horace Thorne—both attorneys —all of Toronto.

21. Barnes, H. H., Diary, cit. C. J. Barnes, op. cit., p. 12.
22. The Brandon Sun, March 2, 1882.
23. Barnes, C. J., op. cit., p. 12.
24. The Brandon Sun, March 23, 1882.
25. Saunderson, H. H., c. 1951, Some Pioneer Townsites Along the Souris River, unpublished manuscript. Copy in Public Archives of Manitoba.
26. Ibid., p. 24.
27. Ibid., p. 22.
28. The Brandon Sun, June 19, 1884.
29. Personal communication with Mrs. O. Orr of Wawanesa.
30. Saunderson, H. H., op. cit., pp. 23-24.
31. Henderson's Directory for Manitoba, 1884, Winnipeg.
32. Saunderson, H. H., op. cit., p. 23.
33. Ibid.
34. Ibid.
35. The Brandon Sun, September 27, 1888.
36. Ibid., October 23, 1884 and December 11, 1884.
37. Saunderson, H. H., op. cit., p. 24.
38. Campbell, D., 1967, Chesley United Church, 1898-1955, p. 3, Altona.
39. McClung, N., op. cit., pp. 78-80.
40. Ibid., p. 134.
41. The Brandon Sun, November 20, 1884.
42. Ibid., February 7, 1884.
43. Ibid., July 9, 1885.
44. Chapman, C., 1952, unpublished manuscript entitled St. John's Anglican Church, Rounthwaite, in possession of Mr. Chapman.
45. The Brandon Sun, March 2, 1882.
46. Ibid., December 26, 1883.
47. Henderson's Directory for Manitoba, 1882. Winnipeg.
48. Personal communication with Miss Ethel Rounthwaite, Thornhill, Ontario.
49. The Brandon Sun, June 12, 1884.
50. Ibid., March 2, 1882.
51. Ibid., April 12, 1884.
52. Ibid., March 23, 1882.
53. Ibid., March 16, 1882.
54. Minutes of East Brandon School Board, 1882-1883.
55. The origin of the name Oakland is not known.
56. Saunderson, H. H., op. cit.
57. The Brandon Sun, April 12, 1884.
58. Ibid., January 16, 1884.
59. Ibid.
60. Ibid.
61. The Brandon Sun, January 21, 1884.
62. Ibid., January 23, 1884.

The Old-fashioned Girl

She flourished 30 or 40 years ago, and was a little girl till she was 15.

She used to help her mother wash the dishes, and was ambitious to make pies so nicely that Papa could not tell them from mama's. Then too, she would darn her own stockings to say nothing of knitting them herself . . . her rag doll and little bedstead and chair that Uncle Tom made were just as valuable as the $20 wax doll and its Paris ward robe are to children nowadays . . .

She did not say "I can't" or "I don't". . . was modest, didn't know any slang phrases, respected her elders. She didn't go to parties by the time she was 10 and stay till midnight playing euchre, dancing, and eating lobster salad and ice cream. She went to bed in season and rose at 6 a.m. happy and ready to give happiness.

The Brandon Sun
December 10, 1885

A Big Time in the Hills

Messrs. Leetham and Daniels have recently been engaged in burning lime on shares, at the Brandon Hills, and a day or so ago a difference arose as to the division of profits, and while the men were in Brandon, their wives began to review the situation. After hurling at one another a few choice, but innocent adjectives they proceeded to more lively demonstrations.

Mrs. Daniels in their encounter secured sufficient of Mrs. Leetham's hair to make a good-sized bird's nest, and Mrs. Leetham managed to throw a stone at Mrs. Daniels. They then closed, Marquis of Queensbury rules, and eventually threw one another into the lime kiln.

Brandon Daily Sun
June 6, 1884.

Lake Clementi Picnic

The visitors, who were all in excellent humor, rowed on the lake, played lawn tennis, or sat in the shadow of the barbed wire fence and listened to the band, just as they felt inclined.

Some, and these were noticed, were mostly youthful, strolled, apparently lost in thought, away from the busy hum of the multitude, to some sweet secluded spot where they could whisper sweet nothings in each other's ears, (they couldn't whisper sweet nothings in their own ears, you know,) and be quite, quite alone.

What to them was "Ice cream and lemonade! Ten cents a glass"! Nothing; or what significance had the hoarse cry of "Cigars and lights!" "Cigars and Lights!"—None, whatever!

Sometime the young men would bend forward to whisper something, and the young women would do ditto, to hear what they had to say more easily, and then the young men's lips would come in contact with the young woman's cheek, and there would be heard a faint, circulatory sound, something like the swish of a mule's tale through the air, only much more subdued.

The Brandon Sun
July 4, 1889.

Wedding Bells

One of the most notable social events which has ever challenged Stratherne society's admiration, occurred in the nuptual ceremony of Miss Mary Jackson and Mr. E. Stady at the residence of the bride's father.

The bride, the daughter of Mr. Wm. Jackson, bears the impress of physical and intellectual beauty, ever characteristic of society's chosen queens. With a complexion rivalling nature's fairest picture in its parity, with eyes of a soft brown and a wreath of rich tresses to match, constitute a picture which Praxiteles might worship.

The groom is one of Stratherne's most promising young men, of an excellent character, and possessing the attributes of a noble manhood.

The interest taken in the contracting parties was manifest in the large and brilliant assemblage in attendance at the ceremonies.

Shortly after two o'clock the bridal party made its appearance, and took their stations. Artistically the scene was complete, and sentimentally speaking it was solemnly impressive. The stillnessed expectancy was at last broken by the first words of the short but impressive ceremony of the Methodist faith, pronounced by the officiating minister, Rev. George Roddick of Brandon Hills. There was little manifestation of excitement on the part of the bride and groom. The responses were made in clear and distinct tones, and nothing occurred to mar the beauty of the scene.

At the conclusion the usual time was devoted to congratulations by friends and relatives of the newly wedded couple, after which the bridal party and immediate friends and relatives sat down to a sumptuous and magnificently-served dinner, while Miss Jenny Reynolds, assisted by M. C. Gray, performed a brilliant wedding march at the organ, the strains of which floating through the apartments added enchantment to the splendour which reigned supreme.

The Brandon Sun
November 3, 1887.

Salt on the Applesauce

The West is the country of infinite possibilities. Thither go the knights errant of this age—not to rescue distressed damsels, for damsels are distressingly scarce there, and are more apt to distress the knights—but to conquer every kind of difficulty and to solve every kind of riddle which Nature presents to her sturdier children.[1]

This statement from a handbook on Canada compiled for the British Association for the Advancement of Science in 1884 reflects the bright-eyed spirit that reigned over the Prairies in the settlement era.

For example, while visiting his former home in Huron County, Ontario, early in 1888, Chesley district pioneer Joseph Townsend had strong praise for the "area of thrifty and prosperous people" he had helped to establish in Manitoba eight years before. He remarked that his hundred acres of fall wheat had produced an average of 40 bushels to the acre the previous autumn, and that, although Chesley was "expressly grain country and will never be adapted to stock on account of the scarcity of grass and hay", the farmers there had experienced "very little trouble with frost". Regarding the amenities of life, Townsend mentioned that he lived close to Chesley School, and said that Thomas Cory (once a resident of the same part of Huron County as himself) had "as good farm buildings as can be seen on most farms in the County of Huron".[2]

In a similar vein, Oakland's John Taylor confided to a newspaper reporter who interviewed him on Brandon's Rosser Avenue in 1889, that he had emigrated from Bruce County, Ontario, with $10 in his pocket, got himself in a position to purchase NW 25.7.19 from the C.P.R., cultivated eighty acres, and built a good frame house, stable, and outbuildings on the quarter section. He further disclosed that he was homesteading NE 20.7.19, where he had a house, stable, and granary. Taylor claimed he had "a complete outfit, three horses, a yoke of cattle, a cow, pigs, poultry, etc., and all the machinery I require . . . I am very pleased with the climate, and believe this is just the country for a young man with any go."[3]

After only a year in the vicinity of Millford, a settler from the Old Country told yet a third tale of the opportunities awaiting Nature's "sturdier children" in the West:

Like it, why of course I like it! It is the finest country in the world. It has no drawbacks to the man that means to work. I like the country so much that I am on my way back to England to bring out the rest of my family . . .

Farming must pay and those who think otherwise had better try farming four hundred acres in England and pay the high rents I had to pay there. Wait and see if I don't bring out a number of well-to-do farmers with me. That is the class we want here, and I will induce a number to come. I like your people. I like their ways. I like the freedom you enjoy. Nothing would induce me to try farming in England again.[4]

It was also true that the "knights" had a great deal of trouble with "damsels". The battle of the sexes was distressingly fierce (and fun) in the Chesley district early in 1886 when the eligible males formed an "offensive and defensive alliance" known as the Oakland Bachelors' Club. "Never say—marry" was the stalwart war cry of this high-minded little army; and posterity is indeed fortunate that The Brandon Sun of July 1, 1886, saw fit to print such terribly serious items as:

THE CHESLEY BACHELORS
Men Who Might and Should Get Married

We have repeatedly been requested to publish a list of the eligible bachelors in Chesley for the benefit of the different Ladies' Aid and Guild Societies in Oakland. Having recently taken out an accident policy for a large amount, we now comply with the request. It will be noticed that no attempt at classification in order of age or beauty is made. The first on the list is

Mr. Duncan Gray

Mr. Gray is president of the Oakland Bachelors' Club, whose members are all sworn not to get married inside of sixty days. He has resided here for a number of years, drives a good horse, and is well-fixed financially. Duncan is regarded as a "catch" by the ladies, and we hope to see him occupying his mansion shortly.

Mr. Samuel Townsend

This gentleman was formerly quite a ladies' man and could often be seen dashing around the country with his fast horse always accompanied by a lady teacher generally the latest arrival. Of late he has reformed in this respect, and we are now afraid he is drifting into becoming an incorrigible old bachelor.

Mr. Sam'l Miller

This enterprising young man is one of the slickest men in the club. He can talk quickly and give more taffy than any man in the business. He favours the brunette style of beauty, and insists on it. We hope to hear of Sam coming to the front shortly and doing his duty like a little man.

Mr. Neil Peter Gray

Here we have a good looker, a fine singer, and a good all around musician. Neil is quite a society man and generally takes in all that is going on. He was formerly inclined to be a little giddy in his attention to the ladies, but of late he has settled down to farming. He now likes to look at the bright side of life, and before many months roll by he will probably be struck off the bachelors' roll call.

Mr. R. F. Martin

"A very sly young man," remark the ladies as Dick dashes down to Pelican Lake at a 220 clip, behind the fastest horse in the country. Dick is fond of horses, but it is reported that he does not waste all his attention on trotters. He is quite a traveller, and it is rumored that he will visit Pelican Lake in the fall on an important mission.

Mr. Noble Smith

Is one of the most happy-go-lucky, good-hearted dare-devil young men on the plain. He is generally into mischief, and when not actually engaged in it is thinking up some reckless undertaking. Notwithstanding his pranks "Uncle" Noble is popular with the ladies, but we are reliably informed that Chesley has no charm for him in this respect. Brace up "Uncle" and we will see you through.

Mr. Frank O. Fowler

Genial light-hearted Frank is a special favourite with the girls. He has a weakness for Souris City, but is a regular church goer, and sings in the choir. One of his lungs is weak and he is obliged to go to

A. E. Rome

Richard Cory, Jr.   F. O. Fowler

Souris City every week or so to sniff the sweet scented breezes from the Souris river. It seems to agree with him as he always looks happy when he returns.

Jas. Townsend

Is a recent arrival and has so far kept a little quiet. We have been given a pointer that he will tender his resignation to the bachelors' club before 1886 has rolled away.

Mr. Guss Cory

Is a knobby dresser and a reformed masher. The girls say "Ah there's Guss!" as he passes by, but Guss pays no attention as his mind is fixed on a more distant subject. It is whispered around that Guss presented his lady love with a set of rubies the other Saturday evening, but we are not prepared to vouch for the fact.

Mr. A. E. Rome

Like all other young men, is quite a favourite in society. It is said he thinks the scenery around London the finest in the world, but we trust that some of our local belles will be able to remove this erroneous impression.

Mr. Joseph Townsend

This young man prides himself on being the son of an Italian Count, and gets himself up regardless of expense. He never has less than two girls on the string, and at one time, it is said he had no less than six. Joe lacks concentration, and in future should confine himself to a single subject.

Mr. Richard Cory

Here is a young gentleman we wish to warn susceptible maidens against. He is a notorious flirt and has recently emerged from a little affair in which a returned engagement ring figures prominently. He is very fickle in his attentions and is "hardly off the old love until he is on with the new". The report that he is to marry the daughter of an Irish peer is entirely without foundation.

Mr. John Martin

Is the carpenter's son. It is reported that he is heir to a large fortune, and it would be a good policy for the ladies to cultivate John's acquaintance.

Mr. William Noble

It is hardly necessary to place this gentleman's name on the roll call as it is only a question of time when he will tender his resignation. Wm. flies high, and only steps on the high places. It is reported that he was to have been married to a daughter of the late Wm. Vanderbilt, but owing to the recent death of that gentleman, the wedding has been postponed until the family go out of mourning.

Mr. Alexander Fowler

Everybody knows "Sandy" from the smallest school girl to the venerable matron. Sandy was disappointed in love, and has never fully recovered from the shock. The lady who is fortunate enough to secure his second-hand affections is sure of a good home and a loving husband, provided she lets him have his own way.

Mr. Maxwell Murray

Is the only bald-headed man in the party, and as he doffs his hat to the ladies they admire his noble brow and toboggan slide. Maxwell used to be quite a rustler, but now he attends to his business. He is waiting for an heiress, and is not particular how long he waits.

We might add a dozen names to this list, but "sufficient for the day is the evil thereof", or words to that effect. Our duty to the ladies has been performed as promised, and we are prepared to stand or fall on the records.

Seven months later, the league of wise young bachelors suffered its first major setback: "Everything passed along as smooth as a school trustee election until a bombshell was thrown in the camp when Jas. A. Hector deserted ranks and went over to the enemy". The next defector was Noble Smith. "Then F. O. Fowler wheeled into line and tendered his resignation. Messrs. [Gus] Cory and [Samuel] Martin left [granted 'travelling certificates'] further reducing the ranks to a corporal's guard. Messrs. R. Martin, S. Townsend and [Dick] Cory are under surveillance for 30 days, and if they remain steadfast in faith will be reinstated in good standing".[5]

There was still hope, though; and this particular bit of intelligence went on to relay the good news that over the New Year the "Old Guard" had regrouped "for the next campaign" under the veteran command of Duncan Gray (second term of office), with A. E. Rome as revising bachelor; R. W. Hector, scrutineer; and an investigating committee composed of S. Townsend, F. Morrison, and C. Rogers. President Gray, however, allowed that the situation was so critical "it was hard to tell where lightning would strike next" and cautioned the brethren against indulging in "overconfidence and carelessness".

Yet spirits were not always as high as the British Association handbook would have them. The glowing success stories quoted above and the heart-rending misadventures of the bachelors' club were also deceptive. In fact, the future looked so black during the winter of 1883-4 that certain Manitobans were considering armed rebellion against the Dominion government.[6]

Political feeling did not reach this degree of warmth in Oakland. Nevertheless, there, too, many felt that Manitoba was getting unfair treatment from Ottawa; and believing their rights as British subjects were being scorned, a group of Rounthwaite pioneers led half the municipality

116

in a loud chorus of protest that quickly spread through much of the settled area of the province.

One of the causes of this dissatisfaction was Dominion land policy, and among the dissatisfied were the Flemings of Carroll.

During their land hunting expedition in the spring of 1881, the brothers William and Robert and their cousin James inspected "practically every section" north of the Souris in what is now the rural municipality of Glenwood. Then, after choosing in order of preference four locations to which they were particularly attracted, they walked to the land office at the mouth of the Souris. There they arrived—not without nearly drowning in the course of crossing Black Creek near today's Nesbitt—only to discover that the office was closed for the day. "Two Englishmen who were running the office refused to give them anything to eat or a place to sleep. They, therefore, ate their bannocks with bacon which had become soaked in crossing Black Creek, and slept in a hay stack".[7]

In the morning, they made inquiries about homesteading the section of land that had appealed to them most; it was already taken. The same applied to their second and third choices. Angered, William Fleming asked the land agent why these homesteads were unavailable. Why, "they had walked all over the country and had scarcely seen a human being . . .", he was amazed. The official's reply was that the Sowden party, the group who founded the settlement at Plum Creek, had reserved rights to the land in question; and that the members of the party had been permitted to enter for their homesteads back East at Millbrook, Ontario. On account of this the Flemings were forced to be content with their fourth choice, 24.7.20.

This episode convinced William Fleming that if his father, who was hoping to come West that fall, wished to settle on a homestead near 24.7.20, the older gentleman would have to make entry in Ontario. So Fleming entered into correspondence with the federal member for Stormont County on his father's behalf, requesting that the matter be broached with the Minister of the Interior.

The latter refused to grant Fleming, Sr., the same privilege he had given Squire Sowden. Consequently, when his father reached Manitoba, William "had to abandon his own pre-emption in order to get him a place in the district".[8]

The wrangle that developed in 1881 when the C.P.R. was guaranteed $25,000,000 and 25,000,000 acres of land in return for the construction of Canada's first transcontinental railroad affected Oakland. Under this agreement the company received the odd-numbered sections within a twenty-mile belt on either side of the main line. Since Oakland lay within this belt, it seems some squatters in the Elliott Settlement were worried about losing their claims. Tradition tells of old Dicky Cory shingling his first, frame house on NW 19.7.17 when a stranger with a top hat and a pair of handsome drivers reined up and inquired whether he had clear title to the land. Well, Mr. Cory replied, he'd just come West, squatted, and intended to homestead as soon as the official survey was properly registered. Apparently the stranger made a remark to the effect that it was an odd-numbered section and therefore belonged to the C.P.R., whereupon Mr. Cory got upset, hurried down from the roof, and chased the slicker away with an axe![9]

The first provincial election campaign in the Brandon area was then in progress, and Dicky's son, Gus, recalled that John W. Sifton "promised to fix things up if elected".[10] This commitment probably was rather easy to fulfil, considering that the C.P.R. had been expressly forbidden to interfere with the prior rights of squatters.

A more common complaint was the yardage of red tape a settler had to cut through to qualify for a homestead—especially after the Dominion Lands Act was tightened in 1883. The new regulations were meant to ensure that actual settlers and not mere speculators were entering for homesteads. This was not altogether practical, and the editorial page of The Brandon Sun carried a number of letters from irate settlers who believed the bureaucrats had gone too far.

Under the revised scheme, a homesteader carrying out his duties was obliged to sleep on his homestead a minimum of six months (183 days) of each year. A party, who signed his letter to the editor "Public Opinion", grumbled that a Dominion land agent had told him: "I don't care whether you have a house, tent or dug-out, or whether you sleep in your well, but sleep somewhere!" The tough thing about this ruling was that, unless a man could prove he had slept on his land 183 days, someone who either disliked him or coveted his land might appeal to have the government nullify his homestead entry.

Public Opinion's further claim that a man who happened to be away from his homestead on business could be robbed before his return simply "by the complaint of a neighbour", may have been an exaggeration. But there is no doubt that the residence ruling alarmed Oakland settlers. A Stratherne district pioneer had to arrange for pressure to be brought to bear in Ottawa to prevent his homestead being "jumped" under this regulation.[11] Some bachelor settlers kept lights burning at night in their shanties to give the impression that they were obeying the regulation—though they were actually keeping each other company elsewhere.

Public Opinion considered the regulation a "ridiculous inconvenience" for these young men who bached together or who lived with relatives not far from their homesteads. Furthermore, he wondered, what homesteader had time to record where he slept each night? The "old timers", or original settlers of the Oakland area, had not been informed that they had to sleep on their homesteads, he recalled. "When we remember the pledge given by Sir John A. [Macdonald, Canada's first prime minister] that the Act should be most liberally interpreted in favour of bona fide settlers, we are astonished and dismayed."[12]

Another Sun reader, who was not surprised by Public Opinion's outburst, quipped:

I fancy Public Opinion has not been in this country long else he would as quickly search for kneebuckles on a Highlander as look for "common sense" or even "profundity of wisdom" in the decrees or decision of the Land Board. I have the conviction

119

that there is neither common sense, justice, dignity or consistency in the decisions of that body and that Sir John A. is really not aware of the extent to which settlers are being tortured and becoming disaffected by its administration.[13]

Also criticized were rules regarding homestead patent applications. The Department of the Interior at one point required a witness—almost invariably the prospective patentee's neighbour—to answer the following questions:

1. What is your occupation?

2. How long have you known the applicant, and where have you resided since he perfected his entry to the above homestead?

3. Was he entitled to the entry for this quarter section?

4. When did he build his house thereon?

5. When did he perfect his entry to this homestead by taking on his own person possession of the land and beginning continuous residence thereon and cultivation thereof?

6. What portion of each year since that date has he resided thereon? State each month.

7. When absent from his homestead, where has he resided, and what has been his occupation?

8. Of whom does his family consist: when did they first commence residence upon this homestead; and what portion of each year since that date have they resided on it?

9. How much breaking has he done upon his homestead in each year since he obtained entry, and how many acres has he cultivated each year?

10. How many horned cattle, horses, sheep and pigs has the applicant had upon his homestead each year since date of perfecting his entry?

11. What is the size of his house, and what is its present cash value?

12.   What extent of fencing has he made, and what is the present cash value thereof?

13.   What other buildings has he erected? What other improvements has he made, and what is the cash value of the same?

14.   Are there any indications of minerals or quarries on his homestead? If so, state nature of same, and whether it is more valuable for agriculture than for any other purpose.

15.   Has he had any other homestead entry? If so, when and where and what became of it?

16.   Has he assigned or transferred or agreed to assign or transfer his homestead or pre-emption right or any part thereof? If so when and to whom?

17.   Have you any interest, direct or indirect, in this application?

18.   Do you believe the claimant has acted in good faith in obtaining his entry, and in his application for Patent?

19.   Is the applicant married, and have his children had the mumps, the whooping cough, measles, and all the diseases incident to children of a youthful age?

20.   Is there any prospect of there being a large contingent of homesteaders in the family?

21.   If unmarried, is the applicant's house swept out carefully once a month, and the cobwebs removed from the attic window every spring? [14]

The Brandon Sun was not impressed by this procedure. Among other things, complained the newspaper, to answer these questions a witness needed "the faculty of putting his nose most determinedly and impertinently in his neighbour's business!" [15]

Economic factors, such as the tariff barrier erected in 1879 to shelter Canadian industry from bearing the brunt of international trading competition, frustrated the pioneers more than Dominion lands legislation. To avoid paying large freight bills on goods manufactured in Ontario and Quebec, Manitobans wished to deal with mid-Western American cities. But while lime, clays, gravels, sands and other items readily available in Manitoba could cross the border duty-free, there were import charges of between twenty and thirty-five per cent on stock, anvils, grindstones, muskets, cartridges, stoves, hardware and agricultural implements.[16] People struggling to settle the West thought this concession to Eastern Canadian commercial interests inexcusable. As an unnamed Rounthwaite district pioneer put it:

> . . . we are all handicapped with the crushing tariff, heavy . . . [freight rates], and the absence of competitive markets, while the needful currency brought in by new settlers is swept into the Dominion treasury by the avaricious maw of the Ottawa insatiates.[17]

Similarly, it looked as if the older provinces held Manitoba in a financial vice when it came to the thorny question of transportation. Efficient transportation was the life-blood of settlement on the Prairies, and three words summed up most economic problems of those days: NOT ENOUGH RAILROADS. The situation would probably have been less acute if the C.P.R. main line had preceded the course of settlement. Instead, not knowing exactly what route it would take, the original homesteaders settled over a larger area of Manitoba than a single set of tracks could possibly have serviced. Such was already the case when the C.P.R. reached Brandon in 1881.[18] With this arrival, Brandon became established as a wheat city, and on some occasions grain was even teamed from as far afield as Gainsborough, Saskatchewan—at least a nine-day round trip of nearly 250 miles![19] It was no wonder that a hue and cry went up for more branch railroads.

Standing in the way of branch railroad construction was a much disputed clause in the C.P.R. contract stipulating:

> For 20 years from the date hereof (October 1880) no line of railway shall be authorized by the Dominion

122

parliament to be constructed south of the C.P.R. from any point at or near the C.P.R., except such line shall run S.W. or W. of S.W., not within 15 miles of latitude 49 . . .[20]

Designed to free the C.P.R. from the direct competition of American railroads until the turn of the century, this so-called "monopoly clause" was justified by the Dominion government on the ground that the company deserved special consideration in exchange for undertaking huge risks. The clause was defended, too, as a means of saving the Canadian West from American economic domination. According to a contemporary Eastern Canadian business-man:

> The businessmen of the Eastern Canadian prov-inces may be excused if we fail to comprehend all the railway manoeuvring that has been in progress for several years in the Canadian North-West; but we do not need to go deeply into the subject to understand that there is at this moment a conspir-acy in existence composed of two parties, one, within our own country, that hopes to profit by delivering to the United States the commerce of our North-West; the other, a party that is prepared to accept this steadily increasing commerce and to pay in hard cash for this great service to United States railway interests, United States trade centres, and United States seaports.[21]

In contrast, Manitobans tended to see the monopoly as part of a plot hatched against them by Eastern politi-cians and big businessmen. Again Sir John A. Macdonald was under fire:

> Manitoba is the only province within the British possessions that is denied . . . [the right] . . . to build railroads within her borders . . . Does the ima-gination of the Dominion lead . . . [Sir John] to anticipate himself as the chief of the Clan Mac-donald with the farmers of the Northwest as his vassals and the whole territories his domain by right of vassalage?[22]

The Brandon Sun agreed on the grounds that "the C.P.R. company are under a moral obligation to the people of the Northwest to build branch lines as fast as the requirements of the country demand them; that was the implied condition of their monopoly privileges. They are breaking faith with the people; they are not building them; they evince no disposition to build them, and they refuse to permit others to build them".[23]

The C.P.R.'s elevator policy was another bone of contention. "In 1883 the management of the Canadian Pacific . . . placed a minimum of 25,000 bushels of capacity on elevators and warehouses on its lines. The result was to create local monopolies which buyers exploited and to produce an outburst of anger from the farmers and the demand that the restrictions be removed".[24]

Charles Whitehead, an influential Tory who farmed near Brandon, was among those opposed to the company on the elevator issue. In his capacity as vice-president of the Provincial Agricultural Society, Whitehead recommended that the C.P.R. abolish its size minimum for elevators and allow grain to be stored for shipment in flat warehouses. Since flat warehouses, then a common sight in Ontario, were less expensive to construct and maintain than elevators, the number of grain buyers would multiply, competition would become keener, and consequently grain prices would improve, he argued.

Others reckoned the company's freight rates were unfair and that they would drop considerably if only the monopoly were ended and the Canadian transcontinental received a run for its money from United States lines.

Despite this, not everyone faulted the C.P.R. When the first freight arrived at Brandon by rail in 1881, the bills of lading were higher than expected, and an "indignation meeting" was held that night in an unfinished store on Rosser Avenue. "Someone was in every place where one could sit or stand or hang", wrote an early Methodist minister in the area. Several speakers held forth on the evils of "heartless syndicates" and "soulless corporations", until a supporter of the railroad inquired:

What if the C.P.R. had not been built? . . . Where would the people of the country have been if it had not been for the C.P.R.?—whereupon a theatrical voice piped up: "In Huron and Bruce [two Ontario counties]" . . . everyone burst out laughing and the meeting broke up with no vote of condemnation.[25]

Had the weatherman co-operated, protective tariffs that seemed discriminatory, controversial freight rates, and poor marketing facilities might have been bearable. But the economic picture changed dramatically in 1883 when a dry summer and early frosts hastened the collapse of the once-spectacular Manitoba boom. In the wake of hard times, choice Winnipeg lots depreciated drastically in as short a time as a week. An estimated three-quarters of the businesses in Portage la Prairie failed. Banks and other lending institutions hurriedly withdrew lines of credit and seized goods, chattels, and farms from persons unable to meet their obligations. Machinery firms increased prices, and the C.P.R. "mercilessly exploited its monopoly" by raising rates and threatening punitive action when Manitoba complained.[26]

Of course, Oakland was enmeshed by this ominous turn of events. The depression ensured that Charles Stewart's plans for his East Brandon townsite were still-born, and dealt a telling blow to the development of Souris City. It also knocked the bottom out of the Brandon wheat market so that, seeing no option, a number of Oakland settlers helped launch Western Canada's first farmers' alliance, the Manitoba and North West Farmers' Co-operative and Protective Union. The objectives were "the sale and disposal of farm products, the procuring of grain supplies and implements, the building and operation of grain warehouses, elevators, and grist mills, and generally the promotion of farmers' interests".[27]

Precisely where the union movement originated is debatable.[28] That Oakland farmers played a leading role in its establishment there is no doubt. Charles Stewart of Rounthwaite was very active at the preliminary provincial meeting in Brandon on November 26, 1883, and at the founding convention in Winnipeg on December 19 and 20, where

129

George Purvis, also of Rounthwaite, was elected secretary of the organization. Others in attendance at the founding convention were Lindsay Marmont of Rounthwaite and James Hector of Souris City. At the union's second convention in March, 1884, (to which G. G. Harley and A. J. Killam, both of Rounthwaite, and Richard Kinley of Souris City were delegates) Stewart became one of the directors. Later that year, James Elliott of Souris City also became a director.

Since four branches of the union flourished in Oakland early in 1884, it seems reasonable to infer that towards the close of 1883 the majority in that area sympathized with the union's "Declaration of Rights" that:

Whereas, in view of the present depression in agricultural and commercial industries in the province of Manitoba, the farmers of the Province have assembled for the purpose of expressing their views upon the causes of the said depression and the means of removing the same;

And, whereas, the present and future prosperity of this Province depends both commercially and otherwise upon the successful prosecution of agriculture;

And, whereas, numerous and embarrassing restrictions are placed upon the efforts made by the settlers to extend their operations and improve their condition;

And, whereas, such restrictions are unjust and unnecessary, and have been continued in defiance of the just rights of Manitoba;

And, whereas, some of the said restrictions consist of the oppressive duty upon agricultural implements, the monopoly of the carrying trade now enjoyed by the Canadian Pacific Railway Company, and the improper and vexatious methods employed in the administration of the public lands of Manitoba;

And, whereas, the inhabitants of Manitoba are British subjects, and have made their homes here upon the representation that they would be allowed all the privileges which, as such subjects, they would elsewhere in Canada be entitled to, and it appears that by the terms of the admission of Manitoba into Confederation they should be allowed such rights and privileges;

And, whereas, they are denied such rights, and they find that the representative system of the Province is such that they are practically denied the privilege of securing the redress of their grievances through their representatives in the Provincial or Dominion Parliaments;

And, whereas, a large proportion of the business of the Dominion Government is wholly connected with Manitoba and the Northwest, especially the important Departments of the Minister of Railways, Public Works, Immigration and Agriculture, which should be controlled by our provincial legislature;

And, whereas, it is the right of every British subject to call the attention of the constituted authorities to the existence of abuses and wrongs;

Therefore be it resolved that . . . [we demand]:

1. The right of the Local Government to charter railways anywhere in Manitoba, free from interference, and

2. The absolute control of her public lands (including school lands) by the Legislature of the Province, and compensation for lands sold and used for Federal purposes.

3. That the duty on agricultural implements and building materials be removed, and the customs tariff on articles entering into daily consumption be greatly modified in the interests of the people of this Province and Northwest.

4. The right of representation in the Dominion Cabinet. And that . . . the Hudson's Bay Railway should be constructed with the least possible delay.

Finally, consideration of this discouraging period in Oakland's history would be incomplete without again mentioning the sudden death of Rev. J. F. Rounthwaite on Christmas Eve, 1883. The passing of this man left a feeling of discontent in his parish, for no clergyman could be found immediately to succeed him. Soon this became a source of grievance and frustration, not unlike that characterizing the farmers' union in 1884.[29]

With headquarters in "The Wheat City", the executive of the union systematically stumped the surrounding countryside to organize local centres of protest. Oakland was responsive to this campaign.

Charles Stewart's district of East Brandon probably established a branch first, closely followed by one in the Rounthwaite district late in 1883. The latter branch re-organized on January 19, 1884, at Delton School, where G. G. Harley was re-elected president, J. M. Sherk was elected vice-president, and Lindsay Marmont became the secretary-treasurer. A council, including A. G. Killam, Robert Dobson, W. S. Moody, E. A. Lockhart and Alfred Birch, also was formed.

No details of the founding of the Stratherne branch have been discovered but some information is available on the "large and enthusiastic" meeting on February 2, 1884, at the Souris City School, which resulted in the inauguration of the Oakland Branch Farmers' Union. James Hector was made president; James Elliott, vice-president; W. G. King, secretary; and Dick Kinley, treasurer. Councillors of the branch included (W.O.?) Fowler, Joseph Wells, Amos Smith and Stewart Robertson.

In further business, King, seconded by Kinley, pronounced a two-part motion calling for the adoption of the union's Declaration of Rights "in its entirety" and

That this meeting is of the opinion that full and open free trade with all the world is of the utmost necessity and indispensible for the prosperity of this Province; and though connected with and embraced in the Canadian colonies, should for all purposes whatever be considered as independent

132

Flumerfelt & Co.

Try our patent Rubbers, ladies.
    Walk this way, ma'am, if you please.
Very good we find the trade is
    For such articles as these.
Large, ma'am? not a bit!
They're a lovely fit!
Now you'll find you'll walk with perfect ease.

Mitts, sir?, yes sir. Take your pick, sir!
    Calf- skin. Buck-skin, here's a host!
    Wanting something warm and thick, sir?
We are selling now at cost.
Here's a dandy pair,
    That's a suit to wear
Mister, hesitate and you are lost!

Ask a gent, or ask a lady,
Walking gracefully and gay
Up and down a sidewalk shady
    Who's your shoemaker, I pray?
    From the he or she
Comes the answer free:
Bought at Flumerfelt's across the way!

Not a boot store in the city
Can compete with us we find
Don't it seem almost a pity
They should lag so far behind
Flumerfelt and Co.
All the people know.
Only keep the best of every kind!

S.B.F.
The Brandon Sun
March 6, 1890.

Brandon 188

An Enigma

Young Thomas bids my first farewell
And strains her to his manly breast;
"Adieu, dear heart!" he fondly cries,
"I seek my fortune in the West!"

My country! though compelled to roam,
When next I view thy welcome shore,
My pockets with my second lined
Oh! never will I leave thee more.

Then turning slowly towards the ship,
He blew his nose with mournful squeak,
And dashed with bitter smile away
The tear that gambolled o'er his cheek.

He gains the deck: how proudly now
She cleaves the glittering green expanse;
Young Thomas stands abaft the bow
His spirits rise, his pulses dance.

Alas! a change too soon appears—
His cheek is pale—his senses swim,
Young Thomas staggers down below;
My third is all too much for him!

"Why did I leave my native land?"
He faintly cries, while on his brow
Large beads of perspiration stand:
"Oh! Could my mother see me now!"

Poor Thomas pitching in his bunk,
Makes feeble moan and plaintive cry!
"Scuttle the ship and let her sink!
Oh burn her up, and let me die!"

And did so die, that gallant lad?
Oh no! He managed to pull through.
No doubt he felt extremely bad;
But so have I and so have you!

. . . the author prefers to leave the solution . . . to the ingenuity of the gifted reader . . .

A copy of THE BRANDON SUN will be mailed free to anyone forwarding the correct answer to the above enigma to the editor in a sealed envelope, containing also, as a matter of form, one year's subscription in advance.

S.B.F.
The Brandon Sun
January 23, 1890.

Brandon Man

and free to contract commercial treaties with whom she pleases, and to carry on her internal government as the majority of her citizens may see fit; subject, of course, to Imperial interests and consent.[30]

The motion carried without a dissenting vote.

The same assertion of rights received the formal approval of the East Brandon branch on February 12, 1884. Other business was the election of the following slate of officers for the year: Charles Stewart, president; E. Donaldson, vice-president; D. Mitchell, secretary-treasurer; T. M. Babington, assistant-treasurer; and Wm. Bertram, John Stady, D. Shields, W. Andrews, W. Lamb, A. Quarrie, and Rev. J. Mowat on the governing council.

Having listened to Stewart's explanation of his conduct at the founding convention, the meeting gave its formal and "hearty approval of the manly way in which he expressed himself there . . ."[31] This refers to the stir Stewart created at the convention by advocating that Manitoba secede from Canada.

Stewart had told those who were branding his resolution treacherous demagoguery that he favoured secession only in a "limited sense":

I have been stigmatized in various quarters as a secessionist, rebel, annexationist, &c . . . I deny that I have on any occasion advocated secession or rebellion. At the recent convention I did certainly advocate secession, but not secession from British rule, and I am anxious . . . to explain why I did so —a declaration of rights had been prepared by a sub-committee and was approved by the convention. This declaration was drawn up in such imperative language, that in my opinion its terms could hardly be complied with by the Dominion Government without considerable loss of dignity. It was, in fact, an impeachment of the Dominion Government by the people of Manitoba. Now, though I heartily agreed with the declaration of rights in every particular, I failed to see how it could

139

be presented to the Dominion Government with any hope of its demands being conceded. Again, on the other hand, to approach the Government by a petition would have been an act of humiliation, because it is not customary for anyone who has been robbed of his rights to petition the offending party for redress. The proper and only course would unquestionably be to submit his case to a proper tribunal . . . It is, moreover, admitted by many that the interests of Manitoba and the Eastern Provinces are so dissimilar as to be actually conflicting, and that the legislation that would be beneficial to the Western Provinces would be injurious to the Eastern Provinces and vice versa . . . I maintain, therefore, that I was perfectly justified in moving that a petition be presented to the Privy Council of England praying for a Confederacy of the Western Provinces, and I must emphatically deny that in doing so I was activated by any motives of disloyalty to the British or to the Dominion Governments . . .[32]

Although Stewart had injured his reputation in some quarters by speaking out on the secession question, he was certainly not alone in his opinion of Confederation. The combined membership of the union and its sister association, the Manitoba Rights League, about January, 1884, was estimated at 100,000 and growing steadily.[33] Trying to calm the situation, the C.P.R. lowered freight rates a little and the Dominion Government opened for settlement some hitherto reserved lands in Manitoba.[34] But union supporters were in no mood for token moves. Here is how The Brandon Sun described the state of mind:

Just now . . . the agitators are settlers, and the settlers agitators. They will continue to be agitators until the reforms demanded are secured to them. There can be no more settlement until those grievances are redressed . . . What the Northwest wants is fair, honest treatment by the Dominion; we want our shackles struck off; we want liberty to live. To make of the great Northwest a great and prosperous

140

country is a tremendous task to undertake. It can be done, but we can't do it with our hands tied.[35]

Even more blunt was the report of a union rally in the Turtle Mountain district:

Loyalty is a beautiful sentiment, but the farmers are beginning to realize that it will not provide for the family, and the Government will soon realize the fact that they have placed burdens on the people that cannot be borne by free men, and they may yet learn, when too late, that their utter disregard of the sacred right of the people has lost them the fairest province of the Dominion.[36]

Hence, when Sir John A. Macdonald appeared to be ignoring its representations in Ottawa, the union staged another, stormier convention in Winnipeg on March 5. There it was agreed unanimously that "immigrants couldn't be advised to come to Manitoba as long as the burdens imposed on it precluded profitable agriculture"[37]—a resolution which created hard feelings between Charles Stewart and the Brandon city fathers.

Prior to the March, 1884, convention, the union was generally supported by Manitoba businessmen, who, like the farmers of the province, were critical of the C.P.R. freight structure and of the monopoly clause.[38] They could not, however, endorse the union's immigration policy. An influx of more clients and customers was essential to the success of their burgeoning businesses. Anything aimed at discouraging immigration, even temporarily, was viewed as a challenge to their bank accounts. Consequently, the mayor and aldermen of Brandon wasted no time in condemning both the union's anti-immigration manifesto and Stewart, whom they singled out as its author.

Stewart denied having drafted the controversial resolution, but made it clear that he was in general agreement with the union's approach to the subject of immigration. He called the Brandon council's move to blackball it as "one of the boldest untruths that has ever been passed" and a "deliberate insult to the whole farming community".[39]

Another public quarrel involving Stewart began with his alleged arrest for treason at Winnipeg's Brunswick Hotel, where he stayed during the March, 1884, convention. Stewart claimed he had been arrested and kept in confinement by "a man whom I knew to be a detective and who was accompanied by a policeman", and that the warrant for the arrest had come from the attorney-general's department.

"A number of detectives and government spies [had been] posted at all hotels frequented by farmers' union men and on all trains in and out of Winnipeg", Stewart further stated. Although no members of the provincial government had attended the convention, "the attorney-general had his own private secretary at the reporters' table to take shorthand of any private conversation between members of the [union] council". Stewart also charged that four cannon from Fort Garry had been placed at strategic points in the city while the convention was on, and that a supply of rifles had been hidden mysteriously in a Winnipeg church. Evidentally the government was trying to intimidate union members, he concluded.[40]

The attorney-general's public explanation of the incident was that Stewart had been the victim of a practical joke on the part of some of his friends.[41] Whereupon an infuriated Stewart wrote an open rebuttal in which he repeated his accusation that the attorney-general's office had been responsible for the so-called joke. Perhaps the concerted efforts of Premier John Norquay to arrange better financial terms for Manitoba with Ottawa were just "another joke being played on the poor, unsuspecting and unsophisticated farmers of Manitoba", he suggested, but:

I have never been able to see anything particularly comical in the Manitoba situation. On the contrary, I believe that the men composing the Farmers' Union are terribly in earnest, and I venture to predict that if Mr. Norquay returns from Ottawa without . . . [having arranged better terms for Manitoba] . . . future pilgrimages to that capital will not be necessary.[42]

142

What truth there was in Stewart's version of the Brunswick Hotel incident is difficult to ascertain; apparently nothing further came of the affair. His accusations may not have been entirely exaggerated, because Norquay's government did take security precautions against an outbreak of violence at the time of the convention. Clearly, the provincial authorities were unnerved by the strength of the farmers' movement. Meanwhile, Manitobans were becoming increasingly impatient with the poor economic climate —especially south of Brandon where even some petticoats got into the act.

News that the ladies of the Glen Souris district met at the Glen Souris School on March 10 and formally voiced their "deep disappointment with the Dominion government in [its] failure to concede to the people their just and reasonable rights and privileges" made extraordinary front-page fare in The Brandon Sun. The brief which the ladies voted to send to Ottawa read in part:

A gloom hangs over our homes, our husbands and brothers are thoroughly disheartened; we are unable to comfort them on account of the hard circumstances in which we ourselves are placed. Our utmost attempts at economy are insufficient to feed and clothe our household as we would wish . . .

We have borne hardships and suffered many discomforts and there has been no end to our hard toil. We have done so with the earnest hope that we should have a reward to maintain us in comfort, keep us out of debt, and make us happy and contented.[43]

While professing "every sincere feeling of loyalty and patriotism", the ladies said they had decided that their only salvation was to support the farmers' union.

If this feminine flirtation with politics made Sir John A. blush, it probably could not have been detected—the Old Chieftain's face was already smarting from the blistering opposition to his $22,500,000 C.P.R. relief bill. Preoccupied with other problems, he dismissed the disturbance in the Northwest as largely the snivelling of "speculators who were ruined by the collapse after the boom of three years ago, and are of desperate fortunes", and confidently predicted, ". . . the reaction has set in . . . at the opening of spring, when the people are on their farms, the agitation will be forgotten".[44]

But cries for help continued to come from Western Canada, and excitement mounted in Oakland "at the opening of spring" when the Rounthwaite union branch declared itself in favour of secession unless redress were speedily obtained.

The threatening pronouncement was made at Delton School on May 8, 1884, and angry words flew thick and fast. G. G. Harley made a speech condemning the union officials for lobbying in Winnipeg and Ottawa "like beggars" rather than as representatives of a powerful body of free people. The climax came when W. H. Gammon and E. A. Lockhart condensed the clouds of heated air into the resolution that:

> this meeting views with alarm the policy of procrastination pursued by the Manitoba Legislature in appointing another delegation to proceed to Ottawa after the failure of . . . [previous attempts] . . . and the urgency of the Manitoba situation demands immediate appeal to England for redress or by petition for independence under imperial control.[45]

Shortly thereafter, some Stratherne farmers carried the matter a step further by throwing themselves at the imperial mercy of Queen Victoria. In a formal supplication dated May 26, the farmers' union members of that district besought Her Majesty's agreement that because the Canadian government had contemptuously refused to grant the loyal people of Manitoba their due rights as set forth in the British North America Act, "the keystone province" should be permitted to secede. The petition stressed, however, that Manitobans infinitely appreciated the advantages of the imperial connection and wished to remain under British rule. To further the cause, The Brandon Sun editor ran the petition in the newspaper, and called on all like-minded readers to copy it out on sheets of paper, collect as many signatures as possible, and mail them to him for forwarding to Windsor Castle.[46]

144

LET THE BIG CHIEF BEWARE!

There was even a hint of annexationism in Oakland. William Cleveland, Jr., told an audience at Delton on June 7, that to expect Premier Norquay to cure Manitoba's ills "savoured strongly of a hopeless race after very wild game". He maintained that the settlers would have either to "seek protection from our kinsmen across the border, or to begin a British colonial life on our resources". Obviously, they could not count on assistance from the team of "taskmasters" at Ottawa, which "periodicaly treats us to doses of political rubbish so unequally mixed with justice in infinitesimal grains as to sorely afflict our stomachs rising our bilious inclinations to the exploding point!"[47]

Western grievances were clearly more than teapot tempests. But, after reaching a peak in the spring of 1884, the Manitoba farmers' union soon fell into disfavour. One reason for this, giving rise to speculation that the organization was a mask for Grit party tactics, was that some of its prominent members were active Liberals.[48]

The union executive strongly denied this allegation. The secretary, George Purvis of Rounthwaite, who referred to himself as a Tory, told the Conservative association of the electoral division of Brandon in a letter of April 10, 1884, that it was an "insult . . . to state, as has been done in some quarters, that the union had its inception at the behest of the so-called Grit political leaders . . . nor is anyone as a politician connected with the Union today".[49]

Conservatives could hardly be blamed for ignoring Purvis' non-partisan assurances, as long as the pro-union press editorialized in this manner:

> The entire Conservative vote of Manitoba bids fair in a short time to be divided up between justices of the peace and game guardians. When the enormous labor of the appointments is concluded it is proposed that the two divisions shall meet somewhere on the prairies and play a match at football, the ball to be composed of Manitoba's rights—[50]

Out of respect for party, therefore, many original backers of the union withdrew their support.

146

One such Tory was Edward Cliffe, editor of the Brandon Mail, whom union member William Cleveland, Jr., of Rounthwaite scornfully termed a "political acrobat". Cleveland said that in his vocabulary the coined word "Cliffe-like" was synonymous with all things "mean and despicable". The union's failure to form a branch in the western half of Oakland suggests that Cliffe's views had a healthy following there.[51]

The union being tarred with a Grit brush may also have been disadvantageous in the Souris City district. Although the majority in Township 7.17 was Liberal, "The Toronto Company" probably exerted an opposite influence.

On the other hand, party considerations did not blight the union's prospects at the east end of the Brandon Hills. G. G. Harley reported to the provincial convention of March 5, 1884, that a number of his Tory neighbours were "fully in sympathy with the objects of the Union"—which, if true, largely explains why Rounthwaite was the centre of agitation in the municipality. Moreover, it seems that Oakland farmers from both sides of the political fence were attracted by the union grain marketing deal that James Elliott, of Souris City, helped negotiate later that year.

The scheme, which the Oakland Council unanimously endorsed after an interview with the union secretary on June 21,[52] apparently operated as follows: The union arranged to buy grain from its members on a two-payment basis, not unlike that now used by the Canadian Wheat Board. Elevators handling union grain charged two cents per bushel (a quarter-cent less than the standard fee for the same service at non-union elevators); and the grading of all such grain was scrutinized by a superintendent whom the organization hired when the government refused to name an official grain inspector. The union also offered its customer-members the choice of shipping through Port Arthur or over American lines. The latter was an important stipulation to those who resented the C.P.R. monopoly.

In time, though, this marketing venture further undermined the union's popularity. A splinter group was formed of former union members who felt the organization had impaired its usefulness for reform by entering the grain business. W. G. King of Souris City and W. T. Hunter of Rounthwaite were among the leading lights of this group, which was called the Manitoba and North West Farmers' Alliance and People's Rights Association.

This process of internal decay was greatly hastened in the spring of 1885 in the face of Riel's armed uprising in what is now the province of Saskatchewan.

REFERENCES:
1. Dawson, S. E., 1884, Handbook for the Dominion of Canada, p. 327. Montreal.
2. The Brandon Sun, March 8, 1888.
3. Ibid., March 14, 1889.
4. Ibid., July 21, 1887.
5. Ibid., February 3, 1887.
6. Hill, R. B., 1890, Manitoba; A History of its Early Settlement. Toronto.
7. The Souris Plaindealer, April, 1926.
8. Ibid.
9. Personal communication with Mrs. Frank Turnbull of Brandon, Manitoba.
10. Cory, A., Memoir.
11. Personal communication with Arthur C. Wright of Stratherne district.
12. The Brandon Sun, January 24, 1884.
13. Ibid., January 26, 1884.
14. Ibid., February 11, 1886.
15. Ibid.
16. Henderson's Directory for Manitoba, 1879. Winnipeg.
17. The Brandon Sun, June 19, 1884.
18. MacIntosh, W. A., 1934, Prairie Settlement; The Geographical Setting, Vol. I, p. 55. Toronto.
19. Reekie, I. M., 1965, Along the Old Melita Trail. Saskatoon.
20. Robertson, F. B., 1887, Railway Monopoly, p. 1. Winnipeg.
21. Disallowance of Manitoba Railway Charters, 1887, p. 3.
22. The Brandon Sun, January 3, 1884.
23. Ibid., April 4, 1884.
24. Morton, W. L., 1957, Manitoba: A History, pp. 209-210. Toronto.
25. Bridgeman, Rev. W., 1920, Breaking Prairie Sod, pp. 43-45. Toronto.
26. Warner, F., 1960, The Idea of Continental Union, p. 163. University of Kentucky.
27. Manitoba Gazette, January 30, 1884.
28. According to W. L. Morton (1957 Manitoba: A History, p. 221. Toronto), the movement originated in Lang's Valley, and the leadership was then taken from "men like James Long of Langvale, a rugged Ontario farmer, by excitable men like Charles Stewart of Rounthwaite and budding politicians like Clifford Sifton". The Brandon Sun of January 4, 1884 states: "The first to suggest public meetings for a redress of the grievance which all admit was Mr. Chas. Stewart of Rounthwaite".
29. The Brandon Sun, June 26, 1884.
30. Ibid., February 11, 1884.
31. Ibid., February 19, 1884.
32. Ibid., January 28, 1884.

33. Warner, D. F., op. cit., p. 166.
34. The Brandon Sun, February 19, 1884.
35. Ibid., January 14, 1884.
36. Ibid., February 5, 1884.
37. Warner, D. F., op. cit., p. 170.
38. Morton, W. L., op. cit., p. 212.
39. The Brandon Sun, March 12, 1884.
40. Ibid., May 8, 1884.
41. Ibid., April 22, 1884.
42. Ibid., May 8, 1884.
43. Ibid., March 12, 1884.
44. Letter from Macdonald to ex-governor-general Lorne dated March 26, 1884, cit. D. G. Creighton, 1955, John A. Macdonald—The Old Chieftain, p. 380. Toronto.
45. The Brandon Sun, May 10, 1884.
46. Ibid., May 29, 1884.
47. Ibid., June 19, 1884.
48. Morton, W. L., op. cit., p. 212.
49. The Brandon Sun, April 14, 1884.
50. Ibid., May 15, 1884.
51. Presumably the fact that the Carroll area was settled about two years later than the eastern half of Oakland meant that grain surpluses were not an acute problem there in 1883-1884. Fred H. Carroll of Flin Flon, Manitoba, thought he recalled that one or two meetings were held at Robert Fleming's homestead by union organizers, but that nothing came of them.
52. The Brandon Sun, June 21, 1884.

A Rural Drama

recently enacted at Rounthwaite

ACT I. Hour 1 a.m.

MIDNIGHT ORATOR. Hello.

FARMER. (At chamber window.) What is all the noise about? What are you doing here anyway?

M.O. Descend thou profligate, thou son of Noah; come within the radius of my outstretched arms; thou vilest of creation, till I twine the remnants of thy vulgar soul about my feet.

F. Get out of this! Out of my—

M.O. Answer me not; I know what thou would'st say. Keep silence, and remember that vain mortals tremble when I pour forth. Know then that I — I the future successor to the Duke of March, have been elected by a spirit (?) above and beyond mine own, to disclose to the eyes of justice the secret and villainous workings of thy heart. Where are they whom thou so foully murdered? Ha! Why dost thou not tremble?

F. I do; you confounded imbecile. I'm deucedly near frozen.

M.O. Hark! What cries are these? Whence come those sounds? Ogre! It is children whom thou hast imprisoned. I will be their valiant rescuer. (Proceeds to goose pen and releases occupants.) Villain thou art; come from within thy fortress till I thrash thee.

F. If you don't leave out of this, I'll let the dog loose on you.

M.O. I am an oracle, and when I ope my lips let no dog bark.

F. Sic him. Put him off, Sailor.

M.O. Unbaptized dog, be civil; brawl not in my presence, or I will do a deed misbecoming of me on that caitiff corpse of thine. My friend it grieves me I am obliged to leave thee now of a reason which I shall explain hereafter.

(Exit M.O. trolling forth . . . a jolly tune . . .)

ACT II. Hour 1:30 a.m. Scene next neighbour's house.

M.O. . . . So, ho! Whom have we here? (Approaches a couple of cows.) Aw, really; good evening, gentlemen. Can you put me on the right trail to Brandon or home. You do not answer. Perhaps you would like an address, an exhortation, from he whom men call nature's miracle. You do not ask me to be seated, gentlemen; so, perforce, I must attend mine own wants; though you must know I am wholly unaccustomed to doing so; yet to prove to you the innate magnanimity of my disposition I will not be offended at your lack of courtesy, but will repose myself upon this seat, which, though somewhat lacking that graceful magnificence to which I have always been accustomed, is yet substantial withal. (Attempts to sit down on three-legged milking stool, but loses his balance and is precipitated among the cows.) Ha now! Thou art but canting varlets. I scorn to converse or associate with the authors of such premeditated irreverence. (Fires the stool violently at the cows.)

(Owner approaches.)

M.O. Thy name, young man.

OWNER. Hilarious Admiratus . . .

M.O. Sir, I have lost my way, all owing to that little dog Punch. I am endowed with an unusually trustful and childlike nature, and centred my hopes in him, thinking he would guide me home; but he has most foully betrayed my trust, and you now see him, I am ashamed to say, in a high degree of intoxication. I repeat my request, will you put me on the right road to Brandon, or home? . . .

H.A. This is my servant . . .

SERVANT. What appears to be the trouble with thy pedal extremities, my friend?

M.O. (Singing) I have stockings, 'tis true,
            But the devil a shoe.
Punch, go home and to bed, and be sick like a gentleman. I'll follow my dog; he'll take me home; he is er—perfectly trustworthy. Home; sir—shoot—

(Then followed a scent of the wildest confusion; angles and triangles, circles and semi-circles, were traced in a most fantastic style in an adjoining wheat field, Punch ahead, M.O. close in the rear.)

My kingdom for a horse!

(He then entered a small building and seized upon an unfortunate member of the swine family, balancing himself with a deliberation not participated in by his unhappy victim, judging from the ear-splitting sounds it emitted, as they emerged from the building with a rapidity altogether unprecedented in the annals of history. Punch again played a prominent part by persisting in a propinquity in the rear of this noble steed, that must have been somewhat distracting. After vainly resorting to several stratagems this much persecuted animal at last succeeded in ridding himself of our midnight hero, and speedily betook himself "far from the haunts of men", giving vent to a succession of prolonged grunts of satisfaction.)

H.A. Come, my friend, will you not allow me the inexpressible delight of steering you home?

M.O. Urge me, no more; your prayers are vain; I shall sleep this night beneath the smiling moon and er—twinkling stars. So depart my friend, and leave in peace yours truly . . .

H.A. I fear your ardour will be somewhat cooled before the night is gone. My business calls me to your residence this evening, and I would be highly gratified if you would honour me with your company.

M.O. I ever yield to the demands of hospitality. We will away at once. Punch, thou graceless cur, begone.

(Exit Hilarious Admiratus, Midnight Orator and Punch.)

We will draw aside the curtains for a few moments after the return to the lordly castle. Sad indeed was the sight displayed. The remainder of the party, so recently participants in the songs, wagers and merry carousals, all gallant youths in knee britches and jaunty "Tam O'Shanters", were strewn about the floor in a most promiscuous manner. Our loquacious hero was gently deposited beneath the counter pane, a perfect picture of childlike purity and innocence.

The Brandon Sun
December 8, 1887.

The 'Monster' Picnic

The farmers' union movement in Oakland failed to gain the sympathetic ear of Ottawa. However, the capital was soon forced to heed the stir created by the return of Louis Riel from a Jesuit mission school in Montana.

Having accepted an invitation in June, 1884 to lead the agitation in the Prince Albert region, the Metis "martyr" believed that the Northwest was "one pile of tinder and that it required but a single match to set it all aflame".[1]

Riel's view, though tragically exaggerated, was not totally blind. For weeks stretching into months, Prairie politics had been marked by threats of insurrection, and even the relatively moderate Brandon Sun saw no alternative to violence as a last resort. "It would mean open rebellion", if Manitoba's grievances were ignored by the British Privy Council, warned the newspaper. Nevertheless, "the risk of failure must be taken . . . To surrender now would result in making our condition more intolerable than ever . . . 200,000 British subjects are not to be suppressed with impunity . . ."[2]

An annexationist attempt to involve the Manitoba farmers' union in a coup d'état further indicated the gravity of the situation. As outlined in an intercepted letter to Rounthwaite's George Purvis, the plan was first to borrow $150,000—it was hoped from lenders in the United States. Some of these funds were to be for the purchase of Winnipeg's three newspapers. The balance was tentatively earmarked for ensuring "the co-operation and assistance of some public men who have offered under certain circumstances to aid . . . by their influence and political positions to bring about the state of things set forth". Next, late in the year when snow and ice could be expected to complicate communications with the rest of Canada, Premier Norquay would be induced to "proclaim practical independence . . . A convention would be held, and officers elected for the new republic",[3] which would issue $30 million in bonds. A prominent "Romish religious order" under the influence of St. Boniface Archbishop A. A. Taché would buy most of the bonds, negotiations would be opened in Washington for annexation, and the United States government would be persuaded to guarantee the interest on the newly issued bonds, bringing them to par. Those who advanced the initial $150,000 would then receive their reward in the form of $5 million worth of the new bonds.[4] In addition to Archbishop Taché, prominent Grit leaders such as Sir Richard Cartwright were said to have promised to assist the conspirators. Although the authorities promptly squelched the plot, Sir John A. privately confessed that he feared a revolt in the province.[5]

The Dominion cabinet was, therefore, aware of an impending crisis. Yet a commission of inquiry was not appointed until March 30, 1885, and by then it was too late. At Duck Lake and Battleford, Metis and Indians already had taken the law into their own fists; and troop trains soon were bound westward to restore peace, order, and good government to the British North American frontier.

As it happened, Riel had made several major miscalculations — not the least being his alliance with the Cree

156

chieftains Big Bear and Poundmaker. Tabletalk turned to Indian atrocities when in April the white population of Manitoba and what is now Saskatchewan learned that a Cree war party had tortured and murdered a group of settlers at Frog Lake Creek. "Up to that time the 'trouble' was a vague and abstract state, far away and impersonal", explained Millford-raised author Nellie McClung in her first volume of autobiography. "But now the menace had come out in the open, and the evil had assumed shape and image; painted savages, brandishing tomahawks and uttering blood-curling cries had swarmed around the lonely and defenceless farm houses. . ."[6]

Shocked reaction to the massacre at Frog Lake Creek dashed rebel hopes of winning widespread support. Embittered by protective tariffs, the C.P.R. monopoly, and other millstones, white settlers had recently held meetings and declared themselves ready to shoulder Winchesters or to do anything to free the West from Eastern Canadian domination.[7] But damned if they were going to be associated with gangs of blood-thirsty savages—not to mention the Yankee Fenians who were reportedly eager to clamber aboard Riel's bandwagon.[8]

Predominantly Anglo-Saxon areas such as Brandon scrambled to surpass Old Ontario's devotion to the Crown. In an effort to out-God-Save-The-Queen the descendants of United Empire Loyalists, they even turned to ardent doggerel:

Who are these bully boys,
Clothed in a uniform,
And rifles bearing;
Making a dreadful noise,
Humming like bees in a swarm,
Shouting and tearing?

These are our Brandon troop,
Part of the Ninety-first,
Marching to meet the foe,
Meet the red Injun,
Who with his curdling "whoop",
Throws off the yoke accurst,

157

Scalping the whites, and so
Burning and singing,
Digs up the tomahawk,
"War to the knife", he cries;
Venting a deal of talk
Venting a pile of lies,
Scowling, but cringin'.

So Canada says, "My glorious sons,
We can't have such a thing as rebellion!
Volunteers march! Charge for the guns!
It will cost half a million!
But no matter for that! Eyes right! Left wheel!
Let the band strike up the cotillion,
We'll make it unpleasant for Mr. Riel,
If it does cost half a million! . . . "

Onward they move to the front,
Scenting the battle afar,
Eager to bear the brunt
And win the laurels of war.
What if they lose an arm or a head?
Does it matter to them if blood be spent?
And in Canada's cause they are put to bed,
Nailed, confined, coffined and dead,
Do they shrink or care? — not a cent . . .[9]

Fortunately for the enemy, these dauntless souls never stirred in the heat of battle. The "poet" concluded:

So back we go to Brandon town,
Hurroo! Hurroo!
There wasn't a chance of winning renown,
Bahoo! Bahoo!
But if there had been
You would all have seen
How we serve our country and honour our Queen;
We are the stuff
Without any bluff
And don't you never forget it.

Neither were Brandon girls bluffers when it came to doing duty in times of distress. They became famous for their serving of refreshments to troops on trains heading west. A private from Ontario recalled "tasting" their warm hospitality:

About forty girls got on the train at Brandon to serve coffee. The boys were uproarious and were seized with a "sort of spontaneous combustion", for everyone seemed to start at the same time to kiss and hug the girls. And the girls were just as keen for it as we were and kissed us as often as we kissed them. It was something terrific! the boys yelling and hugging, the girls screaming and the men of Brandon looking black in the face.[10]

In the light of this, it was perhaps well that the C.P.R. did not run through the Chesley district for did not the die-hards of the Oakland Bachelors' Club know in their hearts that the young ladies on the neighbouring farms were the fairest in the Dominion? And who knows, if troop trains had stopped for refreshments in such scenic surroundings, lonesome lads from the East might have been tempted to end their soldiering then and there?

Aside from any ideas their daughters might have had on the matter, Oakland settlers probably would have welcomed an influx of muscle that spring. Hired hands were scarcer than usual, as the rebellion had reduced the flow of immigrants to the Prairies.

A number of early residents of the municipality answered the call to arms. A detailed list of those who went to the front is not available, but it is known that part of the contingent from the Rounthwaite district included Richard Pope, S. B. Flower, a McDonald, and gentlemen surnamed Minchin, Wilson, Grant and Kirkman — most of them graduates of Oxford Military College in England.[11]

It did not take long to round up volunteers, the son of a Carrolton district pioneer recalled. "I remember that in March, 1885, a man came to us at noon on horseback and took one of our horses and went south and came back in the afternoon, and that with him were Andy and Alex Shaw and Bill Ballintine and Bill Lambie. They caught the 90th [Battalion] that night and were under fire at Fish Creek three days later. [The battle of Fish Creek was fought

159

April 25.] Not bad for a country with no communications. Father was quartermaster sergeant of the 33 Bruce Rifles and they were ordered out, but camped at Owen Sound [Ont.] for a month and never did get west, but father had to be continually ready to leave."[12]

Homesteaders volunteering for active service were allowed to deduct time spent in uniform from the period they otherwise would have been obliged to spend in residence on their land while "proving up".[13]

Many expected the rebellion would touch off a full-scale native uprising in Western Canada. Although it was about 400 miles from the scene of the fighting, Brandon became jittery on March 2, 1885, after a young Indian disguised as an old man was caught bypassing the city, heading west with a load of rifles.[14] Inside of a week, nervousness increased when heavy pieces of iron were discovered laid across the C.P.R. tracks not far from the Oak Lake Reserve. This was presumed to be an attempt to delay westbound troops.[15]

Brandon's fears seized the surrounding communities, where, with dwellings so much farther apart, people had even greater cause for concern. One of those who panicked was Mrs. William Fleming, of Carrolton. Mrs. Fleming insisted that her husband keep a "get away" team harnessed at all times, and more than once scurried to the A. H. Carrolls with the horrible news that Indians were razing Plum Creek. The "disasters" always proved to be straw stacks being burned by farmers.[16]

If neighbours snickered at Mrs. Fleming's antics, it appears they took no chances either. Indian messengers seldom passed through the district without being treated to a meal.

Kitchen diplomacy also was practised in the Millford district, according to Nellie McClung. She recalled an occasion during the rebellion years when a boy, who had been home helping his father put in the crop, rushed to school to proclaim the approach of a mile-long procession of Indians — "all in war paint and feathers and their carts creaking like ten thousand wolves howling". It was just

160

as well that the teacher managed to calm the excited pupils. Instead of a procession a mile in length, there were only three carts of harmless Indians, who "went the rounds of the neighbourhood, and were so well fed, and showered with gifts of flour, potatoes, eggs and butter that they must have wondered . . . at the sudden warming of hearts that had taken place. Houses that had been closed and locked to them, on former visits, while the owners had looked out from behind the edge of factory cotton blinds, now were opened hospitably and kettles were boiled and meat was fried for the visiting delegates. So it came about that the misdeeds of their brethren in the North-West brought gifts and friendliness to the Indians at Pelican Lake . . ." [17]

Though something of a boon to hungry Sioux in the Oakland area, the rebellion discredited Charles Stewart and others whose left-of-centre political opinions were linked with Riel in the flag-waving public mind. The minute Snider Enfields and Gatling guns blazed in the valley of the North Saskatchewan, The Brandon Sun's former hero became a laughing stock.[18] Also rejected was the organization which Stewart had been instrumental in founding, the farmers' union. By the fall of 1885, it had virtually disintegrated.[19]

Thus the ill-fated Riel Rebellion precipitated the fall of a declining western Canadian reform movement. Yet the conditions that had given rise to the movement remained basically unchanged. Furthermore, when the flush of victory over Riel's forces had faded, many Canadians came to regard the three-month conflict as a tragedy that could have been avoided. Sober second thoughts are reflected in a Western journalist's comment on a contemporary joke:

> One of Sir John A.'s "witty" and considerate stories is told apropos of the Northwest outbreak. It is said that Indian Commissioner Dewdney telegraphed to Sir John the news of Riel's revolt and the probable Indian rising and asked what was to be done about it. Sir John replied, "Whatever else is done you had better keep your own hair cut short". A joke like this will be thought by some to be worth all the lives lost and suffering caused.[20]

As another example of Ottawa's negligent administration, the rebellion was consequently added to the lengthening list of Western grievances.

The difficulty of marketing mounting grain surpluses without adequate railroad facilities was Oakland's main grievance in the 1880's. This was not an overriding concern for the first harvest or two, because initial crops were generally small and used almost solely for seed and feed.

But by 1884—the year the council gave its blessing to the farmers' union marketing scheme—the more settled parts of the municipality were beginning to produce healthy surpluses. A newspaper report noted in May that Thomas Nichol, newly arrived resident overseer of Souris City, had profited handsomely from the sale of 70,000 bushels of grain, and that he stood to do even better "on the balance of his large holdings".[21] A marked increase over 1883 in the acreage of cultivated land and the "surprising . . . number of top buggies that flourish in the vicinity" were signs of the district's material progress. Appropriately, a load of "thirty-to-the-acre" wheat grown on W. S. Foster's farm (SE 3.7.17) was the first teamed to Brandon that fall.[22]

Still staggering from a poor harvest the previous year and inclined to pessimism by "the present political situation", Rounthwaite district farmers did comparatively little breaking of land during the first six months of 1884. Continuous dry weather strengthened their resolve to "wait and see"—but "genial" June rains "changed the aspect of affairs . . . very materially, giving a healthy appearance to the crops and a still more healthy tone to the feelings of the settlers who can once again look forward to the future".[23] As a result the crops were "looking magnificent" at Rounthwaite towards the end of August and, in due course, a number of farmers there were able to boast of remarkably good yields.[24]

Such successes made it clear that Oakland contained some of the finest grain fields in the province; and settlers "whose energy and perseverance have not been checked by the hardships of Manitoba, but who are still hopeful of making this country what it should be—the granary of the world".[25]

The following statistics as at December, 1884, spoke for themselves:[26]

Township	Estimated Crop Acreage	Number of Inhabitants	Number of Ratepayers	Number of Schools
7.17	6,107	151	57	1
7.18	4,290	129	59	1
7.19	1,408	88	40	2
8.17	3,091	145	67	2
8.18	3,042	299	67	2
8.19	2,350	130	61	1
Totals	20,288	942	351	9

A year later the total estimated crop acreage had increased to 29,757 acres, which (multiplied by an average yield of twenty bushels, less odd thousands needed for local purposes) meant about half a million bushels for export. "I question, Mr. Editor, if any other municipality can give such a good showing", a proud Oakland resident wrote The Brandon Sun with regard to this projected surplus.[27]

Threshing costs were another variable to be considered, and allowances had to be made for the risk of inefficient trip after trip over rough trails to a fickle market. Accordingly, although Oakland took impressive strides forward during the first half-decade of settlement, the feeling grew that it would be folly to gamble on expanding operations until steel tracks brought elevators closer than Brandon.

Fortunately the reeve for two or three terms from January, 1885, was James Hector, a man determined to improve the precarious economic position. It was a triumphant day for the ratepayers when his persistence eventually paid off.

Reeve Hector was not alone in tackling the problem of insufficient branch railroad lines. Municipal councils were unofficially held responsible for courting railroad construction within their judicial boundaries and Oakland's was no exception. In fact, the election for reeve in January, 1884, may have, so to speak, turned on a roundhouse.

According to a post-election analysis, the leading candidate for chief magistrate had been Richard Kinley of Souris City, "one of the strongest men in the municipality". But those who considered the incumbent reeve, Samuel Rounthwaite's brother-in-law, Robert Dobson, "safer on the railway question" are said to have nominated George Stewart of Stratherne to split the vote. This explanation, although impossible to verify, seems at least plausible. Kinley was involved about that time in plans to build a branch line from Brandon via Millford to the Crystal City-Pilot Mound area of the province.

Perhaps farmers in the western two-thirds of the municipality foresaw a neglect of their welfare in the process?

If putting forward Stewart's name was a stratagem, it worked well. Dobson virtually swept townships 7 & 8.18 and 7 & 8.19. Meanwhile some ninety percent of the votes cast in Township 8.17 were in Stewart's favour.[28]

Candidate	Total	7.17	7.18	7.19	8.17	8.18	8.19
Dobson	70	—	8	9	1	37	15
Kinley	50	39	8	—	3	—	—
Stewart	43	9	—	—	34	—	—

If not the deciding factor, the "railroad question" almost certainly had a bearing on the reeve's re-election. By then the lack of branch lines had become a major political problem in Manitoba. It was in 1884 that one member of the provincial legislature went so far as to move that the Dominion government be asked to postpone construction of the Rocky Mountain section of the C.P.R. until sufficient C.P.R. branch lines had been built in southwestern Manitoba.[29]

The same year Thomas Nichol of Souris City, presumably on behalf of "The Toronto Company", offered to supply the necessary rails, if the municipalities of Cornwallis and Oakland would do the grading for a railway from Brandon to Souris City. Mr. Nichol's offer was not accepted.

Illustrating the panic that growing grain surpluses were beginning to cause, was Whitewater municipality's scheme to relieve the farmers in that area of the burden of teaming grain to the C.P.R. main line. Their proposal called for an apparatus consisting of a thirty-mile-long rope conveyor belt mounted on A-shaped poles one hundred yards apart.[30] Suspended from the rope at regular intervals would be hoppers and there was to be an engine at each end of the line: one to draw full hoppers to the elevator, the other to return emptied hoppers to Whitewater. Estimated cost of construction was $1,000 a mile; a similar one was then operating across the Elbe River in Germany. The "rope road" idea was short-lived, but sparked interest at the time.

A rope road was also mooted briefly at Plum Creek in Glenwood municipality. There, in addition to wishing for better marketing conditions, the settlers were worried that the surrounding supply of wood would soon be exhausted. What would they do for fuel unless a branch line were built to furnish the district with coal from the area of the present Bienfait, Saskatchewan?[31]

Thus, depending upon the shifting winds of local self-interest, Oakland found itself alternately co-operating and competing with neighbouring municipalities to find a way out of the marketing dilemma. When and where branch lines would be built had become a major question.

The hub of the trading area naturally played the politics of these steel "spokes", too. When, on January 21, 1884, James Hartney of Plum Creek asked the Brandon council to endorse the promotion of a line connecting Brandon and Plum Creek with the Souris coal fields farther southwest, this was one alderman's reaction:

> If farmers out there could be made to work and do their trading with us; it would be better to keep down railways; but that could not be done . . . [Any way] Plum Creek would never be a large place, and Brandon would have the principal trade.[32]

By the same token, Brandon was less enthusiastic about a branch line project that promised to be much more beneficial to Oakland than the "coal fields branch". This was the proposed extension of the former Manitoba South Western Colonization Railway[33] to Millford, Souris City, and Plum Creek. In 1882 the C.P.R. took over management of the bankrupt Manitoba South Western (which had only been able to lay track from Winnipeg to Elm Creek, Manitoba) and South Cypress, Oakland, and Glenwood were among the municipalities hoping to profit from the transaction. But "The Wheat City" was loath to lose its nickname. Although "there is no doubt that remunerative traffic would be supplied from the outset", The Sun warned that it would be preferable if the districts south of Brandon were served by railroads running out of Brandon.[34]

Of the municipalities in the country immediately south of Brandon, Glenwood appears to have been in the best position to get a branch railroad. Having been colonized by Squire W. H. Sowden, an influential Tory, at a time when Tory governments were in power in both Winnipeg and Ottawa, Glenwood presumably had some means of seeing that its ambitions came to the attention of the appropriate C.P.R. authorities. Besides, even if Brandon threw its political weight against the proposed extension of the Manitoba South Western, Glenwood could be sure it would benefit from the C.P.R. branch line to the coal fields.

Brandon's objections and Glenwood's apparent advantage did not, however, deter Oakland and South Cypress from pressing their respective cases.

Anxious lest Oakland's good grain-growing cards be lost in a political shuffle, Reeve Hector took the initiative in calling "one of the most enthusiastic meetings ever held in the municipality" late in November, 1885, at Chesley School.[35] After the reeve relayed the "latest news" that the C.P.R. was in the process of deciding whether to extend the "old Manitoba South Western" either to Plum Creek or south of the Tiger Hills across Lang's Valley, a number of prominent ratepayers expressed their agreement with the reeve that Oakland was, indeed, at a "parting of the ways".

Oakland must present a forceful brief to the railroad company in order to make sure that the extension was to Plum Creek and not south of the hills, the ratepayers contended. "We must have it, they said, or there was no telling what the result might be". Reeve Hector and Francis J. Clark (N 10.7.19) were consequently delegated to interview the C.P.R. authorities with a view to persuading them that the Manitoba South Western should run through Township 7 to Plum Creek.

But the mission was in vain. Hector and Clark reported to a ratepayers' meeting in about ten days' time[36] that they had been given "no definite information".

Indeed, straight answers from the C.P.R. became rarer and rarer as the Manitoba South Western slowly neared Oakland. Its western terminus was Holland one year; Treherne the next. And always the sparks from the farthest west locomotive started prairie fire rumours in districts just a little farther west.

Hopes were stirred in Oakland in June, 1886, for insance, when Dick Kinley sighted engineers in the Souris City district "trying to locate the route of the extension of the C.P.R. southwestern . . ."[37]

The next month The Brandon Sun reported the C.P.R.'s famous engineer, W. C. Van Horne, as having said that the much-discussed branch line would never cross the Souris River in the Brandon area.

Contradicting this immediately, Thomas Nichol, of Souris City, claimed the route west of Glenboro had not yet been determined. The Brandon press was simply fabricating news to discourage promotion of branch railroads that did not terminate in Brandon.

The scramble to secure the services of the Manitoba South Western was part of a broader political struggle, namely the knock-down, drag-out disallowance debate. Disallowance—the repeated Dominion veto of Manitoba railway charters on the pretext that they interfered with the C.P.R. "monopoly clause"—was the running sore of Winnipeg-Ottawa relations in the 1880's. Moreover, Manitoba Premier Norquay's manner of dealing with the problem was equivocal. Seemingly torn between loyalty to Sir John A. Macdonald's National Policy and obligations to the population of Manitoba, Norquay did justice to neither.[38]

A number of Manitoba Tories joined in the struggle against the federal government over the disallowance question in January, 1887, a spokesman for the Conservative Anti-Disallowance Association (of Manitoba) gave this view of the C.P.R. monopoly:

The Company received from the Canadian people:

Completed road, costing	$35,525,444
Cash subsidy	35,000,000
From sale of lands (cash)	12,000,000
Municipal bonuses	370,000
Total	$82,895,444

and have land remaining to the extent of more than 13,000,000 acres which, if sold at an average price of $1.25 per acre, would make the total gift to the Company upwards of $100,000,000.

The company claims that the right of way, construction and equipment of the road cost them less than $80,000,000, and the administration of the land grant some $300,000; so that the company gets a road which practically costs them nothing, and a bonus of $20,000,000 for building it. The land grant was originally proposed as a means of recouping the losses it was estimated would occur on traffic, but as no losses have occurred, it may be considered as a bonus. Now, what do we get for our generosity? Excessive freight and passenger tariffs! . . . But somebody benefits.

The spokesman also commented on a despatch from San Francisco which stated that a cut had been made in the price of railroad passenger fares from San Francisco to New York as a result of the C.P.R.'s having bid to supply first-class transportation between those two cities for $50 a ticket:

170

That is to say, we have bonused the C.P.R. to the extent of $100,000,000 to enable them to carry American travel from San Francisco to New York for $2.85 more than they charge for taking a Winnipegger to Montreal, and $29.50 less than they will charge for taking him to Victoria, B.C.? . . . To think that this state of things must endure for the next fifteen years under the monopoly clause of the C.P.R. contract would be intolerable . . .[39]

Manitobans in increasing numbers agreed with the aims of the Anti-Disallowance Association. In October, 1887, the Oakland council stood up to be counted on the disallowance matter by fully endorsing and supporting the association's constitution, and by publicly stating its belief that "the agitation at present existing in Winnipeg regarding the disallowance extends throughout the rural portions of the province".[40]

The council's disallowance resolution was only one manifestation of the rising tide of opposition to Premier Norquay's government. Thomas Greenway of Crystal City, leader of the Liberal opposition in the Manitoba legislative assembly, capitalized on this widespread frustration. Many of the planks of Greenway's platform were, in fact, reworked slogans of the Manitoba and North West Farmers' Co-operative and Protective Union. This was not surprising as the liberal, if not Grit, bias of the union had been one of its distinguishing characteristics. The union had collapsed amid charges of extremism, but Greenway's party flourished—mainly, perhaps, by letting it be known that, if elected, it would build railways in defiance of the C.P.R. monopoly.[41]

The eastern half of Oakland was one of the strongest areas of Greenway Liberalism in the province. There the memories of the farmers' union movement were still strong, and the demand for a railroad was particularly urgent in view of the grain trade. This had been clear during Reeve Hector's campaign for the Manitoba South Western; and was again extremely evident in the provincial election of December, 1886.

171

Earlier that year, touring Western Canada, Sir John A. Macdonald put his foot in his mouth in the lion's den when he told a crowd at the Brandon station:

Rome was not built in a day, neither was Brandon, neither are the railways . . . Every man can't have a railway at his door, nor every township have one . . . you must be ready to put your hands in your pockets.[42]

At the Brandon roller rink later the same day, August 20, 1886, Sir John A. revealed the true colours of his "Rome was not built in a day" address by admitting that he would be "greatly disappointed, grieved and mortified" if the railway question should adversely affect his Tory party candidates' chances at the polls.

From the Oakland returns of the December provincial election, it would appear that the settlers in townships 7 and 8.17 and 7 and 8.18 heeded Sir John's advice at the station, but ignored what he had to say at the roller rink. They put their hands in their pockets, all right—to help finance the local Grit candidate, J. W. Sifton.[43]

Township		J. W. Sifton	J. N. Kirkhoffer
7.17		19	16
8.17		35	16
7.18		24	18
8.18		21	16
7.19		10	24
8.19		17	25
Totals		126	115

Kirkhoffer lost Oakland, but he won the riding as a whole by the small margin of fourteen votes. The Tory majority in the legislature was, however, substantially reduced.

With power apparently within reach as a result of the 1886 election, Greenway's followers continued building and mending political fences. Meanwhile, Premier Norquay tried in vain to recapture public confidence by commencing construction of a railroad from Winnipeg, south along the

172

James Smart

H. C. Graham

Thomas Greenway

west bank of the Red River to the American border. Although this official defiance of the C.P.R. monopoly was a significant departure in policy, it did not win the respect of other areas of the province which badly needed marketing facilities and which felt the premier could no longer be trusted on the branch line question.

Increasing the political tension was the famous bumper crop of 1887. That season one could "believe almost any crop story that may be told you", claimed The Brandon Sun.[44] Among the Oakland farmers who had large surpluses for export in 1887 were James Bremner (20,000 bushels), James McFadden and Thomas Nichol (18,000 bushels each) and Jabez Elliott (14,000 bushels)—all in the Souris City district. The Millford district also reported a large harvest that required "grace, grit, and greenbacks" to market. There, too, railways were badly needed, and the crop of 1887 undoubtedly convinced many hitherto undecided farmers to seek political help from Grits or "Greenwaybackers".[45]

It seems it was the combination of Greenway's rising expectations and the bumper crop which in September, 1887, convinced the C.P.R. to lower its freight rates to twenty-five cents per hundredweight from thirty cents. Like Norquay's stopgap Red River Valley Railway gamble, however, this belated freight reduction came too late to rescue the monopoly privilege.

The excitement of provincial public affairs towards the end of the 1880's seems to have had a corresponding impact on municipal politics. At least this would appear to be a reasonable interpretation of the "Oakland Wants to Know" controversy late in 1887.

The first one reads of the controversy is in The Brandon Sun of November 12, 1887, where, under the title "Oakland Wants to Know", is printed the following letter from Dr. H. Aubrey Husband of the Souris City district:

Sir — In a local contemporary [Brandon Times] under the above title, I have read a guarded letter in which the writer states that since the foundation

174

of the municipality there has been no statement as to the amount of interest received on arrears of taxes collected. An attempt was made this year to publish for the first time the accounts of the municipality, and of this attempt we have been favoured with three editions, each as misleading and incomprehensible as the first, only more so. The clerk seems to have a method of bookkeeping peculiar to himself, for we find assets and liabilities so exquisitely mixed up as to render all attempts [at understanding them] almost impossible.

There is a general feeling in the municipality that a public meeting should at once be called, not a hole and corner affair, but one fully advertised throughout the district, so as to give the electors time to carefully weigh the important issues at stake before the day of the [municipal] nominations; for if one half of the statements made in the letter of the correspondent to whom I have alluded are true, a most disgraceful state of things exists in the municipality, which is incumbent on those implicated to at once explain.

Replying about a month later, the Oakland secretary-treasurer, W. S. Moody, Rounthwaite, stated that Dr. Husband's letter and the previous anonymous one in the Brandon Times had been "mere maresnests" — simply the municipal "election gimmick of a gentleman who hasn't the character to run on his own merits".[46]

Moody went on to identify the spineless office-seeker as Thomas Nichol, of Souris City, who, he claimed, had at the December 6 council nomination meeting in Chesley School owned up to having started the controversy. At this meeting Nichol had unsuccessfully attempted to explain his charges to a "weary and patient audience" by means of a "blackboard and chalk", Moody stated:

Many think him a poor speaker but no doubt he's a poor calculator, because after an hour, the assembled voters came to the conclusion that Mr. Nichol knew no more about the deficit than they

175

themselves did and . . . doubted the existence of such a thing as a deficit altogether . . . [Nichol] could not show it, nor could he trace it. The slippery figures under his hands were always adding up to something quite different from what he had intended.

Moody further stated that he was worried lest Nichol's slanderous attack had shaken public confidence in the municipality, because "once shaken" it would be "exceedingly difficult to re-establish".[46]

It would appear Moody was not too far off the mark in suggesting that the controversy had a distinct "election gimmick" ring. Nichol successfully sought the position of Oakland reeve in the forthcoming municipal election. The fact that the provincial political fight was reaching a peak at the time probably accounted for the vigor of the dispute, however, since Moody was secretary-treasurer of the Oakland Conservative Association, whereas Nichol and Dr. Husband both strongly supported Greenway.

The climax of the push to topple Norquay's government came in 1888. Norquay himself had been obliged to tender his resignation in the wake of scandal; and it was not long before the successor was forced by an ever-harder-hitting opposition to appeal to the electorate. Seizing their opportunity, Oakland Grits rallied behind the banner of unanimously nominated H. C. Graham of Hayfield. The target was to defeat J. N. Kirkhoffer, the Plum Creek resident who had barely managed to win the seat in December, 1886.

Making no bones about its choice, The Brandon Sun warned that Kirkhoffer supported the Tory party that had "crowded this province out of its natural position for years, materially retarded its growth, and done everything possible toward its injury".[47] In contrast, the newspaper hailed Graham as a true representative of the people. Unlike the politicians "of the office seeking kind" with their "flighty pretensions", the newspaper said, Graham's "only ambition" was to serve his constituents "honestly and independently".

Graham, needless to say, did not beg to differ with The Sun's analysis of his character. In an open letter to the "Free and Independent Voters of South Brandon", which was printed and reprinted several times in The Sun of May, 1888, Graham pointed out that he was a farmer "in one of the most important districts in a predominantly farming province". Being a tiller of the soil enabled him to sympathize with the current demand "for adequate railroad facilities and reduced freight rates". He said that consequently he would promote "every legitimate railway enterprise".

The election of a Greenway government was necessary if Manitoba citizens were to get value for their tax dollars for a change, Graham's advertisement continued. With Greenway at the helm "rigid economy shall characterize every department in the administration of our affairs", in striking contrast to the "lavish and indefensible extravagance" and "extreme recklessness" of the Tory governments that had previously controlled the destiny of the province. It emphasized that Graham felt obliged to have the "present excessive school rates materially reduced, and the burden of taxation with its unfair mode of distribution relieved as far as possible and equitably adjusted". Above all, it maintained, as a member of a Greenway government, Graham would do everything in his power to put Manitoba's welfare first.

The election was in July, 1888, and Graham's defeat of Kirkhoffer was representative of the fate that befell the majority of Tory candidates elsewhere in the province. Indicating Greenway's rapid gain in popularity since the previous election, moreover, Graham did much better in Oakland than had J. W. Sifton in December, 1886.[48]

Township		H. C. Graham	J. N. Kirkhoffer
7.17	....	31	15
7.18	....	20	24
7.19	....	23	24
8.17	....	36	31
8.18	....	21	15
8.19	....	22	17
Totals	....	153	126

Whoop

Cock-a-doodle-Doo!

Worse than a CYCLONE !

UP SHE GOES.

The Sweep a Clean one !

Since Hanna Died !

The Government sustained by
an overwhelming Majority.

The Opposition not more than
six at best.

Norquay and his Party Snowed
away under.

The Three Brandons pronounced
for Provincial Rights.

The result of the
the province was a

DISASTER
Hon. Thos. Green
Hon. J. Martin. P.
Finlay Young. Kil
Wm. Winram. Ms
Alex. Lawrence. W
Thos. Smith. Spri
C. J. Mickle. Birth
R. P. Roblin. Deff
F. W. Colcleugh,
A. F Martin. Mor
All supporters of t
NORTH WINNIPEG
(govt). Maj. 460.
Golden, lost his dep
BRANDON CITY—H
govt). Maj. 62.
CENTRE WINNIPEG
Millan (govt). Maj.
Mr. Gilroy, lost his
SOUTH WINNIPEG—
beil govt). Maj. 2
SOURIS—Mr. A.
Maj—
TURTLE MOUNT.
govt. Maj.—
KILDONAN—Hon.
Maj. 2
ROCKWOOD—S. J.
36.
LAKESIDE—Kenne
maj 75.
BEAUTIFUL PLAIN
(govt) maj 17.
NORFOLK—S. J. T
—2.
DENNIS—D. McLe
LANSDOWNE—E
111.
NORTH BRANDO
govt) maj 42.
SOUTH BRANDON—
maj. 16.
ROSENFELT.—E
maj. 48.
EMERSON—Jas.
maj. 12.
LORNE—R. O. Ma
ST. BONIFACE—R.
6
CYPRESS—E. Woo
tween Burnett and
MINNEDOSA—J. S.
The Liberal vote
Hean and Myers.
WOODLANDS. Hon
(Government) 57 in
hear from.

LAT

special to the SUN

Full returns have
from Carillon, Cartier
Turtle Mountain or
the results show that
have been elected in c
sums up the result as f
Government 32

Although Graham's 18-vote majority over the constituency as a whole was not in striking contrast to Kirkhoffer's 14-vote margin of the previous election, The Sun interpreted the victory as a "most exciting" one for the Liberal cause. Graham, "an ordinary every day farmer" fought the "battle against odds", said the newspaper— especially considering that Kirkhoffer considered the constituency "as being a pocket borough for himself". But Graham was "determined to win", and win he did "with both hands down!"

In addition, the Greenway triumph, and the success of Graham in particular, turned out to be a turning point in Oakland's history .It was not without significance that by then, ex-reeve James Hector had been Graham's campaign manager, because before long the new Grit government had negotiated the abrogation of the C.P.R. "monopoly clause". Soon, too, the Brandon-Morris branch of the American-based Northern Pacific and Manitoba Railway was completed. And on August 1, 1889, the settlers in the eastern half of the municipality threw a huge picnic at Souris City to celebrate the fact that at last they were to be seviced by a railroad.

Picnics had been held in the Souris City district from the earliest days of settlement.[49] But the picnic held there that August 1, was something the like of which the settlers had never seen before, and which Oakland has not seen since. Indeed, it was hailed as the best picnic that Manitoba had ever seen prior to that time; and from contemporary Brandon Sun accounts, it would even seem that statement may not have been an exaggeration.

"The people of Souris City are only expressing a natural gratitude in holding a railway picnic today", explained the newspaper in an editorial of that date:

> There is no event that can be suggested in which all classes can join with more sincere sympathy and cordial enthusiasm than this securing of transportation facilities. Their inability to get them sooner will create a just appreciation of them now . . .
> The satisfaction of the Souris City people in being

able to deliver their crops with a reasonable haul, will only be intensified when they recollect the struggle and effort expended in securing the advantage. Had they and their friends not joined in a fierce and sustained struggle against a combination of forces and great odds, they would have less occasion to appreciate the signal of victory they have achieved, and which they will joyously celebrate. They will recollect how in the early days of this province the Dominion government, doubtless at the instance of the C.P.R., made a violent attack upon our rights and liberties. An attempt was made to rob us of our rights. What was accorded us under the distinct provisions of the British North America Act Sir John and his friends sought to rob us of.

This act of grand larceny was successfully committed year after year . . . Men revolted at the thought that a whole province could be pillaged for the benefit of a powerful corporation . . . A Moses in Mr. Greenway was found to lead the people up out of the galling bondage that a paternal government at Ottawa had imposed . . .[50]

It is in reading the next edition of The Sun, however, that the present citizens of Oakland may fully realize what the Souris City picnic meant to those who laid the foundations of the municipality.[51] For even Brandonites had their eyes opened when they piled into their rigs and followed the trail southwest, around the beautiful hills after which their city was named, and continued on among some of the cream of the crops on which the prosperous development of the country depended.

As they passed "wheat field after wheat field" on their way to the picnic, they discovered that rumours of drought damage in the area had been false. "Instead of a poor dilapidated condition, with carrion filling the air", they found the crops that August "as good as in the very best years"; and that their interest was "all the time increasing", as "the great wealth of the country, as mile after mile were passed, showed to greater and greater advantage". Until finally they reached the lovely "grove" at

180

Ode to the Elevator at Rounthwaite

So the die at length is cast,
And monopoly is past,
And an elevator vast
    Beating time
Towers aloft to reach the cloud
And the voices of the crowd
Led by Yankees slick and loud
    Sound sublime.

And the foreman, with his square,
Moving here and moving there
Keeps a sharp eye everywhere
    On the men;
For he knows there's not a man,
Since the universe began
But will shirk it if he can
    Now and then.

There's a tea pot with a spout
Which he always takes about—
It would hold a quart of stout,
    At a guess;
And frequently it goes
To his mouth; and like a rose
Is the colour of his nose
    More or less.

When the elevator's done
Lots of beer and lots of fun
The Yankee "takes the bun"
    For a spree!
When all his cash is spent
This enterprising gent
Is perfectly content
    Up a tree.

Mr. Martin and his crew
Who have put the building through—
Most likely with a view
    To buy wheat—
Great promptitude displayed
(As the Brandon papers said)
And deserve a serenade
    For a treat.

When the winter is no more
We can start a rifle corps;
See us marching to the stare
        From the farms.
And each hardy volunteer
Feels the exercise severe
When the order echoes clear,
        "Shoulder arms!"

Halt recover—form to line
Hold your head up number nine!
Number three you're doing fine—
        Steady there!
Turn your beetle crushers on!—
By your right! you clumsy lout—
What the devil are you about?
        As you were!

And when the wheat is sold
And we've pocketed the gold;
We can gather to the fold
        Once a week.
How delightful it will be!
The symphony in C—
Or any other key,
        So to speak!

There are flutes and whistles, too,
In the window of the Jew
And I think he'll sell a few
        Cheap for cash.
So we'll work the loamy land,
We've a market right at hand
And we'll knock the Brandon band
        All to smash.

                    S. B. Flower
                    The Brandon Sun
                    January 9, 1890.

A Plea

Sweet Rounthwaite, loveliest spot upon the plain,
Soon to be rattled by the railway train,
Still stands supreme for raising perfect wheat
Razor-backed hogs and cattle hard to beat.
"Smart place," the immigrant observes, "is this!
To settle here, indeed, were scrumptious bliss.
Mark how those hills reflect the sunset glow;—
There's nothing like it in Ontario,—
And note that rivulet a glittering streak,
Which the old moss backs here have named 'Spring Creek'
This is the spot, sir, for a future town:
We'll buy our land, and here settle down."
So speaks the immigrant who knows what's what
And marks the beauties of this fruitful spot.

But now the N.P.R. has hove in view,
And cuts the good old settlement in two;
And lands look up and speculators frown,
And in the heart of Rounthwaite springs a town.

A town, by thunder! twang the glorious lyre!
And play the organ, farmers, till you tire!
Ring out the bells and strike the wild guitar!
We'll have an elevator and a bar.
Long time ago, the farmers drew their grain
Some fifty miles, and then returned again.
Expenses took all profits from the load,
But still the trip was doubtless of some good.
They met their friends and talked of prices slack,
And left their wheat but brought a bottle back.

Now times are changed. No more with weary feet
We trudge to Brandon with a load of wheat;
No more we travel at the ox's tail
We find it pleasanter to go by rail;
And our young town shall rival Brandon's fame,
And everything's perfect but the name.
"Naughton we'll call it! Naughton it shall be!"
Remarked the man who works the great N.P.
Let it not be so! Hear, ye magnates; hear!
Spurn not so ruthlessly remembrance dear.
The town should take it's nomen from the place;
Grant us, ye rulers of the road, this grace!
'Tis a small boon not meriting a frown—
We made the place, then let us name the town.
Let it be Rounthwaite as it was lang syne;
And the next station, higher up the line,
Can be Naughton, since it has no name,
And the result to all intents the same,
Despise not this petition, well begun
In the fair columns of THE BDN. SUN.

The Brandon Sun
December 5, 1889.

Souris City, where people from twenty, thirty, and forty miles away were gathering "to picnic and hear speakers".

An estimated 2,000 settlers were on hand for the grand event and, after a "well-arranged program of sports", they settled back to enjoy the speeches.

There could be no doubt why the crowd had assembled. At the entrance ot the "grove" hung "suitable mottoes", one declaring, "RAILWAY COMPETITION HAS COME". Forming a colourful background to the speakers' platform was a large swathe of bunting, bearing the words, "GOOD-BYE MONOPOLY". And above this were featured pictures of the Northern Pacific's "Engine No. 1" and of a Northern Pacific coach.

Reeve Nichol launched the torrents of stately words in a brief speech which stressed the importance of the railroad to the municipality.

Next on his feet was popular ex-reeve Hector, a fitting choice to read the following welcome to a very special guest:

> The people of the Souris City district most heartily join in extending to you a very cordial welcome on this occasion. Your presence, and that of your colleagues, with us today, enhances very greatly the gratification we all experience in celebrating the advent in our midst of the Northern Pacific and Manitoba Railway.

The guest of honour was none other than the premier himself, Hon. Thomas Greenway, the bearded symbol of everything that the picnic had been organized to applaud. Was he smiling, or did he remain stern, as Hector continued:

> We need not point out to you, who are one of the pioneers in this great country the disabilities and difficulties encountered by those at a distance from a shipping point. The people of this district have found by sad experience the necessity of having satisfactory transportation facilities, in order to enjoy aright the fruits of their labor.

185

The political hero's attention next was drawn to the "scenery of rare beauty" and the "soil of extraordinary fertility" of the district. It was hoped he recognized the "industry, perseverence and confidence in the country" that the Souris City district settlers had shown when there had not been a railroad nearby.

Now that the district was to benefit from the Northern Pacific, the farmers there would save an average of ten to fifteen cents per bushel on haulage alone. "This factor alone will mean a clear annual gain of many thousands of dollars to the district". Thus, Hector stressed:

> We desire to recognize and acknowledge the obligations to yourself and your colleagues under which we, in common with the rest of the country, have been placed for your patriotic defence of the rights of this province, for your heroic and sustained efforts in contending with those who sought to defeat our wishes and to fasten upon us more firmly the shackle that monopoly and tyranny had forged, and for the brilliant victories you have achieved on our behalf.

> We remember that powerful combinations were united in opposing you and that no means were too unscrupulous to compass your defeat. We have been made unwilling witnesses of the malicious assaults upon you by calumniators and slanderers, and have been gratified with the complete vindication that time and the logic of facts have brought.

Finally, after again thanking the premier and his colleagues for having delivered Oakland and particularly the Souris City district "from the thraldom of disallowance and monopoly", the ex-reeve expressed the hope that the members of the new Liberal government would "live long to enjoy the distinction and honor" they had acquired for their "patriotic devotion and brilliant success in defending, securing and promoting the highest interests of our beloved province".

In reply to the address of welcome, Mr. Greenway paid tribute to the district, and said he wished it could be used as an example to show the "eastern croakers" that, unlike Ontario, Manitoba was going to have a fine harvest this season. He noted the refreshing effect that railroad competition had had upon Manitoba's agricultural prospects. He reviewed his government's policies, spoke by way of contrast of the degenerate record of the previous government, and emphasized that he was not talking politics, but rather philosophies of public administration. In fact, there were few topics of Manitoba public life to which the premier did not refer in the nearly one and a half hours before he "took his seat amid cheers".

Next to speak was Hon. James Smart of Brandon, Greenway's minister of public works. In a speech which was the new government's official mention of what was to become known as the Manitoba School Question, Mr. Smart proposed to speak some "common sense'" about the provincial system of education.

He did not wish "to be speaking disparagingly of Roman Catholics by speech or inference—they were entitled to their rights as any other people and he would defend them as energetically as he would those of Protestants". Nevertheless, the maintenance of separate school administrations, one Protestant and one Catholic, as had been the case since the formation of the province, was too expensive. Since the "cost of this was borne by the people" . . . he believed but one system should exist. (HEAR, HEAR.)"

After tracing some of the financial injustices that he thought were being wrought on Manitoba Protestants by special considerations that had in the past been given to Roman Catholic school boards in the province, Mr. Smart stated that the government realized that the amalgamation of the two systems "might be very unwise from a political standpoint". However, the government felt reform was "in the interests of the people of Manitoba", so it had conscientiously determined to "let the chips fall where they may".

When Mr. Smart took his seat, it was the turn of South Brandon's member of the legislature, Herbert Graham. Mr.

Graham congratulated the organizers of the picnic, and commented upon how nice it had been to hear the political questions of the day "discussed from the fountainhead". He rehashed the railroad question, underlining how fortunate Oakland was that the Greenway government had assumed power. Before concluding with the comment that his "only desire" was to serve his constituents "in an honest manner and to the best of my ability", he made the following predictions:

> I believe our darkest days are over; I believe that we have a grand future before us, and that our course will be a rapid one and afterward one of progress; I believe you have all the elements of success here now, I believe the crossing of the Souris will be the best place in the Morris and Brandon line. You will start with a thriving village, which will grow in importance until it will be no small rival to that place up here [gesturing] behind the hills called Brandon.

Some predictions seem made to be proved false, and Mr. Graham was wrong about Wawanesa, the modern-day Souris City that was founded about three miles downstream from "The Toronto Company's" flats, during the winter of 1889-90. But he was right about what the coming of the railroad would mean to Oakland's' future.

Thus the "monster" Souris City picnic was much more than raisin buns and "cinnamon rolls, curled up like snail shells" or doughnuts and cookies or "lettuce cut up in sour cream, mustard and sugar". It signalled the end of the settlement days for a picturesque and productive Manitoba municipality.

REFERENCES:
1. MacKintosh, W. A., 1934, Prairie Settlement, The Geographical Setting, Vol. I, p. 95. Toronto.
2. The Brandon Sun, February 2, 1884.
3. Warner, D. F., 1960, The Idea of Continental Union, p. 175. University of Kentucky.

4. Ibid., pp. 171-172.
5. Ibid.
6. McClung, N., 1964, Clearing in the West, p. 183. Toronto.
7. Hill, R. B., 1890, Manitoba: History of Its Early Settlement, Development and Resources, p. 487. Toronto.
8. The Brandon Sun, April 7, 1885.
9. Ibid., June 13, 1889.
10. Coleman, M., 1957, The Face of Yesterday, p. 58. Brandon.
11. The Brandon Sun, April 9, 1885.
12. Fred H. Carroll of Flin Flon, Manitoba, in a letter to Mrs. M. E. Franklin of Carroll, March 13, 1957.
13. The Brandon Sun, April 2, 1885.
14. The Brandon Sun, March 28, 1885.
15. Coleman, M., op. cit., p. 47.
16. Fred H. Carroll to Mrs. M. E. Franklin, op. cit.
17. McClung, N., op. cit., p. 190. In her book, The Mere Living (1957, p. 58, Altona, Man.), Mrs. H. M. Parkinson of Hartney, Man., states that the mood of the normally docile Sioux bands changed during the rebellion. She states that, with the Cree fighting farther west, the Sioux, too, grew restless, tended to become insolent, and occasionally slashed at settlers' horses with whips.
18. The Brandon Sun, August 12, 1886.
19. MacKintosh, W. A., op. cit., p. 95.
20. The Brandon Sun, April 23, 1885.
21. Ibid., May 24, 1884.
22. Ibid., September 4, 1884.
23. Ibid., June 26, 1884.
24. Ibid., August 28, 1884 and October 9, 1884.
25. Ibid., December 24, 1885.
26. Ibid.
27. Ibid., November 26, 1885.
28. Ibid., January 9, 1884.
29. Ibid., June 5, 1884.
30. Ibid., August 28, 1884.
31. Ibid., May 5, 1884.
32. Ibid., January 22, 1884.
33. This railway was chartered by the Manitoba government in 1879, prior to the C.P.R. monopoly clause.
34. The Brandon Sun, April 8, 1886.
35. Ibid., November 26, 1885.
36. Ibid., December 23, 1885
37. Ibid., June 17, 1886.
38. According to D. F. Warner, op. cit., p. 170, Sir John A. Macdonald tried to "buy off" Norquay without remedying Manitoba's political grievances.
39. Robertson, F. B., 1887, Railway Monopoly, p. 8. Winnipeg.
40. The Brandon Sun, October 13, 1887.
41. Holmes, J. L., 1936, Factors Affecting Politics in Manitoba: A Study of the Provincial Elections, 1870-1899, p. 68, published M.A. Thesis at the University of Manitoba.
42. The Brandon Sun, August 26, 1886.
43. Ibid., December 3, 1886.
44. Ibid., September 8, 1887.
45. Ibid., January 5, 1888.
46. Ibid., December 22, 1887.
47. Ibid., June 28, 1888.
48. Ibid., July 12, 1888.
49. Saunderson, H. H., 1951, Some Pioneer Townsites Along the Souris River, p. 26, unpublished manuscript in the Public Archives of Manitoba, Winnipeg.
50. The Brandon Sun, August 1, 1889.
51. Ibid., August 8, 1889.

Rev. J. F. Rounthwaite

Rev. John Frederick Rounthwaite was the son of a Liverpool, England, shipping magnate friend of former British prime minister William Gladstone. His achievements at St. John's College, Cambridge University, included a master of arts degree in mathematics and a rowing trophy. He was an accomplished pianist and violinist, besides having a splendid tenor voice. Before ordination in the Church of England in 1867, he was tutored on the continent.

Humanitarian concern marked his parish work in Lancashire and Chester. Later he served with distinction as headmaster of Witton Grammar School in Norwich. Prior to leaving England he also was school inspector for Manchester and grand master of the Masonic Order for the province of Chester.

Rev. Rounthwaite's health had begun to slip; but, rather than retire, he decided his Christian duty lay on the Canadian frontier. He arrived at the postal settlement of Rounthwaite (named after his brother, Samuel) in 1882. St. John's Church of England building, which he finished, had been started there that year; and he brought with him gifts of money, a stained glass window, and other gifts for the church. The conscientious cleric threw himself into pastoral and educational work in the community, and his sudden death in 1883 was much lamented.

Dr. H. A. Husband

Dr. Henry Aubrey Husband, M.B., C.M., B.Sc., F.R.C.S.E., M.R.C.S.E., was born in Jamaica in 1843. He received his professional education at Edinburgh University, where he later taught. Royalties from medical books written while an instructor at the university helped him settle in the Souris City district in 1885.

The presence of a doctor in the eastern part of Oakland was greatly appreciated. In winter his sleigh and cutter were a familiar sight in the surrounding countryside — even as far south as Pelican Lake.

Fancy carpentry was Dr. Husband's hobby, but his chief interest was the building of a better world. An outspoken advocate of social justice, he reportedly ran afoul of Old Country authorities when he proposed that museums and botanical gardens remain open on Sundays for the benefit of the working classes. While in Manitoba he kept a critical eye on the conduct of public administration. On one occasion, appalled by the Brandon sanitation system, he suggested through the Brandon Sun that "for every five cases of typhoid fever, one of the aldermen, beginning with the mayor and ending with the medical officer of health, should be publically whipped".

In 1905, Dr. Husband returned to Jamaica, where he championed equal opportunities for all, regardless of colour.

T. E. M. Banting

One of Oakland's first big farmers, Thomas Edward Meredith Banting — an uncle of Sir Frederick Banting of insulin fame — moved to the Sourisburg district from Newton Robinson, Ontario, in 1887.

The Sourisbourg district already contained many of his immediate family, including his father, Benjamin, a member of the Anglo-Irish gentry forced to flee Ireland during the great potato famine. So Thomas apparently did not have too much trouble getting settled. When the C.P.R. branch line crossed Oakland in 1892, a siding was laid near his home. The elevator at Banting Siding and the large brick house he had built in the 1890's were among the landmarks of the countryside.

Thomas Banting had a Methodist's determination to prosper and enjoyed doing things in a big way. As they said in the heyday of the big harvesting crews, he was one of those who had "one gang going, one gang coming and one gang working".

An inventive streak was part of his somewhat aristocratic nature. He tried to make economical fuel from a rig that rolled moistened straw into "wood", was one of the first Canadian farmers to experiment with a cement-floored barn, and pioneered the "automatic" method of watering cattle indoors.

"Prof." Alfred Grainger

"Lovely Souris River is the title of a new work for pianoforte and violin by Professor Alfred Grainger of Souris City. The composition will appear next month". This local news item from an 1888 Brandon Sun is one of the rare mentions of the mysterious itinerant music teacher who gave dozens of Oakland children a grounding in music that they would not have had otherwise.

Present residents of the municipality say the eccentric "professor" was tight-lipped about his past. He travelled from farm to farm with his practice piano keyboard in the 1890's; then disappeared, and was not seen again until the 1920's and 1930's, whereupon he suddenly left never to return. He also is remembered as having been "as English as all get out", and for his remark that he had walked "as far as twice around the world and from here to Winnipeg desides".

A visit from the musician often entailed extra chores for the woman of the household. He tended to arrive just in time for a meal, stayed several days to a week, and, before moving on, usually left some article of clothing to be washed and mended before his next visit. At first he gave only piano lessons, but later taught the violin to boys who wanted to play at community dances.

A. L. Kempton

Wagon seats, a hemmorrhoid cure, and honing paste for straight razors were several of the products once manufactured in Wawanesa by Alonzo Fowler Kempton. But the enterprising native of Nova Scotia is best known as the founder of one of Canada's largest and most innovative fire and casualty insurance companies.

The Wawanesa Mutual began in 1896, when twenty district farmers met in Wawanesa, and put up $20 each to launch a company which was prepared to offer low-premium fire insurance on wooden threshing machines. Kempton, whose experience as an insurance salesman had led him to propose the scheme, was elected secretary-treasurer. The farmer directors provided the financial stability that saw the firm through the initial lean years — a link with the past that has been retained. The sleepy village of Wawanesa still boasts the head office, and "The Mutual" continues to recruit officers and directors from the Wawanesa district.

The Wawanesa Mutual's imaginative methods — for instance, an astute decision in 1952 to give old pensioners policy writing positions in the Montreal branch office — may be traced to the flair of its founder. Kempton was fond of whiskey, Turkish cigarettes, oysters, salt cod, automobiles and business sidelines. It is said that he became irrascible as time went on, however, his many acts of generosity have not been forgotten.

Epilogue

Along the Northern Pacific and Manitoba Railway (now a Canadian National Railway branch line) grew up the villages of Wawanesa and Rounthwaite. Also, by 1892, the C.P.R.'s Manitoba South Western branch was finally extended through Oakland. This resulted in the founding of Methven, Nesbitt and Carroll. Since then, Wawanesa became incorporated as a town, thereby legally leaving the municipality. Meanwhile, economic competition killed Methven and this is now slowly curtailing the size and influence of Rounthwaite, Nesbitt and Carroll.

On the other hand, the acreage of improved land in the municipality is more than five times what it was in 1885.[1] Grain production has greatly increased, and some Oakland farm land was recently sold for more than 2,000 times the price of an original acre of homestead land! Moreover, the municipality now boasts all-weather roads to every farmer's gate.

As a result there has developed an enormous admiration for the settlers and for the foundations that they laid.

This legitimate admiration unfortunately is often tinged with nostalgia and one may well inquire of those who refer to Oakland's "glorious pioneers" — Why gild the lily? Why should the early settlers be forever bound and gagged by the emotional hindsight of their descendants?

For instance, two sons of a man named Richard Cory nearly starved to death in a shanty near the mouth of the Souris River ninety winters ago. Why glorify that? Perhaps, on their way from having harvested that crops of oats at High Bluff the preceding fall, they realized that they had forgotten to purchase sufficient provisions at Portage, and had not bothered to retrace their steps. Or perhaps someone familiar with Manitoba winters had warned them to take more supplies, and they ignored the advice.

Surely the point of the story is that the Corys were in the vanguard of a progressive settlement which was determined to develop the fullest potential of what became the Wawanesa district.

Similarly, the obituary of William Fleming, the "first" of Carroll's "first settlers", does not present a balanced enough analysis for the interested modern reader. Quoting in part:

> Of limited schooling he became one of the most widely read and best posted men in the country. His wonderful memory and pungent Irish wit put many a budding theologian and politician to rout. His anecdotes and tales of the past, many of them tinged with Celtic mysticism enraptured many a gathering.

> He was an ardent Conservative and a devout Anglican, one of the founders of the church at Carroll. A man whose Christianity glowed through his daily living, a character pure and unsullied, whose lightest word was as good as any man's bond.

202

And now he has taken the long trail to the sunset towards the land

> "Where falls not hail, nor rain, nor any snow.
> Nor ever wind blows loudly, but it lies
> Deep meadowed, happy, fair with orchard
> lawns,
> And bowery hollows crowned with summer
> sea".

May God in His infinite mercy give him rest. He was a very gallant gentleman whose like we shall not see again.[2]

This is a good attempt at description in the context of the times; but the "pioneer" tends to emerge larger than life, and the obituary implies that those following in his footsteps are moral degenerates. Rivalry between generations is a misleading yardstick with which to measure historical change.

The fairest interpretation of what motivated people to settle Oakland was given by the late William Bertram, of Rounthwaite—one of those who wintered in the municipality in 1879-80—when he wrote in 1932:

> Sometimes a recent arrival conceives the idea of praising the early settlers, and speaks of them as heroes and heroines. They only expose their faulty information regarding the early times and those who took part in them. As for being heroes and heroines, they never were, and never thought they were anything save earnest workers, striving advantageously to make a go of shaping their own lives and making it easier for those who might come after them.[3]

In other words, the significance of Oakland's settlement era has become encrusted, and hence tarnished, with sentimentality.

Present and future generations should appreciate this, but not forget that the municipality was once an almost exclusively Anglo-Saxon community, with proudly transplanted traditions.

Although means of agricultural production and social mores have changed greatly since the 1880's, the basic outlook of the population seems to have remained relatively constant.

It is not yet apparent whether the demands of increasingly technical twentieth century society, and the influence of a number of men and women with other historical backgrounds who now farm in the municipality, will alter basic attitudes.

REFERENCES:
1. Dominion Bureau of Statistics, Agricultural Census for 1961, Ottawa.
2. Souris Plaindealer, August 20, 1941, Souris.
3. Bertram, William, 1932, A Story of The Brandon Hills, pp. 25-26.

Acknowledgements

More than three years have passed since the Oakland council commissioned this written tribute to the men and women who laid the foundations of the municipality. The occasion was the availability of senior government publishing grants for Canadian centennial histories, and the intention was to produce an account that would be readable and historically relevant.

It was felt by the author that such a centennial undertaking should relate local events to the mainstream of Canadian history. As there has been a tendency to romanticize the agricultural pioneering era in Western Canada, the author also believed that Oakland had an opportunity to present a more balanced view of the settlement days — despite almost a total lack of early municipal records and other documents that could have made the task easier. On the other hand, the author was privileged to receive kind co-operation from many interested individuals, and it is a pleasure to acknowledge formally this valuable assistance.

The Oakland council, of course, deserves credit for initiating the project. Unfortunately this manuscript did not meet with the council's approval, and other arrangements were made for its publication. The author is happy these arrangements were completed in time for Manitoba's centennial celebration.

A good deal of the research for the book was done through personal interviews with descendants of the Oakland pioneers (a number of whom now reside in the Vancouver area) and other persons familiar with the early history of Manitoba. These individuals gave generously of their time — often at short notice. In this context the author recognizes the special interest shown by the following:

Mrs. Elsie Blakely, Toronto; Miss Evelyn Brandon, Souris; Mrs. H. B. Donaldson, Treesbank; Mrs. A. J. Elliott, Wawanesa; Frank Ferris, Wawanesa; Mrs. J. L. Grossart, Brandon Hills; Hilton Harper, Winnipeg; Mrs. Georgina Husband, Wawanesa; C. R. McFadden, Winnipeg; Ivor Rogers, Toronto; C. F. T. Rounthwaite, Toronto; Miss Ethel Rounthwaite, Thornhill, Ontario; Canon R. L. Taylor, Winnipeg; Mrs. Jemima Webster, Winnipeg.

It is difficult to give a complete list of all who contributed information. But, with apologies to any sources inadvertently omitted, the author makes this grateful attempt:

Brandon area (including the Brandon Hills, Carroll, Glen Souris, Hayfield, Nesbitt, Rounthwaite, Souris, Stratherne, Treesbank and Wawanesa districts) — Mr. and Mrs. Herbert Abbott, Mrs. Herbert Atkinson, the late Donald Bain, Mrs. N. L. Baker, Dick Bell, Mrs. Lucy Boneham, George Brockie, Mrs. Charles Brooks, Mrs. E. A. Burton, Mrs. Mary Buscarlet, Mrs. Ada Cameron, Dan Cameron, Mr. and Mrs. D. A. Campbell, the late Mrs. D. H. Campbell, Mrs. N. Carrothers, Mrs. E. Carscadden, Mr. and Mrs. J. H. Chalmers, Mr. and Mrs. Stanley Chalmers, Cliff Chapman, Norman Chapman, Mrs. George Christie, Carroll Clark, Russell Clark;

Miss Beulah Cory, Clare H. Cory, Dion R. Cory, Ethelbert Cory, Miss Frieda Cory, Jim Cory, Miss Ruby Cory, Cameron Couling, Lloyd Couling, Russell Couling, Talbot Criddle, Mrs. Edith Crosbie, A. L. Cunningham, Miss Lottie Currie, Miss E. A. Doyle, Miss Hazel Dunseith, Mr. and Mrs. Carroll Eamer, Stewart Eastley, Mr. and Mrs. Graham Elder, Mr. and Mrs. Wallace Elder, Mr. and Mrs. Rich Elliott, Oliver English, Mrs. F. W. Fenwick, Noel Fisher, Mrs. Perry Fisher, Mrs. Margaret Flewitt;

Mrs. M. E. Franklin, Mrs. B. Giles, Miss Mabel Glendenning, Fred Granger, Mr. and Mrs. John Granger, W. P. Groves, Mrs. Elsie Gullett, James Hampton, J. W. Harding, Bill Hardwick, Mr. and Mrs. Harold Hawkins, Mr. and Mrs. Syd Hawkins, R. W. Hector, Mrs. John Hopwood, the late Jack Kent, Miss Agnes Knudson, H. B. Knudson, T. W. Knudson, Herb Lawrence, Mrs. Frank Lawson, Charles Lewis, Mr. and Mrs. Charles Little, Mr. and Mrs. Dave Lovatt, Mr. and Mrs. George A. MacKay, George Maher, Howard Maher;

Mr. and Mrs. Charles Mann, Josiah Martin, Miss Pearl Martin, Mrs. Dunc McAdam, Mr. and Mrs. E. M. McCulloch, Mrs. G. E. McCulloch, Angus K. McDonald, Mrs. Maud McFadden, Mrs. Frank McFarland, Mr. and Mrs. Dugald McKellar, Earl McKellar, Miss Kate McKellar, Mrs. Merle McKellar, George McPherson, the late Jack McPherson, Alvin Miller, Mrs. George Miller, Mrs. Syd Miller, Mr. and Mrs. Hugh Munn, Mr. and Mrs. R. D. Munn, Alex. Naismith, Mrs. Ralph Nicol, Mrs. O. Orr, J. E. Osborne;

Herb Patterson, Mrs. Alice Payne, Albert Pettit, Mrs. James Pringle, Mrs. Amy Raison, Bill Rice, Harvey Rogers, J. B. Rome, R. M. Sanderson, Jerry Scott, Mrs. Ruth Scott, Mr. and Mrs. Harris Simpson, Mrs. Mary Smart, Mr. and Mrs. Reuben Smith, Sam Somersall, Mrs. Ron Sopp, Eric Sundell, Mrs. Mary Sweeney, Raymond Townsend, Mrs. Frank Turnbull, Mrs. Hope Turner, Harry Vane, Percy Vint, Mrs. Robert Wallace and the late Robert Wallace, Albert Watson, Mrs. C. Wickett, Mr. and Mrs. Arthur C. Wright;

Greater Vancouver — Mrs. Sara Banting, Mrs. Bessie Battison, Miss Lazelle Boake, Miss Laura Brander, Mrs. M. E. Cole, Alison E. Fawcett, Bert Granger, Miss Hilda Granger, Jim Graves, J. D. Harrower, Dr. Benjamin Harry, Miss Lena Henderson, Mrs. Luanna Hunter, Mrs. Sherwood Lett, Claude Marmont, Mrs. J. S. Mawhinney, Miss Myrtle McKenzie, Mrs. C. Lyle McPherson, Stewart Rutledge, Roland Storey, the late Mrs. Mae Stubbs;

Greater Winnipeg — Mrs. C. H. Burnell, J. A. Casemore, Mrs. Helen Downie, Mrs. W. O. Graham, Gwain Hamilton, Miss Iva Jackson, Miss Kathleen Kinley, Mrs. Clifford Leech, Mrs. J. S. Mc-Arthur, Mrs. Ed McDonald, Mr. and Mrs. John T. McKenzie, Mrs. Alice Morley, Mrs. P. R. Pollock and the late P. R. Pollock, Chris Vickers.

Elsewhere — Dr. J. O. Banting, Ladner, B.C.; R. G. Birch, Cloverdale, B.C.; Fred H. Carroll, Flin Flon; Mrs. J. L. Carter, Toronto; Mr. and Mrs. Alf Cory, Glenboro; Miss Maida Criddle, Sidney, B.C.; Mrs. Talbot Criddle, Miami, Manitoba; Mr. and Mrs. Russell Cunningham, Killarney; Mrs. Earl Dickey, Revelstoke, B.C.; Miss Shelagh Dickey, Sicamous, B.C.; Edgar E. Elliott, Newton, B.C.; Mrs. Claude M. Grace, Phoenix, Arizona; Mrs. John Hopkins, Haney, B.C.; Mrs. Harold Lindsay, Flin Flon; Mrs. H. K. Manuel, Sardis, B.C.; Elsie L. Moe, Regina; Tom Munk, Margaret; Frank Presunka, Glenboro; Mrs. S. L. Rodgers, Morden; Mrs. John Stady, Sardis, B.C.; Mrs. Gilbert Storey, Toronto; W. A. Witherspoon, Glenboro; Mrs. Grant Wheeler, Sardis, B.C.

Research also was conducted at the following: Public Archives of Canada, Ottawa; Manitoba provincial archives, Winnipeg; Ontario provincial archives, Toronto; British Columbia provincial archives, Victoria; Library of Parliament, Ottawa; post office department library, Ottawa; Manitoba provincial library, Winnipeg; Brandon Public Library and the libraries at Brandon University, University of Winnipeg, Hudson's Bay House, Winnipeg, and The Brandon Sun; also Brandon University geography department; the Canada North West Land Company office, Winnipeg; the Manitoba government departments of education, industry and commerce, mines and natural resources, and the provincial land titles offices at Brandon and Winnipeg. The staffs were most helpful.

The author would especially like to thank the Governor and Committee of the Hudson's Bay Company in London, England, for permission to publish extracts from the Brandon House journal for 1793-94; the Glenbow Foundation in Calgary for research assistance and the permission to reproduce a number of photographs.

The author is particularly obliged to the following for encouragement, advice or technical assistance: Mr. and Mrs. A. C. Bateman, J. D. Dick, A. H. N. Griffin and John Tyman — all of Brandon;

Miss V. Denham of Glasgow, Scotland; G. T. Robinson of London, England; Mr. and Mrs. R. C. Fisher of Nesbitt; Miss B. A. McLean and J. M. Gray — both of Toronto; Hans Arnold, Dr. T. C. B. Boon, Miss C. Gunnarsson, Rev. V. J. Jensen, S.J., J. S. Lamont, Mrs. Marion Lepkin, D. St. J. Magnus, B. P. McDonald, Mr. and Mrs. David McDowell, Miss Mary Scorer and A. H. Sackmann — all of Winnipeg.

Finally, the author is indebted to W. H. Brooks of Winnipeg, who made many suggestions from an historical point of view, and to Jill Brooks, who did the graphic design.

December, 1969.   J. A. D. Stuart,
                                                           Winnipeg.

List of Illustrations

62	Ferry across the Souris River south of Brandon, c. 1890; courtesy of Manitoba provincial archives.
63	Remains of Gregory's Mill, south of Nesbitt, before it was destroyed by natural decay and vandalism; courtesy of Raymond Townsend, Nesbitt.
65	Richard Cory, Sr., Chesley district; courtesy of Mr. and Mrs. Dugald McKellar, Nesbitt. R. Fred Cory (aged 14), Chesley district, 1879; courtesy of Misses Beulah, Frieda and Ruby Cory, Wawanesa.
66	John Smith and his children, Reuben and Linda, Souris City district; courtesy of Mr. and Mrs. Reuben Smith, Wawanesa.
67	Mr. and Mrs. Richard Kinley, Souris City; courtesy of Mrs. Jemima Webster, Winnipeg.
68	William Fleming, Carrolton; courtesy of Mrs. M. E. Franklin, Carroll. William Bertram, about 25 years of age, Brandon Hills district; courtesy of Mrs. J. L. Grossart.
71	Sod hut near Plum Creek, c. 1882; courtesy of Miss Evelyn Brandon, Souris.
72	Two lads in front of log shanty; courtesy of L. A. Stuckey, Brandon. Norman Criddle and Vane families at "St. Alban's", Aweme district, 1895; courtesy of Glenbow Foundation.
80	Bill from Thomas Harrison's store at Souris City (Sourisbourg post office), Aug. 6, 1881; courtesy of Frank Ferris, Wawanesa.
91	Brandon county council, possibly 1884; courtesy of L. A. Stuckey, Brandon.
93	Hayfield School, about 1900; front row: Stirling girl?, Tilly Cameron, Cora Cunningham, Phoebe Miller, Pearl Cunningham, Minewie Miller, Rathwell girl; back row: Stirling boy?, John Rathwell, A. C. Miller, Clinton Cunningham, Russell Cunningham, Wellington Rathwell; name of teacher unknown; courtesy of J. R. Cunningham, Killarney.
94	East Brandon School, about 1888; front row: Bill Kelly, Mary Kelly, Jim Doherty, Daisy Hill, Ben Stady; back row: Miss Preston, Florence Graham, Sally Pringle,

Bob and Dan Pringle, Mary Doherty, Nellie Pringle, Mary Graham, Russell Hill, Harry Graham, Myrtle Hill, George Graham, Annie Graham, Bob Pringle, Mary Maher, Russell Maher, Frank Graham; courtesy of Mr. and Mrs. G. A. Griffith, Rounthwaite.

101   Mrs. Dave Shields, Sr., East Brandon district; courtesy of Mr. and Mrs. John Granger, Rounthwaite.

102   Mrs. William Jackson (left) and her daughter, Mrs. Aggie Gibson, Stratherne district; courtesy of Mr. and Mrs. Alf Cory, Glenboro.

103   Picnic at Lake Clementi, towards west end of Brandon Hills, 1882; courtesy of Brandon Public Library.

104-105 Hayfield district picnic at Lake Clementi, c. 1890; courtesy of Mr. and Mrs. Stanley Chalmers, Brandon.

106   Scene from Rounthwaite district picnic at Lake Clementi; left to right: Miss Jessie Bertram (Mrs. F. R. Jewkes), Mrs. Donald Bain, Syd Hawkins, Miss Sadie Bertram, Donald Bain, Miss Mary Bain, Miss Willa Watson (Mrs. Fred Martin), Miss Bella Bain (Mrs. Roger Harries); courtesy of Mr. and Mrs. Syd Hawkins, Brandon.
Rowboats on Lake Clementi, courtesy of L. A. Stuckey, Brandon.

108   Mr. and Mrs. William Payne, Chesley district, taken c. 1879 in Port Hope, Ontario; courtesy of Miss Alice Payne, Wawanesa.

113   Richard Cory, Jr., Chesley district; courtesy of Mrs. Dugald McKellar, Nesbitt.
Frank O. Fowler, Rounthwaite and Wawanesa districts

(later mayor of Winnipeg), c. 1900; courtesy of Manitoba provincial archives.
A. E. Rome, Chesley district; courtesy of J. B. Rome, Brandon.

123   Breaking prairie, The Dominion Illustrated, Aug. 31, 1889, p. 136; courtesy of Public Archives of Canada.

124-125 Harvesting scene in Plum Creek district, c. 1883; courtesy of Miss Evelyn Brandon, Souris.

126   Brandon wheat market, Pacific Avenue and Tenth Street, 1885; courtesy of Manitoba provincial archives.

134-135 Rosser Avenue and Sixth Street, Brandon, 1883; courtesy of Manitoba provincial archives.

213

Appendix

SECTION, TOWNSHIP, RANGE

Southern Manitoba townships consist of 36 sections, each section being 640 acres (one square mile) in area. A township is six sections or six miles (plus the widths of six, 99-foot road allowances) square. Beginning in the southeast corner of each township, sections are numbered as follows:

SUBDIVISION OF A TOWNSHIP

31	32	33	34	35	36
30	29	28	27	26	25
19	20	21	22	23	24
18	17	16	15	14	13
7	8	9	10	11	12
6	5	4	3	2	1

The word township has a second meaning in this context. "Township" indicates a township's position north of the 49th parallel. In contrast, "range" denotes the distance a township is easa or west of the principal survey meridian, which is located near Winnipeg. Thus Township 7, Range 17 West is the seventh "township" north of the 49th parallel and 17 ranges west of the principal survey meridian.

Sections are subdivided into quarter sections. For convenience, a 160-acre of land in the northeast portion of section one in Township 7, Range 17 West is described as NE 1.7.17 W. Because Oakland municipality lies west of the principal survey meridian, the same parcel of land in this book is identified simply as NE 1.7.17. (The northwest portion of 1.7.17 is identified as NW 1.7.17, the north half is N 1.7.17, the southeast portion is SE 1.7.17, the east half is E 1.7.17 and so on.)

Doubt exists as to the precise location of the trading posts established near the mouth of the Souris River in the last eighteenth and nearly nineteenth centuries. The above map by Mrs. A. E. Brown of Winnipeg gives another interpretation of the sites first mapped about 1930 (below) by the late Dr. David Stewart of Ninette, Manitoba.

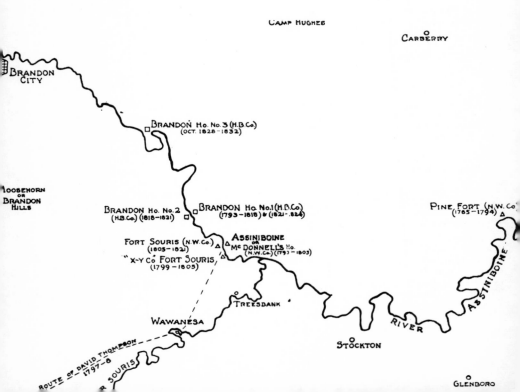

REPORTS OF DOMINION LANDS SURVEYORS

Oakland was first surveyed in two stages. The eastern and northern boundaries of the municipality was established in 1879, and the balance of the township lines as well as the section lines were established in 1880.

The establishment of township lines was referred to as the outline survey; the running of section lines was termed the subdivision survey.

The men who conducted these Dominion Lands surveys in Oakland were J. L. P. O'Hanley of Ottawa, Ontario; W. Beatty of Delta, Ontario; Wm. Wagner of Ossawa, Manitoba, and F. C. Caddy and T. R. Hewson — a team from Cobourg, Ontario. (Caddy prepared the original plan of subdivision for the Millford, Manitoba, townsite in 1879. It appears that Hewson may have intended to settle in Oakland, as a Thos. R. Hewson had done five acres of plowing on each of NE 26.7.17 and NW 25.7.17 by 1880. However, there is no record of Thos. R. Hewson having attempted to homestead or purchase either of the parcels of land in question.)

The following descriptions of Oakland were taken from the surveyors' notes:

Township 7 Range 17

East outline — rolling prairie 1st class except Sect. 26, where ridge of sand hills 70' high — Souris Valley oak & poplar timber & thick scrub (Beatty, July, 1879)

South outline — slightly rolling with scattered bluffs of poplar and oak — soil 1st and second class (O'Hanley, June, 1880)

Subdivision — first class quality — generally heavy black loam with clay bottom — Souris River gives good drainage therefore few marshes — northern tier of sections crossed by fine creek of good quality as fed by springs (Black Creek) — also springfed lake in sections 36, 35, 25, 26 — very little timber of any value, except in river valley and best of it being cut by settlers getting out house tops, etc. (Caddy & Hewson, Sept. 17 to Oct. 9, 1880)

Township 7, Range 18

South outline — 1st class, rolling prairie — some small poplar & oak sections 1 & 2 (O'Hanley, June, 1880)

Subdivision — generally heavy clay loam — better for root crops and grain on east than on west, which is lower & covered with open ponds & marshes — other than Souris River, no timber of any importance (Caddy and Hewson, Sept. 14 to Oct. 23, 1880)

Township 7, Range 19

East and South outlines — along east boundary 1st class rolling prairie — along south boundary land rolling with many small hay marshes or ponds — There is gravel hill in Sect. 5 — Souris runs through deep valley Sect. 6 — sides of valley are timbered (O'Hanley, June, 1880)

Subdivision — mostly class 2 soil — hills of this township outstretches of Brandon Hills and in some parts stony — between hills are swamps & ponds — north eastern part has some timber, but of no great account — "I have no doubt this township will be soon settled; it is well adapted for sheep farms" — Grand Valley is 16 miles north, and a post office (north of Brandon Hills) lately established 9 miles away (Wagner, Aug 31 to Sept. 15, 1880)

217

Township 8, Range 19

North outline — country along this line mostly hilly prairie with number of shallow hay swamps — There are some bluffs of poplar on hills — soil generally 1st class (O'Hanley, Oct., 1879)

East outline — generally through prairie with 1st & 2nd class soil — small poplar & oak in sections 1, 12, 13 & 24 (O'Hanley, June, 1880)

Subdivision — without exception soil number 2 — This township is the western portion of the Brandon Hills — the northern boundary runs through valley of about 2 miles in width which is low and alkaline with but a few hundred (arable) acres at its eastern part — From southern boundary of this valley a range of hills about 150' high rises gently & summit covered with wood but only slope of east corner has timber of any account which is freely used by the few settlers in the township east of this (Township 8.18) — between the ridges and southern boundary of the township on the eastern side a pretty level piece of land of about 4-5,000 acres, part of it overgrown with oak, popuar & hazel underbrush — south easterly corner about 1,200-1,500 acres of poplar and oak which might be subdivided into woodlots and give an advantage for incoming settlers — western tiers of sections are very hilly & the valleys continuing as meadows or swamps yet the soil is excellent on top of these hills and might be good for settlement with fair supply of wood for fuel in vicinity (Wagner, Sept. 22 to Sept. 29, 1880)

Township 8, Range 18

North outline — country traversed by this line rolling & hilly prairie with number of small hay swamps — few bluffs of poplar on hills — soil sandy loam 1st quality (O'Hanley, Oct., 1879)

Subdivision — chiefly fine rolling prairie with fair quantity of good hay land — Brandon Hills on west — in general rough holes with occasional deep ravines — soil generally gravelly, particularly on summits, though soil good in most of valleys— greatest height of this range of hills 300-350' above level plain — small quantity of timber on west part of township chiefly on Brandon Hills but none larger than 10'' & what good timber there is is being rapidly taken off by settlers in this & adjoining townships for all purposes — no large streams of water, but water in ponds generally fresh & good — good water had by wells — "a number of respectable settlers in this township" (Caddy and Hewson, Sept. 13 to Oct. 16, 1880)

Township 8 Range 17

North outline — rolling prairie with occasional bluffs of poplar and clumps of willow — some small oak and tamarack near Assiniboine River — first class except Sect. 34 where gravelly and stony (O'Hanley, Sept., 1879)

East outline—sections 36, 25, 12 & 1 undulating prairie 1st class soil — sections 13 & 24 numerous bluffs of poplar & oak scrub — soil light and sandy — 2nd class quality (Beatty, July, 1879)

Subdivision — chiefly level prairie with rolling land on north & west — soil generally rich clay loam with few sections on northeast of light sandy nature — water in streams & fords generally good & fresh — numerous springs of good water on banks of Assiniboine River which abounds in pike, pickerel & smaller fish — timber very scarce — hardly any except on banks of river which is generally small, very little fit for good building timber — oak generally too small for anything but firewood and fencing — in making survey found road allowance on north side of Sect. No. 36 left out and therefore that section was 1 chain and 50 links too short on north side — "I was obliged to carry this deficiency through the range of sections south of this, in order to run my lines parallel to the east boundary of the townships" (Caddy and Hewson, Sept. 23 to Oct. 30, 1879)

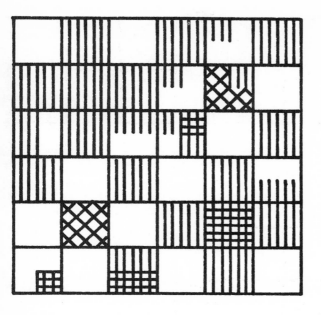

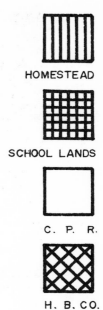

HOMESTEAD

SCHOOL LANDS

C. P. R.

H. B. CO.

TOWNSHIP 7-17W

Normally in each township the Canadian Pacific Railway Company was granted odd-numbered sections, the Hudson's Bay Company was granted a section and three-quarters (in all but townships whose number was divisible by 5, in which case they were granted two sections), two sections were reserved for school purposes, and the balance was retained by the Crown either for granting to homesteaders or for sale.

Owing to prior claims by "squatters" in Township 7.17, the disposition of C.P.R. and school land was contrary to the "normal" pattern. (See text p. 118).

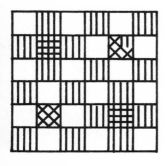

"NORMAL"   219

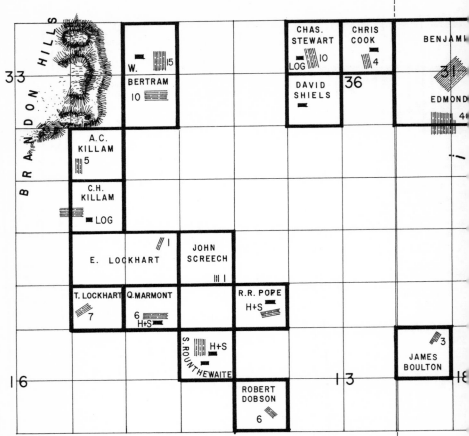

TWP. 8   RGE. 18 W

N

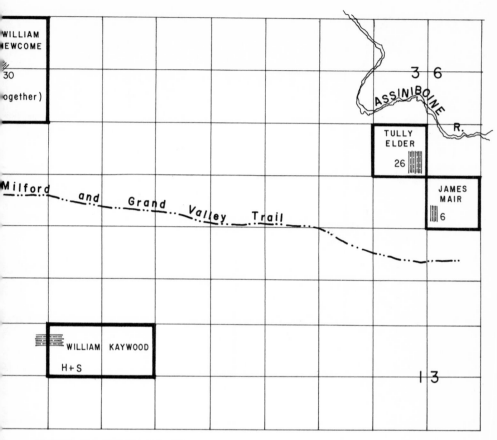

WILLIAM
NEWCOME

30

together)

TULLY
ELDER

26

JAMES
MAIR

6

3 6

ASSINIBOINE

R.

Milford and Grand Valley Trail

WILLIAM KAYWOOD

H+S

1 3

TWP. 8 RGE. 17 W

OAKLAND 1880

This map and the map on the next two pages were prepared from the notebooks of the men who surveyed Oakland in the fall of 1880. The maps show the name and claims of the pre-survey settlers ("squatters"). The spelling has been left unchanged.

The key is as follows:

10 10 acres ploughed

▬ building or buildings

H+S house and stable

221

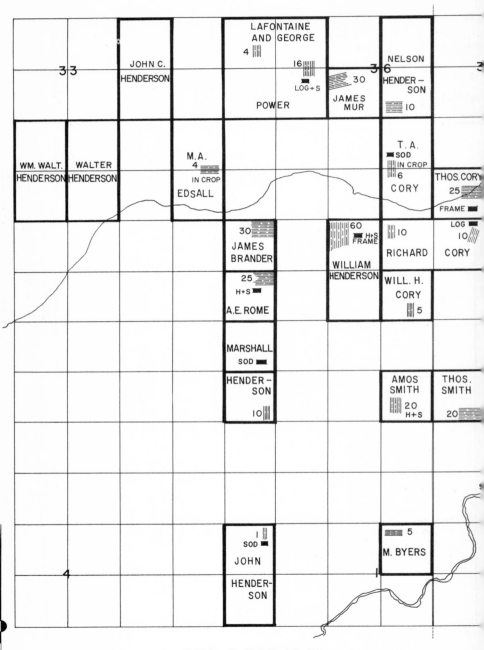

TWP. 7 RGE. 18 W

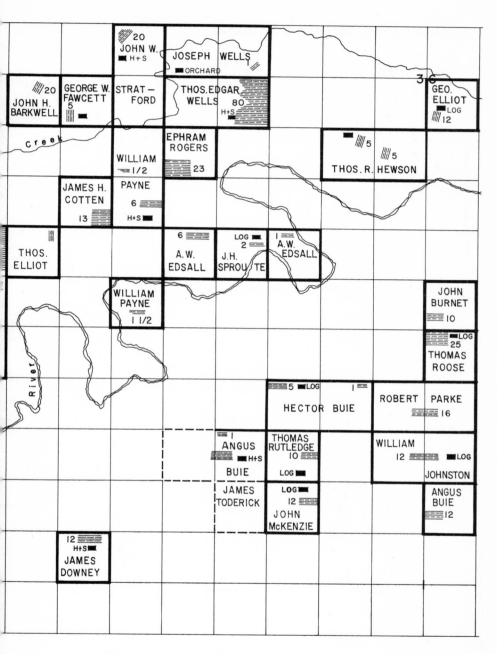

TWP. 7 RGE. 17 W

ORIGINAL DISPOSITION OF LAND

The information below was gleaned from transcriptions of official records. The transcriptions are lodged in the geography department library of Brandon University. In most cases the spelling has been left unaltered.

The following code is used to differentiate the various types of land: H—homestead, P—pre-emptions, CPR—Canadian Pacific Railway Co., HBC—Hudson's Bay Co., S—direct sale of Crown land, SLS—sale of land hitherto reserved for school purposes, MH—military homestead, MUG—Manitoba university grant, FGL—farm grazing lease.

Dates give the month in which the parcel of land was begun to be homesteaded or in which it was first sold.

WARD 1

1.7.17 (CPR) Alex Williamson Jan., 1882

2.7.17 NE(P) Albert E. Lloyd Sept., 1885
NW(H) Albert E. Lloyd Mar., 1882
SE(P) Marmaduke T. L. Lloyd July, 1885
SW(H) Marmaduke T. L. Lloyd Jan., 1882

3.7.17 NE(CPR) Jas. A. Williamson Dec., 1881
NW(CPR) John Brandon Dec., 1881
SE(CPR) William Foster Jan., 1881
SW(CPR) Arch. Speers Feb., 1882

4.7.17 NE(H) James Downie July, 1881
NW(P) James Downie Sept., 1884
SE(SLS) James Downie June, 1900
SW(SLS) James Downie Feb., 1892

5.7.17 N(CPR) Fred E. Nixon Oct., 1881
SE(CPR)
SW(CPR) James Conacher Dec., 1881

6.7.17 NE(H) Donald McRae Jan., 1894
NW(H) Donald McRae July, 1881
SE(SLS) James Downie Feb., 1892
SW(H) Alex. F. McRae July, 1881

7.7.17 E(CPR)
W(CPR) Edward B. Shuttleworth Feb., 1882

8.7.17 (HBC)

9.7.17 (CPR) William Scott Nov., 1881

10.7.17 NE (P) James B. Todrick Jan., 1885

NW(P) Stewart Robertson June, 1884
SE(H) James B. Todrick July, 1881
SW(H) Stewart Robertson July, 1881

11.7.17 (SLS) Wm. Fred Williamson Aug., 1886

12.7.17 NE(H) Wm. T. Johnson June, 1881
NW(H) Wm. T. Johnson Feb., 1895
SE(H) Angus Buie July, 1881
SW(H) Angus Buie Dec., 1894

13.7.17 NE(CPR) Albert Sanderson Apr., 1882
NW(CPR) Thomas J. McBride Dec., 1882
S(S) Robert Park Nov., 1882

14.7.17 NE(H) Hugh Rutledge June, 1881
NW(H) John McKenzie June, 1881
SE(H) Hector Buie July, 1881
SW(P) Hector Buie May, 1885

15.7.17 E(CPR) Alex Speers Nov., 1881
W(CPR) Wm. J. Scott Nov., 1881

16.7.17 E(S) Wm. J. Scott Nov., 1881
W(S) Wm. Scott Nov., 1881

17.7.17 E(CPR) Wm. Scott Oct., 1881
W(CPR) Jabez Elliott Oct., 1881

18.7.17 NE(H) Joshua Elliott July, 1881
NW(P) John Smith July, 1885
SE(P) Joshua Elliott June, 1884
SW(H) John Smith June, 1881

19.7.17 E(CPR) Joshua Elliott Oct., 1881

NW(H) Richard Cory
June, 1882
SW(P) Richard Cory
Jan., 1884
20.7.17 NE(H) Richard Kinley
July, 1881
NW(H) Jabez Elliott
July, 1881
SE(P) Richard Kinley
Nov., 1883
SW(P) Jabez Elliott
Apr., 1883
21.7.17 NE(P) Thomas Elliott
Aug., 1883
NW(H) Thomas Elliott
Sept., 1882
SE(CPR) Wm. J. Scott
Nov., 1881
SW(CPR) Thomas Elliott
Nov., 1881
22.7.17 NE(SLS) James Elliott
Feb., 1893
NW(H) John Craig June, 1881
SE(H) Joseph Telford
Sept., 1882
SW(CPR) John McKenzie
Nov., 1885
23.7.17 NE(CPR) Arch. Speers
Oct., 1881
NW(CPR) John Craig
Dec., 1881
SE(CPR) Arch. Speers
Nov., 1881
SW(CPR) Arch Speers
Sept., 1881
24.7.17 N(S) Chas. G. Johnson
Sept., 1883
S(S) John Burnett Apr., 1884
25.7.17 NE(CPR) Sam Taylor
Feb., 1888
NW(CPR)
SE(CPR) Marg. Jane Taylor
Apr., 1886
SW(CPR)
26.7.17 NE(H) J. E. Green Apr., 1882
NW & S(HBC)
27.7.17 NE(CPR) Eph. Rogers
Sept., 1882
NW(H) Eph. Rogers
Sept., 1882
S(CPR) Clarkson Rogers
Dec., 1881
28.7.17 NE(H) Wm. Payne
Dec., 1892
NW(H) John H. Barkwell
Dec., 1891
SE(H) Wm. Payne June, 1881
SW(H) John H. Barkwell
June, 1880
29.7.17 NE(H) James Elliott
Aug., 1881

NW(P) Thomas Munk
June, 1884
SE(P) James Elliott
Feb., 1884
SW(H) Thomas Munk
Sept., 1881
30.7.17 NE(P) Jas. F. Kinley
June, 1884
NW(P) Thomas Cory
Jan., 1885
SE(H) Jas. F. Kinley
June, 1881
SW(H) Thomas Cory
June, 1881
31.7.17 NE(CPR) Wm. McNaughton
May, 1882
SE(CPR) Wm. McNaughton
Apr., 1882
W(CPR) Joshua Elliott
Oct., 1881
32.7.17 NE(H) Joseph Murray
July, 1881
NW(H) John Weir July, 1881
S(S) Thomas Harrison
Aug., 1882
33.7.17 E(CPR) John W. Stratford
Nov., 1881
W(CPR) John W. Wright
Dec., 1881
34.7.17 NE(H) Jas. Alex Hector
Jan., 1888
NW(H) Thomas E. Wells
June, 1881
SE(P) Maria Fawcett
Nov., 1885
SW(H) Maria Fawcett
Aug., 1881
35.7.17 NE(CPR) Joseph Cornell
c. 1890
NW(H) Robert B. Fawcett
Aug., 1882
SE(CPR) R. W. Ferguson
c. 1885
SW(CPR) Robert B. Fawcett
Sept., 1882
36.7.17 N(S) Edward O. Hobson
Aug., 1882
SE(H) Henry A. Husband
Aug., 1885
SW(P) Henry A. Husband
Aug., 1885

WARD 2
1.7.18 N(CPR) Wm. Patterson
May, 1882
S(CPR)
2.7.18 NE(H) Wm. Patterson
Nov., 1882
NW(H) John Henderson
Feb., 1882

225

	SE(H) John Patterson	15.7.18	NE(CPR) John Gray
	Nov., 1882		Nov., 1881
	SW(P) John Henderson		NW(CPR) Arthur Sifton
	Dec., 1887		Nov., 1881
3.7.18	(CPR) Sextus Kent		S(CPR) Caleb N. Griffin
	Feb., 1882		Jan., 1882
4.7.18	NE(H) Chas. F. Kent	16.7.18	NE(H) John Martin
	June, 1882		Mar., 1883

SE(H) John Patterson
Nov., 1882
SW(P) John Henderson
Dec., 1887

3.7.18 (CPR) Sextus Kent
Feb., 1882

4.7.18 NE(H) Chas. F. Kent
June, 1882
NW(MUG)
SE(H) Sextus Kent Aug., 1881
SW(H) Henry James Scott
July, 1889

5.7.18 (CPR)

6.7.18 NE(H) George Fawkes
April, 1882
NW(H) Thomas English
Dec., 1887
SE(H) James Wharton
Apr., 1882
SW(H) Wm. Reynolds
Jan., 1889

7.7.18 NW(CPR) J. A. Martin
Dec., 1888
SW(CPR)
E(CPR) John E. Thompson
Feb., 1882

8.7.18 (HBC)

9.7.18 (CPR)

10.7.18 NE(H) Caleb N. Griffin
Aug., 1881
NW(H) Frank E. Martin
Feb., 1891
SE(H) Daniel A. Gray
Dec., 1888
SW(H) John Gray July, 1881

11.7.18 NE(SLS) Caleb N. Griffin
Feb., 1892
NW(SLS) John Smith
June, 1900
SE(SLS) Wm. Patterson
Feb., 1892
SW(SLS) Thos. J. Patterson
June, 1900

12.7.18 NE(H) Isaac W. Rogers
Mar., 1882
NW(H) Albert Nich. Smith
June, 1882
SE(P) Isaac W. Rogers
Oct., 1885
SW(P) Albert Nich. Smith
Oct., 1888

13.7.18 (CPR) Amos Smith Oct., 1881

14.7.18 NE(H) Wm. M. Henderson
July, 1881
NW(H) Neil Peter Gray
July, 1881
SE(H) Samuel H. Henderson
Nov., 1887
SW(H) Neil Peter Gray
Dec., 1892

15.7.18 NE(CPR) John Gray
Nov., 1881
NW(CPR) Arthur Sifton
Nov., 1881
S(CPR) Caleb N. Griffin
Jan., 1882

16.7.18 NE(H) John Martin
Mar., 1883
E½ of NW(P) Samuel J. Miller
Oct., 1890
W½ of NE(H) Samuel J. Miller
May, 1886
SE(P) Maxwell Murray
May, 1887
SW(H) Maxwell Murray
Mar., 1883

17.7.18 NW(CPR) Wm. Elliott
Feb., 1882
NE & S(CPR)

18.7.18 NE(S) James A. Lines
Aug., 1888
NW(H) Henry Jull
June, 1882
SE(P) James A. Jull
Jan., 1889
SW(H) James A. Jull
June, 1882

19.7.18 N(CPR)
S(CPR) Edward B. Shuttleworth
Feb., 1882

20.7.18 NE(S) Josiah Martin
July, 1888
NW(S) Wm. L. Henderson
Mar., 1885
SE(H) Francis Fowler
May, 1882
SW(P) Francis Fowler
Oct., 1885

27.7.18 NE(CPR) Edmund Fowler
Apr., 1882
NW(CPR) John Fowler
June, 1882
SE(CPR) Edmund Fowler
Oct., 1881
SW(CPR) John Fowler
Apr., 1882

22.7.18 NE(H) Albert E. Rome
July, 1881
NW(H) Joseph Townsend
July, 1881
SE(H) Albert E. Rome
Dec., 1892
SW(P) Joseph Townsend.
Sept., 1886

23.7.18 NE(H) Duncan Gray
Sept., 1882
NW(H) James Brander
Aug., 1882
SE(CPR) Neil M. Gray
Oct., 1881

SW(P) James Brander
Jan., 1884
24.7.18 NE(H) Richard W. Cory
July, 1881
NW(H) Wm. S. Henderson
July, 1881
SE(H) Wm. Henry Cory
July, 1881
SW(P) Wm. S. Henderson
Nov., 1883
25.7.18 NE(S) Frank O. Fowler
Dec., 1886
NW(P) Orlin Smith Elliott
Nov., 1882
SE(H) Thomas A. Cory
Aug., 1882
SW(H) Orlin Smith Elliott
June, 1882
26.7.18 NE(H) Montgomery Carrothers
July, 1881
NW & S(HBC)
27.7.18 (CPR) Wm. O. Fowler
Nov., 1881
28.7.18 NE(H) Wm. Hume Martin
July, 1881
NW(H) Wm. W. Henderson
July, 1881
SE(H) Richard T. Martin
Aug., 1881
SW(H) Geo. Sherman Henderson Feb., 1888
29.7.18 NE(SLS) Wm. T. Johnston
Nov., 1906
SE(SLS) Malcolm McKellar
Nov., 1906
W(SLS) John Livingstone
Nov., 1906
30.7.18 NE(S) George Whittington
May, 1885
NW(H) Peter McMurchie
July, 1884
SE(P) H. L. Van Luven
Mar., 1890
SW(H) H. L. Van Luven
Sept., 1884
31.7.18 (CPR)
32.7.18 NE(H) Wm. Hoggarth
Nov., 1882
NW(H) James Crosbie
Nov., 1882
SE(H) John C. Henderson
Nov., 1881
SW(H) John Walker
Jan., 1888
33.7.18 NE(CPR) Richard H. Trueman
June, 1882
NW(CPR) David L. Charters
Aug., 1887
S(CPR) Stewart McKay
May, 1889

34.7.18 NE(P) Samuel Townsend
Dec., 1884
NW(P) Walter Henderson
Dec., 1884
SE(H) Samuel Townsend
July, 1881
SW(H) Walter Henderson
July, 1881
35.7.18 E(CPR) George E. Powers
Nov., 1881
W(CPR) L. B. Powers
Nov., 1881
36.7.18 NE(P) I. N. Henderson
Mar., 1885
NW(P) William Noble
Feb., 1885
SE(H) I. N. Henderson
July, 1881
SW(H) William Noble
July, 1881

WARD 3
1.7.19 (CPR) Peter R. Jarvis
Oct., 1881
2.7.19 N½ of NE(H) J. R. Hudson
July, 1884
S½ of NE(S) J. R. Hudson
c. 1890
NW(H) Catherine Donaldson
Apr., 1888
SE(H) David Lockeridge
Mar., 1884
SW(H) Isaac Brock Donaldson
July, 1882
3.7.19 (CPR)
4.7.19 NE(H) Gibson Groves
Nov., 1884
NW(H) John McFarland
Oct., 1888
SE(H) Walter Seafoot
Jan., 1883
SW(P) Walter Seafoot
Nov., 1886
5.7.19 (CPR)
6.7.19 NE(H) Thomas Leadbeater
Dec., 1882
NW(H) Samuel Stinson
Dec., 1888
SE(H) Thomas Leadbeater
Dec., 1894
SW(H) James Copeland
Nov., 1886
7.7.19 NW(CPR)
SW(CPR) Matthew Taylor
July, 1882
E(CPR) Wm. Templeman
July, 1882
8.7.19 (HBC)
9.7.19 (CPR)
10.7.19 NE(P) Francis J. Clark
July, 1886

227

NW(H) Francis J. Clark
May, 1882
SE(H) James Wood
Dec., 1888
SW(H) Albert H. Clark
May, 1882
11.7.19 NE(SLS) John Martin
June, 1900
NW(SLS) Robert H. Campbell
Nov., 1906
SE(SLS) James A. Martin
Nov., 1906
SW(SLS) Robert H. Campbell
Nov., 1906
12.7.19 NE(H) Andrew Martin
Jan., 1888
NW(H) John Martin
May, 1882
SE(H) Jas. A. Martin
May, 1882
SW(H) John Martin
Aug., 1892
13.7.19 NE(CPR) Jas. H. Lines
c. 1895
NW(CPR)
SE(CPR) R. H. Martin
c. 1900
SW(CPR) Alex. Logan
July, 1882
14.7.19 NE(H) Donald Young
May, 1882
NW(H) Arthur Glendenning
July, 1893
SE(H) Alex. Logan Jan., 1888
SW(H) Arthur Glendenning
Dec., 1882
15.7.19 (CPR) Peter R. Jarvis
Oct., 1881
16.7.19 NE(H) Alexander White
Dec., 1882
NW(H) Robert Wallace
Apr., 1882
SE(H) Wm. Christie
Nov., 1887
SW(P) Robert Wallace
Sept., 1886
17.7.19 NE(CPR)
SE(CPR) Wm. Fleming
Apr., 1889
W(CPR) Ezra A. Healy
c. Aug. 1882
18.7.19 NE(CPR) Samuel Stinson
Jan., 1886
NW(H) Wm. Stinson
Oct., 1881
SE(H) Andrew McCormick
May, 1882
SW(H) Isiah Stinson
Aug., 1881
19.7.19 NW(CPR) Wm. T. Stinson
Apr., 1882

E & SW Alfred H. Carroll
May, 1882
20.7.19 NE(H) John Taylor
Nov., 1887
NW(H) Mitchell Lawson
Apr., 1882
S(MH) Thomas Fleming
Apr., 1886
21.7.19 (CPR)
22.7.19 NE(H) Wm. Munn
May, 1882
NW(H) James H. Steinburg
Aug., 1885
SE(H) James Sloan Nov., 1887
SW(H) Henry G. Roberts
Feb., 1888
23.7.19 E(CPR) John McLean
May, 1882
W(CPR)
24.7.19 NE(P) James Long
Mar., 1886
NW(H) James Long
May, 1882
SE(H) John Young May, 1882
SW(CPR) Benjamin F. Lines
May, 1886
25.7.19 NE(CPR) Peter McMurchie
c. 1890
NW(CPR) John F. Taylor
Oct., 1882
Pt. of SE(CPR) Peter
McMurchie c. 1890
SW(CPR) Canada North West
Land Co.
26.7.19 NE(H) Chas. McFarland
May, 1888
NW & S(HBC)
27.7.19 (CPR)
28.7.19 NW(H) Benjamin Neil
July, 1888
E(MH) Edward P. Tew
July, 1886
SW(H) Thomas W. Jones
May, 1882
29.7.19 Pt. NE(SLS) CPR Feb., 1894
Pt. NE(SLS) Elizabeth A. Black
June, 1900
NW & S(SLS) Elizabeth A.
Black June, 1900
30.7.19 NE(H) Copeland Stinson
Dec., 1888
NW(P) James H. Fleming
Aug., 1884
SE(H) John J. Stinson
Aug., 1881
SW(H) James H. Fleming
Aug., 1881
31.7.19 NE(CPR) John J. Laughlin
May, 1885
NW & S (CPR)

228

32.7.19 NE(H) Michael Beyahan
July, 1881
NW(S) Michael Beyahan
July, 1884
Pt. SE(CPR) Peter S. Dawley
Jan., 1892
SW(H) Michael J. Carey
May, 1887
33.7.19 (CPR)
34.7.19 NE(P) Reginald H. M. Tew
Aug., 1889
NW(H) Wm. Hemsworth
June, 1882
SE(H) John Sharp
Aug., 1887
E½ of SW(S) Reginald H. M.
Tew June, 1884
W½ of SW(H) Reginald H. M.
Tew June, 1884
35.7.19 (CPR)
36.7.19 NE(H) Elliott C. Hicks
May, 1882
NW(H) Charles Quarterman
May, 1882
SE(H) Robert Harding
May, 1882
SW(H) Robert Walker
June, 1882

WARD 4
1.8.17 NW & E(CPR) Charles E.
Stephens Feb., 1882
SW(CPR) John Dalzell
Oct., 1881
2.8.17 NE(H) Wm. T. H. Hill
Apr., 1882
NW(H) James Sweeney
June, 1881
SE(H) Charles R. Banting
Apr., 1882
SW(P) James Sweeney
July, 1884
3.8.17 E(CPR) Wm. G. King
Oct., 1881
W(CPR)
4.8.17 NE(P) Alfred Watts
June, 1887
NW(H) James McFadden
Nov., 1882
SE(H) Alfred Watts
Nov., 1882
SW(P) James McFadden
Feb., 1886
5.8.17 N(CPR) Wm. Telford
Dec., 1881
SE(CPR) Joseph Murray
Jan., 1882
SW(CPR) Thomas Telford
May, 1882
6.8.17 NE(H) John Hunter
June, 1881

NW(H) Wm. Henry Hall
June, 1881
SE(H) Wallace Harry
June, 1881
SW(H) Arthur Harry
May, 1882
7.8.17 E(CPR) Robert Lammie
Sept., 1881
W(CPR) Andrew A. Lammie
Sept., 1881
8.8.17 (HBC)
9.8.17 N & SE(CPR) Richard Hector
Dec., 1881
SW(CPR) Thomas M. Harring-
ton Nov., 1881
10.8.17 E½ of NE(H) Alex. Brown
Mar., 1884
W½ of NE(S) Alex. Brown
May, 1888
NW(H) Joseph W. Brown
July, 1881
E½ of SE(H) David E. Brown
Mar., 1884
W½ of SE(S) David E. Brown
Sept., 1887
SW(H) Robert W. Scott
July, 1881
11.8.17 N(SLS) Albert M. Rogers
June, 1900
S(SLS) Thomas E. M. Banting
Feb., 1892
12.8.17 NE(S) Joseph Wells
July, 1891
N½ of NW(H) John Gibson
Oct., 1885
S½ of NW(S) John Gibson
Sept., 1889
SE(S) Thomas E. Wells
July, 1891
E½ of SW(S) James G.
Jackson July, 1889
W½ of SW(H) James G.
Jackson Oct., 1885
13.8.17 NE(CPR) E. L. Stady c. 1890
NW(CPR) James S. Wright
Mar., 1886
SE (CPR)
SW(CPR) David Mawhinney
Dec., 1881
14.8.17 NE(P) Charles Watson
NW(H) Charles Watson
S(S) Horace E. Crawford
15.8.17 NE(CPR) George B. Gordon
July, 1882
NW(CPR) Wm. Jackson
Oct., 1881
SE(CPR) Robert L. Lammie
July, 1882
SW(CPR) Frances H. Stady
Feb., 1882

16.8.17 NE(H) George Stewart
May, 1882
NW(H) Wm. Cawood
June, 1881
SE(P) George Stewart
July, 1888
SW(H) Robert Harrison
June, 1881

17.8.17 NW & E(CPR) Francis H.
Stady Feb., 1882
SW(CPR) W. T. Smith
Nov., 1881

18.8.17 NE(H) Edward E. Bolton
Aug., 1881
NW(H) James Bolton
Aug., 1881
SE(H) Fred. Wright Feb., 1882
SW(P) Fred. Wright
June, 1886

19.8.17 (CPR) W. T. Smith
Nov., 1881

20.8.17 NE(H) George H. Stady
Apr., 1882
NW(H) Wm. Balsdon
Nov., 1882
SE(H) John J. Bolton
June, 1881
SW(H) Wm. D. Bolton
July, 1882

21.8.17 NE(CPR) Robert Torrance
Oct., 1881
SE(CPR) Geo. Landon,
Oct., 1881
W(CPR) Thomas McCullough
Oct., 1881

22.8.17 NE(P) George Jackson
Dec., 1887
NW(H) Edwin H. Morrison
Jan., 1883
SE(H) George Jackson
June, 1884
SW(H) Wm. Jackson
Aug., 1881

23.8.17 NE (CPR
NW (CPR) George Jackson
Aug., 1888
SE(CPR)
SW(CPR) Wm. G. G. Hooper
Oct., 1887

24.8.17 NE(H) George Mair
Apr., 1882
N½ of NW(S) James H.
Jackson Aug., 1888
S½ of NW(H) James H.
Jackson May, 1885
SE(H) Henry Jackson
Aug., 1888
N½ of SW(S) E. L. Stady
Aug., 1888
S½ of SW(H) E. L. Stady
May, 1885

25.8.17 NE(CPR) Allan Bowerman
Mar., 1882
NW(CPR) Tully Elder
Oct., 1881
SE(CPR) James Mair
Nov., 1881
SW(CPR) John T. Forrest
Oct., 1881

26.8.17 NE(H) Andrew M. Wright
Oct., 1881
NW & S (HBC)

27.8.17 (CPR) Chas. E. Stephens
Feb., 1882

28.8.17 NE(H) Samuel Martin
Nov., 1882
NW(P) Wm. Duguid
Oct., 1884
SE(P) Samuel Martin
May, 1888
SW(H) Wm. Duguid
June, 1881

29.8.17 N(SLS) Angus McDonald
Jan., 1888
SE(SLS) James Martin
Feb., 1892
SW(SLS) Angus McDonald
Feb., 1892

30.8.17 NE(H) David Shields
Feb., 1882
NW(H) John Stady
June, 1881
SE(S) David Shields, Sr.
Sept., 1885
SW(H) John Graham
June, 1881

31.8.17 N(CPR) Bartholemew
Edmonds Mar., 1882
S(CPR) John Stady
Dec., 1881

32.8.17 E(S) Alfred T. Clare
Aug., 1882
W(S) Wm. Newcombe
Sept., 1882

33.8.17 (E(CPR) John E. Thompson
Feb., 1882
W(CPR) Robert Taylor
Dec., 1881

34.8.17 NE(H) James A. McManes
Feb., 1884
NW(H) John Wright
Nov., 1894
SE(H) Henry E. Morrison
Mar., 1886
SW(H) John Wright
Aug., 1882

35.8.17 NE(CPR)
NW(CPR) John Anderson
June, 1888
SE(CPR) A. C. Hooper
Sept., 1887

SW(CPR) Fred. Cresswell, Jr.
Sept., 1881
36.8.17 NE(H) Abraham Ake
May, 1882
NW(H) Albert Arnold
May, 1882
SE(H) Edward McVey
May, 1882
SW(P) Henry E. Morrison
Nov., 1889

WARD 5

1.8.18 E(CPR) Canada North West
Land Co.
W(CPR) Wm. Arnott
Sept., 1881
2.8.18 NE(H) Jacob M. Sherk
May, 1881
NW(H) Abel Miller
May, 1881
S(S) Rev. John Kenner
Aug., 1882
3.8.18 NW(CPR)
SW(CPR) Samuel S. Powers
Jan., 1882
E(CPR) Chas. F. Powers &
L. B. Powers Jan., 1882
4.8.18 NE(P) Wm. Taylor
Dec.,1886
SE(H) Wm.Taylor
May,1881
W(S) Robert Little
Dec., 1883
5.8.18 N & SW(CPR)
SE(CPR) Walter Taylor
Aug., 1882
6.8.18 NE(P) Robert Mitchell
June, 1885
NW(H) Robert Mitchell
June, 1885
SE(H) Wm. Crosbie
Feb., 1886
SW(H) John Dalgrain
Oct., 1886
7.8.18 (CPR)
8.8.18 (HBC)
9.8.18 NE(CPR) Fred L. Shaffner
Aug., 1882
SE(CPR) Laeigh R. Schaffner
Aug., 1882
W(CPR)
10.8.18 NE(H) Arthur E. Birch
June, 1881
NW(H) James Flannery
May, 1881
SE(H) Thomas Taylor
July, 1881
SW(H) T. S. F. Taylor
Sept., 1882
11.8.18 NE(SLS) George Pringle
Feb., 1892

NW(SLS) Robert A. Little
Mar., 1930
S(SLS) Henry Meredith
June, 1900
12.8.18 NE(H) Alfred Birch
May, 1881
NW(H) John Screech
June, 1881
SE(P) Alfred Birch
July, 1884
SW(P) John Screech
Oct., 1884
13.8.18 NE(CPR) Robert Bruce
Dec., 1881
NW(CPR) John Powley
Dec., 1881
S(CPR) John F. Rounthwaite
Oct., 1881
14.8.18 NE(P) Robert Dobson
May, 1883
NW(P) Samuel Rounthwaite
May, 1883
SE(H) Robert Dobson
May, 1881
SW(H) Samuel Rounthwaite
May, 1881
15.8.18 NE(H) T. F. D. Walker
Aug., 1882
SE(S) Joseph J. Walker
Oct., 1882
W(CPR) Richard Disette
Jan., 1882
16.8.18 NE(H) C. A. Cleveland
July, 1883
NW(H) C. D. Cleveland
July, 1881
SE(H) Andrew Y. Arnott
Mar., 1889
SW(P) C. D. Cleveland
Oct., 1884
17.8.18 NE(CPR) S. A. Hawkins
c. 1890
NW & S(CPR)
18.8.18 NE(H) Wm. White
July, 1882
NW(H) James Bowen
July, 1906
SE(H) Wm. Crosbie
Mar., 1906
E½ of SW(H) Alex. Waldie
Feb., 1925
W½ of SW(S) Robert J.
Hannah Dec., 1889
19.8.18 NE(CPR) Chas. A. Pratt
June, 1882
NW & SE(CPR) John Pratt
Nov., 1882
SW(CPR) Samuel S. Simpson
Nov., 1882
20.8.18 NE(H) Eugene W. Cleveland
June, 1881

NW(H) Samuel M. Rose
July, 1881
SE(H) Eugene W. Cleveland
Dec., 1891
NW(H) Walter Ford
Jan., 1882
21.8.18 NE(CPR) Wm. S. Moody
Oct., 1881
NW(CPR) John E. Rose
Dec., 1881
SE(H) W. H. Gammon
April, 1882
SW(S) W. H. Gammon
Feb., 1883
22.8.18 NE(H) E. A. Lockhart
July, 1881
NE(H) Walter Birch
Apr., 1882
SE(H) L. E. Marmont
May, 1881
SW(H) Fred L. Lockhart
July,1881
23.8.18 N(CPR) George Purvis
Sept., 1881
SE(P) R. R. Pope May, 1883
SW(H) R. R. Pope
Oct., 1882
24.8.18 NE(H) Levi H. Fisher
May, 1881
NW(H) George Lindlater
May, 1881
SE(H) William Hill
May, 1881
SW(S) Richmond Spencer
Dec., 1888
25.8.18 NE(CPR) John Graham
Nov., 1881
NW(CPR) George Purvis
Nov., 1881
SE(CPR) Levi H. Fisher
Nov., 1881
SW(CPR) George Findlater
Dec., 1881
26.8.18 NE(H) Eben. Donaldson
June, 1881
NW & S (HBC)
27.8.18 (CPR) A. G. Killam
Feb., 1882
28.8.18 NE(H) G. G. Harley
May, 1881
NW(H) James McKay
May, 1881
SE(H) Wm. S. Moody
Aug., 1881
SW(H) Wm. C. McKay
Dec., 1891
29.8.18 NE(SLS) Geo. F. Belaney
June, 1900
NW(SLS) Geo. F. Belaney
Jan., 1888

SE(SLS) Simon Clark
Nov., 1906
SW(SLS) James Watt
June, 1900
30.8.18 NE(P) John Leslie
Mar., 1886
NW(P) Wm. F. Cleveland
Apr., 1885
SE(H) John Leslie
May, 1881
SW(H) Wm. F. Cleveland
July, 1881
31.8.18 NE(CPR) Charles Belaney
Nov., 1882
NW(CPR) Peter S. Taylor
May, 1883
S(CPR)
32.8.18 NE(H) Robert Lindsay
Apr., 1882
NW(P) Charles Belaney
June, 1884
SE(P) Robert Lindsay
Dec., 1885
SW(H) Charles Belaney
May, 1881
33.8.18 (CPR)
34.8.18 NE(H) Wm. Bertram
May, 1881
NW(H) Wm. Wallace Moore
June, 1894
SE(P) Wm. Bertram
Apr., 1884
SW(H) Christian Davidson
administratrix estate of late
George Davidson Aug., 1882
35.8.18 NE(CPR) A. B. Wright & Jos.
G. Owen Feb., 1882
NW(CPR) Edward B. Shuttle-
worth Feb., 1882
SE(CPR) Eben. Donaldson
Oct., 1881
S.W.(CPR) Wm. Bertram
Nov., 1881
36.8.18 NE(H) Christopher Cook
May, 1881
NW(H) Charles Stewart
May, 1881
SE(P) Christopher Cook
Aug., 1883
SW(H) David W. Shields
May, 1881

WARD 6
1.8.19 NE & S (CPR)
NW(CPR) Canada North West
Land Co. c. 1887
2.8.19 NE(MUG) University of
Manitoba June, 1889
NW(H) George A. Miller
Jan., 1895
SE(S) Wm. Brown Nov. 1889

SW(H) Arch. Young
Nov., 1882
3.8.19 NW(CPR) Robert Arnott
Jan., 1883
SW(CPR) Leonard Couling
Sept., 1883
E(CPR)
4.8.19 NE(H) George Roberts
May, 1882
NW(H) James Sherman
Jan., 1882
SE(H) George James Peters
Feb., 1885
SW(S) Enoch G. Shorts
Mar., 1884
5.8.19 NE(CPR) Peter McPhillips
Mar., 1882
NW(CPR) John Carey
Mar., 1882
SE(CPR) Michael J. Carey
May, 1882
SW(CPR) Michael Beyahan
Dec., 1881
6.8.19 NE(H) Fred. B. Gibson
June, 1882
NW(P) Fred. B. Gibson
Dec., 1884
SE(H) Wm. G. Kennick
Mar., 1882
SW(H) George T. Emery
Mar., 1882
7.8.19 NE(CPR) James Millerick
July, 1882
NW & SE (CPR)
SW(CPR) James Beyahan
June, 1882
8.8.19 (HBC)
9.8.19 NE(CPR) George Gilchrist
June, 1882
SE(CPR) Wellington & James
F. Anderson c. 1885
W(CPR) Walter Drew
Mar., 1882
10.8.19 N½ of NE(H) George Miller
Apr., 1884
S½ of NE(S) George Miller
Feb., 1888
NW(P) Wm. Collard
Apr., 1884
SE(H) James F. Anderson
Dec., 1882
SW(H) Wm. Collard
Apr., 1884
11.8.19 NW(SLS) John W. Rathwell
June, 1900
SW(SLS) George Miller
June, 1900
E(FGL) J. R. Cunningham
Jan., 1964
12.8.19 N(MUG) University of
Manitoba June, 1889

SE(H) James Brown
May, 1890
SW(H) Wm. Brown
Dec., 1888
13.8.19 (CPR)
14.8.19 NE(H) Wm. H. Lockwood
Mar., 1888
NW(H) David Black
Jan., 1882
N½ of SE Robert J. Hannah
Nov., 1889
S½ of SE(H) Robert J.
Hannah June, 1886
SW(H) Richard Henderson
May, 1891
15.8.19 N(CPR) David Couling
May, 1882
S(CPR) Wesley Rathwell
Apr., 1882
16.8.19 NE(P) Henry Heal Dec., 1887
NW(H) Henry Heal
Jan., 1882
SE(H) David Couling
Mar., 1882
SW(H) David Couling
Feb., 1892
17.8.19 N & SW(CPR)
SE(CPR) James Beyahan
Dec., 1881
18.8.19 NE(H) Aaron Johnson
June, 1889
NW(H) Hugh A. Cunningham
Sept., 1882
SE(H) Malcolm McKellar
Mar., 1888
SW(H) Peter McKellar
Sept. 1882
19.8.19 N(CPR) Herbert Graham
Oct., 1881
S(CPR) Hugh A. Cunningham
Oct., 1881
20.8.19 N(CPR) Charles C. Hearn
Oct., 1883
SE(P) James Simmon
May, 1886
SW(H) James Simmon
July, 1882
21.8.19 NE(CPR) Albert Tamblyn
May, 1882
NW(CPR) Wm. Chalmers
c. 1885
SE(CPR)
SW(CPR) James A. Stark
c. 1895
22.8.19 NE(H) John E. Thorne
Jan., 1882
NW(H) Leslie P. Bobier
Jan., 1882
SE(H) James Black
Jan., 1882

233

SW(P) Leslie P. Bobier
Aug., 1884

23.8.19 NE & S(CPR)
NW(CPR) Robert Crompton
July, 1888

24.8.19 NE(H) James Chalmers
Jan., 1903
NW(H) Patrick Crogham
Apr., 1882
SE(H) Benson S. Simpson
Oct., 1896
SW(H) Daniel Baxted
Oct., 1898

25.8.19 N(CPR) Phillip E. Durst
Mar., 1882
S(CPR)

26.8.19 NE(H) Wm. Black
Jan., 1882
NW & S (HBC)

27.8.19 NE(CPR) James Cleveland
Feb., 1882
NW(CPR) Thomas Lee
Mar., 1882
S(CPR) Thomas E. Kelly
Mar., 1882

28.8.19 NE(H) Mary Ann Leetham
Jan., 1882
NW(P) Henry McCandlish
Mar., 1885
SE(H) James Cunningham
Sept., 1882
SW(H) Henry McCandlish
Jan., 1882

29.8.19 NE & SW(SLS) Thomas
Hutchinson Feb., 1892
NW(SLS) Daniel A. Harper
Feb., 1892
SE(SLS) Charles C. Hearn
Feb., 1892

30.8.19 NW(P) Benjamin F. Foster
Apr., 1884

SW(H) Benjamin F. Foster
Oct., 1882
E(CPR) Herbert C. Graham
Dec., 1884

31.8.19 E(CPR) Richard Boore &
Wm. R. Getz Nov., 1881
W(CPR) Henry B. Fairfield
Mar., 1882

32.8.19 NE(H) George Irwin
Jan., 1882
NW(S) Wm. Wilson
Nov., 1885
SE(H) Catherine McClue
May, 1882
SW(P) Catherina McClure
May, 1885

33.8.19 NE(CPR) Joseph Quinn
Mar., 1886
SE(CPR) Albert Tamblyn
May, 1882
W(CPR)

34.8.19 NE(H) Charles Belaney, Jr.
Jan., 1882
NW(H) John Crompton
Jan., 1882
SE(H) James H. Cleveland
July, 1883
SW(H) Donald Cameron
June, 1882

35.8.19 NE(CPR) C. A. Woodhouse
June, 1882
SE(CPR) Walter Ford
April, 1882
W(CPR) John E. Ross
Feb., 1882

36.8.19 NE(H) Thomas Beare
Dec., 1882
NW(H) Wm. Beare Dec., 1882
SE(H) Robert Arnott
Jan., 1882
SW(P) Robert Arnott
Apr., 1885

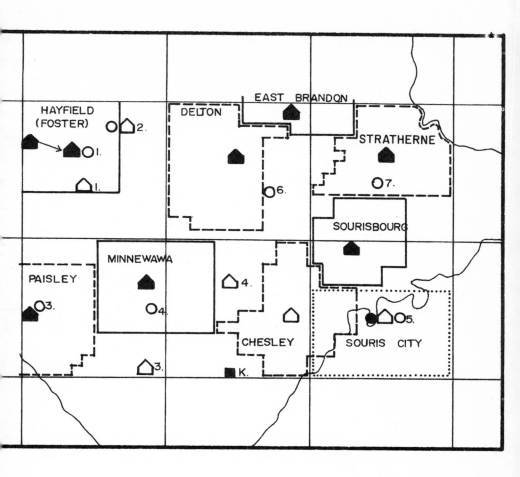

OAKLAND 1885

HOOLS AND SCHOOL DISTRICTS h year first operating) sley #137, 1882 risbourg #136, 1882 ris City #286, 1882 Brandon #165, 1883 ton #188, 1884 ter #200, 1884 therne #349, 1884 newawa #372, 1885 sley #321, 1885	POST OFFICES 1. Hayfield 2. Hazelwold 3. Carrolton 4. Minnewawa 5. Souris City 6. Rounthwaite 7. Stratherne	STOPPING HOUSES 1. David Couling 2. Jas. Cleveland 3. Wm. English 4. W. H. Martin 5. Richard Kinley K—Charles Kent's Store

235

ASSESSMENT ROLL -- 1886

1886.

The following information is taken from the Oakland assessment roll for 1886.

In general the table copies the format used by the municipal assessor, A. E. Rome of the Chesley district. The author usually accepted the assessor's spelling of names, although in some instances these are spelt differently in other contemporary printed sources.

The township by township totals at the end of the table are taken directly from the assessor's notebook, and are not always the same as totals that could be obtained by adding up the columns of the table. One reason for this is that several of the figures in the notebook were illegible and, therefore, omitted.

In the table the letters P and Un are used to indicate whether the land was patented or unpatented.

The names of non-residents are marked with an asterisk.

Except for Aweme, names of school districts have been abbreviated: Ches = Chesley, Delt = Delton, EB = East Brandon, Fost = Foster, Minn = Minnewawa, Pais = Paisley, RB = Riverbank, Sbrg = Sourisbourg, SC = Souris City, Stra = Stratherne. (Neither Aweme nor Riverbank schools were located within the municipality. Aweme was formed by the rural municipalities of Cornwallis and South Cypress in 1885. Riverbank was formed in the same year by the rural municipalities of Glenwood, Oakland, Riverside and Whitewater.)

	NO. OF PERSONS IN FAMILY		NO. OF ANIMALS
	MALES	FEMALES	

Name	Lot	Bearings & Date	Acres	Ten.	Value	Class					Rel.					Total
Buoie, Hector	32	S 14.7.17	100	Un	1660	SC	1	1	1	1	P	3	1	1	3	5
Cory, Richard	55	W 19.7.17	90	P	1620	SC	1	3	1	1	M	2	1	2		4
Cory, Thomas	50	W 30.7.17	130	P	1980	Sbrg	1	7	1	3	P	4	1	2		5
Downie, James	46	N 4.7.17	140	P	1850	SC	1	3	1	1	P	2	2	4	13	10
Elliott, Jabez	40	W 20.7.17	300	P	2480	SC	1	3	1	3	M	8	4	4	5	9
		W 17.7.17	70	Un	1000	SC										
Elliott, James	45	E 30.7.17	138	P	2410	Sbrg	1	2		1	M	8	1	1	1	35
		29.7.17	316	P	2560	Sbrg										
		NW 23.7.17		Un	400	SC										
Elliott, Joshua	37	W 31.7.17	270	Un	1280	Sbrg	1				M					
		E 19.7.17	300	Un	1280	SC										
		E 18.7.17	80	Un	1200	SC										
Elliott, Thomas	33	N & SW 21.7.17	140	P	2305	SC	1	1	1	1	M	4	1	1	1	25
Fawcett, R. B.	42	W 35.7.17	125	P	1715	Sbrg	1	1	1	2	M		2	3	4	10
Foster, W. S.	28	SE 3.7.17	160	Un	2405	SC	1	1	1	1	CE	9	2	4	4	25
		S 1.7.17	130	Un	1120	SC										
Green, J. E.		NE 26.7.17	60	P	765	Sbrg	1	3	1	1	M		2	2	1	12
Hogan, John		SW 5.7.17			560											
Husband, Henry A.	35	S 36.7.17			1000		1	2	2	3	CE					
Johnson, Robert & Charles *	23 & 27	N 24.7.17	140	P	1280	SC	1	2	2	1		2	2	2	3	17
Johnson, Wm.	35	N 12.7.17	160	P	1850	SC	1	2	1	1	M	2	2	2	1	
Kinley, Richard	48	E 27.7.17	100	P	1680	SC	1	2	1	3		2	1	1		
Lloyd, Albert	24	N 2.7.17	100	Un	1620	SC	1	1	1		CE	2				
Lloyd, T.	27	S 2.7.17	100	P	1445	SC	1	1	1		CE	2				
Lomond & McRae		N 5.7.17			1200	SC	1	4	1	1						
Lyle, Samuel	39	NE & S 23.7.17	180	Un	2510	SC	1	1	1	1		5	3	3	3	9
		SW 3.7.17		Un	500											
McBride, T. J. *		N 13.7.17		Un	1200	SC										
McKenzie, John	27	NW 14.7.17	150	P	1100	SC	1	1	1	1	P	4	1	1		2
		Pt. NE 14.7.17		P	240	SC										
		SW 22.7.17		P	480	SC										
McNaughton, Wm.	27	SE 31.7.17	105	Un	950	Sbrg	1	2	1	2	P	2				7
McRae, Alex		SW 6.7.17	60	P	750	SC	1	1	1	7	P	2		1		
McRae, Donald	23	N 6.7.17		P	1050	SC	1	1	1		P		2			

NAME	AGE	DESCRIPTION OF LAND	NO. OF ACRES CULTIVATED	P or Un	TOTAL ASSESSMENT IN $	SCHOOL DISTRICT	MALES MARRIED	MALES SINGLE	FEMALES MARRIED	FEMALES SINGLE	RELIGION	HORSES	MULES	BULLS	OXEN	COWS	COWS UNDER 3 YEARS	SHEEP	PIGS
Murray, Joseph	32	NE 32.7.17	100	P	1050	Sbrg	1	1	1	2	P	2				1	2		8
Nichol, Thomas	50	16.7.17	40	P	2760	SC	1	2	1	6	P	2			2				
		9.7.17	400		2560	SC													
		W 15.7.17	50		1100	SC													
		E 17.7.17			885	SC													
		SE 21.7.17			1306	SC													
Parks, Robert	30	S 13.7.17	140	P	1940	SC	1	3	1	5	P	4				2			6
Payne, Wm.	46	E 28.7.17	100	P	1780	Sbrg	1	2	1	2	M	2				1	3		12
Reid, Samuel	27	NE 31.7.17	100	Un	935	Sbrg	1	1				2				1			7
Robertson, Stewart	31	W 10.7.17	80	P	1780	SC	1	1	1		P				2		2		3
Rodgers, Clark	27	S 27.7.17	160	Un	1685	Sbrg		1			M	2	2			2	3		
Rodgers, Eph.	28	N 27.7.17	100	P	1900	Sbrg	1		1		M	4	2		2	2	3		9
		NW 22.7.17	40	P	560	SC													
Rodgers, Isaac W.	37	NW 33.7.17	121	Un	1140	Sbrg	1	1	1	2	M	2			2	2			5
Rutledge, Hugh	28	S 24.7.17	145	P	1940	SC	1	1	1		P	4				1	1		7
		Pt. NE 14.7.17	70	P	400	SC													
Scott, W.T. *		NW 26.7.17			600	Sbrg													
Scott, J. R.	23	NW 1.7.17	40	Un	890	SC	1	1	1		P	2			2	1			
Shuttleworth, E.B. *		W 7.7.17		Un	1120	SC													
Smith, John	27	W 18.7.17	100	P	1780	SC	1	1	1	1	M	2				2	2		4
Spiers, Alex.	50	E 15.7.17	120	Un	1280		1	1	1		M	2							
Stephens, John	45	E 32.7.17	150	P	1580	Sbrg	1	4	1	2	M	2				1			2
Telford, Joseph	31	SE 22.7.17	25	P	690	Sbrg	1	1	1		M	2				1	1		
Todderick, J. B.	28	E 10.7.17	140	P	1880	(SC)	1	1	1		P	4				2	2		4
																1	15		6

This page is a rotated tabular ledger (a 1918 threshing/harvest return). Columns, left to right: surname/name, No., direction + date, acres, condition (P/Un), yield, grain variety, a group of count columns, a grade letter (M / CE / B), a further group of count columns, and a total. Best-effort reading:

Name	No.	Dir. / Date	Acres	Cond.	Yield	Variety	Counts	Grade	Total
Carrothers, M.	38	E 26.7.18	105	P	1735	Ches	1 1 1 1 … 2 1 2 1	M	7
Cory, Augustus	23	SE 25.7.18	70	P	1880	Ches	1 1 1 … 2 1 2 1	M	4
Cory, R. W.	25	NE 24.7.18	70	P	900	Ches	1 1 1 … 2 2 2	M	5
Cory, W.	26	SE 24.7.18	70	P	940	Ches	1 1 1 1 … 1 1 1	M	5
Crosbie, James	40	NW 32.7.18	30	P	730	Minn	1 1 … 3 3		3
Elliott, O. S.	31	SW 25.7.18	70	P	1025	Ches	1 2 1 … 2 2 1 1	M	3
Elliott, Wm. *	40	NE 17.7.18	40	Un	560	Minn	1 2 … 2 3		
Fawks, George	37	N 6.7.18	80	P	1620	RB	1 1 … 2 2 3	CE	7
Fowler, Alexander	18	E 27.7.18	300	Un	1830	Ches	1 1 … 1 3	CE	2
Fowler, Edward	25	E 21.7.18	170	Un	1560	Ches	1 1 1 … 2 1 1	CE	2
Fowler, F. O.	24	NE 25.7.18	17	Un	1240	Ches	1 1 … 4 1 2	CE	7
Fowler, Francis *	55	S 20.7.18	30	P	960	Minn	1 1	CE	
Fowler, John *	35	W 21.7.18	60	Un	960	Ches	1 1	CE	
Fowler, W. O.	48	W 27.7.18	180	Un	1620	Ches	1 1	CE	7
Gray, Duncan	32	NE 23.7.18	100	P	1015	Ches	1 1 1	B	
Gray, John	45	NE 15.7.18	86	Un	925	Ches	1 1 2 … 2 1 2 1	B	
		S 10.7.18	47	Un	1120	Ches	1 1		
Gray, Neil M.	31	SE 23.7.18	150	Un	1015	Ches	1 2 1 … 2 2 1	B	3
Gray, Neil P.	21	W 14.7.18	70	P	1350	Ches	1 1 … 2 2 1	B	
Griffin, Caleb	62	E 11.7.18	80	Un	1370	Ches	1 2 … 2 1	CE	4
Griffin, Nelson	26	S 15.7.18	120	Un	1120	Ches	1 1		6
		N 10.7.18	20	Un	1120	Ches	1 1		
Henderson, Isaac N.	24	E 36.7.18	85	P	1355	Ches	1 1 1 … 2 1 2	M	
Henderson, J. C.	30	S 32.7.18	60	P	1225	Minn	1 1 1 … 1 1 1	M	
Henderson, John	22	W 2.7.18	40	P	1225	None	1 3 1 … 1 2	M	4
Henderson, W. L.	56	W 24.7.18	250	P	1920	Ches	1 2 1 … 2 2 2 4	M	6
		NW 20.7.18	10	Un	480	Minn	1		
Henderson, Walter	57	W 34.7.18	70	P	1430	Ches	1 1 1 … 2 2 3	M	4
Henderson, Wm. M.	26	E 14.7.18	40	P	1320	Ches	1 1 … 2 2	M	
Henderson, Wm. W.	22	W 28.7.18	70	P	1345	Ches	1 1 1 … 1 1 1	M	
Hoggarth, Wm.	42	NE 32.7.18	65	P	830	Minn	1 2 1 … 2 3	CE	3
Jukes, Andrew		NW 15.7.18			560	Ches			
Jull, Henry	31	N 18.7.18	55	P	1345	Minn	1 1 1 … 2 1 2	M	3
Jull, J. A.	25	S 18.7.18	60	P	1420	Minn	1 1 1 … 1 3	M	3
Kent, Charles F.	36	NE 4.7.18	35	P	1360	None	1 1 … 3 2 3	CE	

NAME	AGE	DESCRIPTION OF LAND	NO. OF ACRES CULTIVATED	P or Un	TOTAL ASSESSMENT IN $	SCHOOL DISTRICT	Males Married	Males Single	Females Married	Females Single	RELIGION	HORSES	MULES	BULLS	OXEN	COWS	COWS UNDER 3 YEARS	SHEEP	PIGS
Kent, Sextus *	66	SE 4.7.18	18	P	560	None	1				CE								
Little, Robert	23	NE 33.7.18	40	Un	560	Ches		1											
Martin, John	22	NE 16.7.18	60	P	800	Ches		1			P	1				1			
Martin, R. T.	45	SE 28.7.18	100	P	900	Ches	1	1	1			2							4
Martin, Wm. H.	36	NE 28.7.18	15	Un	875	Ches		2	1	1	P	2			2				4
McMurchie, P.		NW 30.7.18	25	Un	480	Minn		1			P								4
Miller, S. J.		NW 16.7.18		Un	500	Ches		1											
Murray, Maxwell	38	S 16.7.18	100	Un	1260	Ches	1	1	1		P	2			2				1
Neelands, T. *	28	W 26.7.18	120	Un	1280	Ches		1		1	CE								
Noble, Wm.	30	Pt. W 36.7.18	100	P	900	Ches	1	1		1	P	1				1	2		1
Patterson, John		SE 2.7.18	50	P	1010	None	1	2	1	2		3				2	2		6
		NE 1.7.18		Un	560	None													
Patterson, Wm.	36	NE 2.7.18	80	P	1460	None	1	3	1	2	P	4				3	2		4
		NW 1.7.18		P	640	None													
Powers, George E.	30	E 35.7.18	170	Un	1750	Ches	1	1	1		M	2	2			1	1		7
Powers, L. B.	27	W 35.7.18	160	Un	1700	Ches	1	1	1		M	2	2			1	3		2
Robinson, Ingram	22	Pt. 36.7.18	85	P	735	Ches		1	1		P	2							
Rome, A. E.	27	E 22.7.18	125	P	1580	Ches		1	1		P	2				1			4
Shuttleworth, E. B. *	21	S 19.7.18	100	Un	1280	Minn													
Smith, A. W.	46	W 12.7.18	240	P	1480	Ches	1	3	1	1	M	3				1			2
Smith, Amos	28	NE & S 13.7.18	140	Un	2400	Ches		3		3		2				2	3		4
Smith, Noble	22	NW 13.7.18		Un	1090	Ches		1			M	2							4
Stiles, Arthur	24	3.7.18	345	Un	2720	None		1			CE	6							
Stiles, Edwin		W 4.7.18	18	Un	960	None		1			CE								
Townsend, Joseph R.	28	W 22.7.18	110	P	1500	Ches	1	1			M	2				1	1		
Townsend, Samuel R.	35	E 34.7.18	90	P	1440	Ches	1	1			M	2				1	1		

Name	Age	Bearing / Date	Wt	Un	1120	Pais	1	·	·	·	·	Rel	·	·	·	·	·	·	·	·
Carey, John	23	W 31.7.19	90	P	1545	None	1	1	1			RC	2		1	1			2	2
Carrol, Alfred	40	S 19.7.19	230	Un	1905	Pais	1	1	1	1		P	4		2	2			2	6
		NE 19.7.19		Un	500	Pais														
Clark, A. H.	23	S 10.7.19	45	P	1465	RB	1	1				CE	2		2	2			2	3
Clark, F. J.	25	N 10.7.19	70	P	1485	RB	1	3				CE	2		2	1	1	1	2	3
Donaldson, I. B.	35	W 2.7.19	25	Un	1260	RB	1					P		2	1	2	2	2		5
Fleming, J. H.	27	W 30.7.19	120	P	1500	Pais	1	1	1			CE	2							
Glendenning, Arthur	26	W 14.7.19	40	Un	1280	Minn	1	1				P		2						
Groves, Gibson	26	NE 4.7.19	24	P	480	RB	1					CE								
Guinn, Joseph	26	E 28.7.19		Un	960	Pais														
Harding, Robert	28	SE 36.7.19	40	P	950	Minn	1	2	1			CE	2		2	2		2	2	3
Healy, E. A.	48	W 17.7.19	250	Un	1745	Pais	1	2	1	4		M	3		2	2		1	2	8
Hemsworth, Mr.	45	N 34.7.19	50		1075	Minn	1	1	1	1		P			2					
Hicks, E. C.	37	NE 36.7.19	10		580	Minn	1	1	1	1		CE			2					3
Hudson, Joseph	20	NE 2.7.19	10	Un	480	RB	1	1				P								
Jones, W. T.	28	SW 28.7.19	30	Un	560	Pais	1	1				P								
Kerr, John	26	SE 32.7.19	40	Un	560	None	1	1				P								
Laughlin, John	22	NE 31.7.19	30	Un	640	None	1	1				P								
Lawson, Michael	60	N 20.7.19	44	P	1290	Pais	1	1	1			P			2	1	1		2	2
Leadbeater, Thomas	57	SE 6.7.19	5	P	900	Pais	1	2	1	4		P				1	1	1	2	2
Lines, B.	52	E 23.7.19	150	Un	1420	Minn	1	1					1			1	1		1	1
Lockeridge, David	22	SE 2.7.19	25	Un	560	RB	1	1	1			P								
Logan, Alex.	26	SW 13.7.19	77	Un	875	Minn	1	1	1	1		P	2		1	1	1	2	2	2
Long, James	54	N 24.7.19	75	P	1120	Minn	1	1				P								
		SE 14.7.19		Un	560	Minn														
Martin, James A.	28	E 12.7.19	70	P	1450	RB	1	1	1			P	2		2	1	1	1	2	8
Martin, John	27	W 12.7.19	55	Un	1320	RB	1	1								2			2	8
McBride, J. T. *		N 13.7.19			1280	Minn														
McCormick, Andrew	45	SE 18.7.19	20	P	560	Pais	1	4	1			P								
McFarland, C.	54	NE 26.7.19	14	Un	650	Minn	1	1					2							
McMurchie, Peter	36	E 25.7.19	140	Un	1250	Minn	1	1				M		4						
Minthson, Wm.	21	SE 34.7.19			480	None	1	1				P								
Munn, Wm.	32	E 22.7.19	58	Un	1175	Minn	1	2	1	1					2	2	2	2	2	2
Quarterman, Charles	41	NW 36.7.19	45		730	None	1	3	1	2		CE	3		2	2	3	3	2	4

NAME	AGE	DESCRIPTION OF LAND	NO. OF ACRES CULTIVATED	P or Un	TOTAL ASSESSMENT IN $	SCHOOL DISTRICT	MALES MARRIED	MALES SINGLE	FEMALES MARRIED	FEMALES SINGLE	RELIGION	HORSES	MULES	BULLS	OXEN	COWS	COWS UNDER 3 YEARS	SHEEP	PIGS
Seafoot, Walter	34	S 4.7.19	50	P	1360	RB	1	3	1	2	CE	2				1	1		6
Stinson, John	27	SE 30.7.19	60	P	920	Pais		1			P	2				1	1		1
		NE 30.7.19		P	640	Pais													
Stinson, John H.	23	SW 18.7.19	75	Un	700	Pais		1			P				2				
Stinson, Samuel	21	NE 18.7.19	10	Un	600	Pais		1			P								
Stinson, Wm.	64	NW 18.7.19	50	P	1300	Pais	1		1		P	2				1	3		3
Stinson, Wm. T.	30	NW 19.7.19	82	P	765	Pais	1		1	1	P	1				1			3
Taylor, Alex	33	NW 7.7.19	60	Un	760	Pais		1			P	2			2	1	1		3
Taylor, J. T.	28	NW 25.7.19	65	P	750	Minn	1		1		P	2			2	1	2		3
Taylor, Mat	29	SW 7.7.19	60	Un	800	Pais	1		1		P								4
Tew, R. H. M.	21	SW 34.7.19	25	Un	680	Minn		1		3	CE								1
Walker, Robert	49	SW 36.7.19	20	P	620	Minn	1	2	1		P				2				
Wallace, Robert	41	NW 16.7.19	40	Un	780	Pais	1	1	1		P	2					1		1

Name	Age	Dir	Date					1	4	1	5	P	4	2	5	5	1	12
Arnett, Robert	48	S	36.8.19	30		1480	None	1		1		P	4	2	5	5	1	12
		NW	3.8.19			500	None						2					
Beare, Thomas	23	NE	36.8.19	30		700	None		1			CE	2		1	1	1	
Beare, Wm.	56	NW	36.8.19	30		680	None	1					2	1	1	1	1	10
Belaney, C. M.	21	NE	36.8.19	100		860	Fost		1	1	1	CE	2					5
Beyhane, James	32	S	7.8.19	80	Un	1120	None											
Beyhane, M.	30	SW	5.8.19			640	None	1	1	1		RC		2	1			
Black, David		NE	3.8.19	25		500	None	1	1	1		P						
		NW	14.8.19	100		870	None											
		E	25.8.19			1000	None											
Black, James	22	SE	22.8.19	40		745	Fost	1	1	1								
Black, Wm.	30	NE	26.8.19	25		820	None	1	1	1		P						
Bobier, L. P.	46	W	22.8.19	80	P	1890	Fost	1	1	1	1	CE	2	1	2	2	5	2
Boore, Richard	56	E	31.8.19	160		960	Fost	1	1				1					
Brown, (Mr.?)	36	SW	12.8.19	6		480	None	1	1	1		P						
Cameron, Donald	45	SW	34.8.19	50	P	1025	Fost	1	3	1	2	P	2	2	2	2		1
Canning, James	25	SE	21.8.19	80		600	Fost	1	1			M						
Carey, M. J.	26	NE	5.8.19	60		780	None	1	1	1		RC	1					2
Charters, D. L.	32	SE	12.8.19		Un	480	None	1	1			P						
Cleveland, James	32	SE	34.8.19	15	P	980	Fost	1	1	2	2	B	2	1	1	1	1	4
		NE	27.8.19	90	P	640	Fost											
Collard, Wm.	63	W	10.8.19	45		1480	None	1	1	1	1	M	2	3	1	1		2
Compton, Robert	30	SW	24.8.19			960	None	1	1								1	
Couling, David	45	S	16.8.19	50	P	2480	Fost	1	4	1	5	M	4	9	12		12	6
		N	15.8.19	160		1280	Fost											
Couling, Lenord	23	SW	3.8.19	160		500	None	1	1	1		M						1
Crogan, Patrick	35	NW	24.8.19	6		705	None	1	2	1	2	RC	2	1	2	2	3	4
Crompton, John	57	NW	34.8.19	30	P	780	Fost	1	1	1		CE			1			1
Cunningham, H. A.	26	NW	18.8.19	28		1075	Fost	1	1	1		M	2	2	2			
		SE	19.8.19	135		640	Fost											
Cunningham, J.	64	SW	19.8.19	40		560	Fost											
Cunningham, James	49	SE	28.8.19	130	P	1225	Fost	1	1			P	2	2	1			4
Durst, P. E. *		W	25.8.19			1120	None	1										

NAME	AGE	DESCRIPTION OF LAND	NO. OF ACRES CULTIVATED	P or Un	TOTAL ASSESSMENT $	SCHOOL DISTRICT	MALES MARRIED	MALES SINGLE	FEMALES MARRIED	FEMALES SINGLE	RELIGION	HORSES	MULES	BULLS	OXEN	COWS	COWS UNDER 3 YEARS	SHEEP	PIGS
Emery, George	25	SW 6.8.19	55		600	None		1			M								
Foster, B. F.	23	W 30.8.19	50		1280	Fost						4	2			4	9		6
Gells, Wm. *		31.8.19	160		2400	Fost													
Graham, H. C.	30	N 19.8.19	176	P	2280	Fost	1	2	1		P	3				3	3		3
Hanna, Robert		SE 14.8.19			560	Fost													
Harper, Wm.	53	S 32.8.19	60		1650	Fost	1	2	1	1	M	3				3	3		3
		W 31.8.19			960	Fost													
Heal, Henry	25	N 16.8.19	50		1580	Fost													
Hearne, C. C.	22	N 20.8.19	50		1280	Fost		1											
Hooper, W. H. *		W 35.8.19	90		1200	None						3							
Kelley & Co. *		E 30.8.19			1200	Fost													
Kelley, Thomas E. *	36	E 27.8.19	160		1120	Fost	1		1		M								
Klink, W. G.	76	SE 8.8.19	40		870	None	1		1										
Laughlin, James	22	SE 17.8.19	45		685	Fost		1		1	CE				2				
		SW 6.8.19	8			None													
Leetham, Mary Ann	40	NE 28.8.19	30		600	Fost			1		CE	1				1	1		
Lellan, Samuel *		NE 8.8.19			640	None		1											
Maw, Joseph *		SE 35.8.19			640	Fost		1											
McCandlish, Henry	25	W 28.8.19	70		1120	Fost	1	2	1	3	P								
McKellar, Peter	53	S 18.8.19	60		1380	Fost		1				2				1	1		3
McMurchie, Peter	36	NE 1.8.19			480	Minn	1	2	1	2	RC								
McPhillips, Peter	24	NE 5.8.19	80		720	None	1	1	2	2	M								
Miller, George	56	NE 10.8.19	6		615	None	1	2	1	1	M	2				1			2
Millerick, James	32	N 7.8.19	90		1500	None		1				3							3
Nichol, Robert		NE 9.8.19	80		640	None													
Peters, J. George	38	SE 4.8.19	6		780	None	1	2	1	1	P	2			2	1	1		8
Pringle, Allan		NW 27.8.19			640	Fost													
Quinn, (Jos?)		NE 33.8.19			560	Fost													
Rathwell, W.	36	S 15.8.19	160		1280	Fost	1		1	3									
Roberts, George	50	NE 4.8.19	24		725	Fost													
Sheehy, C.		NW 26.8.19			640	None													
Sherman, James	40	NW 4.8.19	60		940	Fost	1		1	3		2				2	1		3
Short, Ennoc	40	SW 4.8.19	15		640	Fost													
Simmons, James	39	S 20.8.19	20		1265	Fost	1	3	1	3	CE	2				1			6
Smith, C. *		NE 35.8.19			560	None													

Name	Sec	Legal	Acres	T	Value	Dist			Rel					
Birch, Alfred	24	SW 35.8.18	90	Un	560	EB	1		CE	2		1		4
Birch, Arthur	25	NE 12.8.18	45	P	1010	Delt	1		CE	2				
Birch, Charlie (S.?)	25	Pt. SW 22.8.18	40	P	320	Delt				2				
Birch, Walter	21	SE 12.8.18	65	P	840	Delt	1		CE	2		1		5
		NW & Pt. SW 22.8.18		P	1375	Delt								
Bruce, Robert	22	NE 13.8.18	12		600	Delt	1	1	B	3				
Cleveland, C. A.	65	E 16.8.18	45		1120	Delt	1	1 1	B	2	2			2
Cleveland, C. D.	29	W 16.8.18	30		1540	Delt	1	1 1	B	2	1			4
Cleveland, Eugene	24	E 20.8.18	20		1345	Delt	1	1	B	3				2
Cleveland, W. F.	24	W 30.8.18	20		1200	Delt	1	1	B	3				
Coburn, Ed	24	NE 31.8.18	5		680	Delt	1	1	P	2				
Cook, Christopher	36	E 36.8.18	160		1520	EB	1	1	RC	2	2			5
Crosbie, Wm.	19	SE 6.8.18	7	Un	480	Minn	1	1	P					
Davidson, George	48	SW 34.8.18	20	P	730	Delt	1	4 1 3	P	3	2	4	6	3
Donaldson, E.	36	NE 26.8.18	130	Un	1990	Delt	1	1 1	P	3	2	2	2	6
		SE 35.8.18		Un	640	EB								
Findlater, George	26	NW 24.8.18	40	P	965	EB	1		P	2				
		SW 25.8.18	82	Un	560	EB								
Fisher, A. H.	25	NW 13.8.18	27	Un	650	Delt	1	1	M	2	2			1
Fisher, Levi	27	NE 24.8.18	100	P	990	EB	1	1	M	2	1	1	3	2
		SE 25.8.18	10	Un	500	EB								
Flower, W. B.	22	NE 35.8.18	80	Un	640	EB	1	1 5	M	2	1			2
Gammon, W. H.	40	SE 21.8.18	120(?)	P	1510	Delt	1	1		2				
Graham, John		NE 21.8.18	80		640	EB								
Granville, John	23	NW 2.8.18	40	P	900	Delt	1	3 1 2	M	2		3		3
Harley, G. G.	34	NE 28.8.18	65	P	640	Delt	1	1	P					
Hill, Wm.	42	S 24.8.18	60	Un	1185	EB	1	1	M		3			
Kennor, John	40	S 2.8.18		P	1120	Delt								
Killam, A. C. *		NW & S 26.8.18			1920	Delt	1	1	P	2				
		27.8.18			2500	Delt								
Killam, A. G.	24		120	Un	1520	Delt	1	5 3 4	P	2	4	3	6	6
Leslie, John	48	E 30.8.18	50	P	1230	Delt	1	3 1 3		2	1			
Lindsey, Robert	50	E 32.8.18	15	Un	1665	Delt	1	2 1 2	P	2	2		3	3
Little, Robert	45	W 4.8.18	80	P	1170	Delt	1	5 1 3	P	2	3	3		4
Lockhart, E. A.	40	NE 22.8.18	70	P		Delt	1	1 4	CE	2	3	3		6

NAME	AGE	DESCRIPTION OF LAND	NO. OF ACRES CULTIVATED	P or Un	TOTAL ASSESSMENT IN $	SCHOOL DISTRICT	MALES Married	MALES Single	FEMALES Married	FEMALES Single	RELIGION	HORSES	MULES	BULLS	OXEN	COWS	COWS UNDER 3 YEARS	SHEEP	PIGS
Lynn, Robert	30	SW 6.8.18	8	Un	480	Minn	1	1			P								
Marley, John	22	NE 15.8.18	80		640	Delt		1			CE	2							
Marmont, W. T.	25	NE 10.8.18	65	P	760	Delt	1	1			CE				2				8
McDonald, H. E.	25	SE 22.8.18	30		810	Delt	1	1			CE				2	1			
McKay, James	61	NW 10.8.18	40	P	685	Delt	1	1	1	3	CE	2					2		4
Mitchell, Robert	24	W 28.8.18	10		1150	Minn	1	1	1	1	P								
Moody, W. S.	31	N 6.8.18		P	1185	Delt	1	1	1	1	CE	4				1			7
Pope, R. R. *		SE 28.8.18			1135	Delt													
		NE 21.8.18	135		640	Delt													
Powers, C. F.		S 23.8.18	120		1280	Delt	1												
Powers, (Dr.?) *		E 3.8.18	12		1240	Delt	1		1		M								
		SW 3.8.18			560	Delt													
Pratt, J.	63	NW & E 19.8.18	28		1785	Delt	1	1	1		CE	2							2
Purvis, George *		N 23.8.18			1280	EB													
		NW 25.8.18			640	EB													
Rose, J. E.	32	NW 20.8.18	65		1145	Delt	1	1	1		CE	2				2	1		8
Rounthwaite, Mrs.F.	41?	S 13.8.18	150		1590	Delt		2	1	2	CE				4	1	2		12
Rounthwaite, S.	41	W 14.8.18	70	P	1610	Delt	1	4	1	1	CE	2				2	4		4
Selwyne, A.R.C. *	41	W 12.8.18	50	P	1240	Delt	1	1			CE								
		E 1.8.18	24	Un	1050	Delt													
Selwyne, P.	28	19.8.18	300		1935	Delt	1	1	1	2	CE	4				3	5		9
Shields, D. W.	24	W 1.8.18	140	Un	865	EB	1	2	1		CE	2				1		10	3
Shirk, Jacob	40	SW 36.8.18	40	P	925	Delt	1	7	1	1	CE	2				4	4		5
Shuttleworth, E. B. *		NE 2.8.18	40	P	640	EB													
		NW 35.8.18			640	EB													
Simpson, S. S.		SW 19.8.18		Un	480	Delt					CE								
Taylor, Peter	23	NW 31.8.18	10		780	Delt	1	1	1	2	CE				2	2			
Taylor, T.	45	SE 10.8.18	20	P	560	Delt	1	1	1		CE					1			3
Taylor, T. S. F.	27	SW 10.8.18		Un	525	Delt	1												
Taylor, Walter	33	SE 5.8.18	61	Un	1305	Delt	1				M								
Taylor, Wm.	24	E 4.8.18	55	Un		Delt	1				M	2							

Name		Location / Date	Ac.	Ten.	Val.	Soil				Rel.				
Banting, Charles	32	SE 2.8.17	40	P	890	Sbrg	1	1		M	2	1	3	9
Bolton, E. E.	64	N 18.8.17	74	P	1280	EB & Stra	1			CE	2			
Bolton, John	27	SE 20.8.17	100	P	990	Stra	1	1		CE				
Bolton, Wm.	30	SW 20.8.17	45	P	600	Stra	1	1		CE				
Brown, Alex	25	NE 10.8.17	25		560	Sbrg	1	2		P				
Brown, David	40	SE 10.8.17	100	P	1325	Sbrg	3	1	2	P	4	2	3	8
Brown, Joseph		NW 10.8.17		P	480	Sbrg	1			P				
Dale, J. W. *		NE 33.8.17	80	Un	560	Stra			3					
Dalzell, John	39	SW 1.8.17	40		890	Sbrg	3	1	2	M		2		6
Dorsey, Wm. S.	40	W 16.8.17	95	Un	1630	Stra	1	1	1	M	2		2	5
Duiguid, Wm.	36	W 28.8.17	79	Un	1560	Stra	1	1	3	M	2		3	
Elder, Tully	29	NW 25.8.17	70	Un	500	Stra	2	1		P				
Gibson, John	21	NW 12.8.17			480	Sbrg	1			P				
Graham, James	25	SW 17.8.17			600		1							
Graham, John	48	SW 30.8.17	25	Un	1465	EB	7	1	4	CE	4	2	5	12
		NE 25.8.17	120		640	Stra								
Hall, W. H.	29	NW 6.8.17	80	P	940	Sbrg	1				2			
Harry, Arthur	27	SW 6.8.17	80	P	905	Sbrg	1		1	P	2			3
Harry, Wallace	25	SE 6.8.17	80	P	800	Sbrg	1	1		M	2			5
Hector, James A.	25	SW 3.8.17	85		1125	Sbrg	1	1	1	M	4			4
Hector, R. W.	36	N & SE 9.8.17	240		1680	Sbrg	1	1	1	P	5	1	8	100
		E 4.8.17	145	P	2500	Sbrg								
Hill, Wm. T.	35	NE 2.8.17	28		815	Sbrg	1	1	1	M	2			3
Hunter, John	36	NE 6.8.17	70	P	845	Sbrg	1	1		P	2	2		3
Jackson, George	24	E 22.8.17	50		1390	Stra	2	1	1	CE	2		2	3
Jackson, Harry	23	SE 21.8.17			560	Stra	1	1	1	CE		2		
Jackson, James	20	NW 21.8.17	25	Un	640	Stra	1					2		
		NW 24.8.17	60		480	Stra								
Jackson, James G.	22	SW 12.8.17			480	Sbrg	1	2		CE				
Jackson, Wm.	45	SW 22.8.17	24		1540	Stra	5	1	2	CE	7		4	7
		NW 15.8.17	90		560	Stra								

NAME	AGE	DESCRIPTION OF LAND	NO. OF ACRES CULTIVATED	P or Un	TOTAL ASSESSMENT IN $	SCHOOL DISTRICT	MALES MARRIED	MALES SINGLE	FEMALES MARRIED	FEMALES SINGLE	RELIGION	HORSES	MULES	BULLS	OXEN	COWS	COWS UNDER 3 YEARS	SHEEP	PIGS
King, Wm. G.	40	S 14.8.17	10	P	1410	Stra	1	5		1	M				2	2		1	3
Lamb, Henry &	24&	E 3.8.17	60		1120	Sbrg		2			CE	5							6
Wm., Jr.	22	SE 17.8.17	88		1085	Stra													6
Lamb, Wm.	46	NE 17.8.17	120		1115	Stra	1	2		2	M	3			4	3	3	3	
Lammie, Robert	30	7.8.17	175		2590	Sbrg	1				CE								
Mairs, George	70	NE 24.8.17	25		480	Stra	1	1			P								
Mairs, James	25	SE 25.8.17	80		490	Stra		1			P	2				2			
Martin, Samuel	24	E 28.8.17	80		1805	Stra	1	4	1	2	P					2	3	3	7
McDonald, Angus	24	NE 32.8.17	75	P	500	EB		1			P	2				1	1	1	
McDonald, Angus, Sr.	61	W 32.8.17	75	P	1595	EB	1		1		P	2				2	2	2	
McFadden, James &	45&	W 4.8.17	150	P	1985	Sbrg	1	1	1	4	M	4				2	2		6
Wm. J.	23																		
McLean, Wm.	50	E 1.8.17	160		1330	Sbrg									2	2	2		
McLeod, T.	24	SE 32.8.17	50	P	500	EB	1	1			P	2							
McManus, J. A.	21	NE 24.8.17	15	Un	745	Stra		1		2	M	2				2			
McVey, Ed.	52	SE 36.8.17	58	P	980	Aweme		2			M	2					2		6
Morrison, E. H.	24	NW 22.8.17	45		700	Stra	1	1			P								
Morrison, W. E.	24	SE 34.8.17			480	Stra		1			M								
Murray, Joseph	32	SE 5.8.17	40		560	Stra	1												
Rodgers, Albert	25	SW 15.8.17		P	560	Stra													
Scott, J.R. *		8.8.17			2560	Sbrg					CE								
Scott, R. W.	23	SW 10.8.17	50	P	560	Sbrg	1	1			P	4				4	5		
Shields, Charles W.	20	SE 33.8.17	80	Un	920	Stra	1	1			P	3							5
Shields, David	38	E 30.8.17	80	P	1830	EB	1	1	1		P	2				2			25
Smith, A. J.	35	19.8.17	300	Un	2600	EB	1	1			CE								
Stady, Ed.	24	SW 24.8.17	5	Un	500	Stra	1	1			CE	2				2			
Stady, G. H.	21	NE 20.8.17	40	Un	850	Stra	1	1			CE	2				2			2
Stady, John	56	NW 30.8.17	35	P	1010	EB	1	6		2	P					2			2
		S 31.8.17	160		1280	EB													
Stewart, George	39	E 16.8.17	70	Un	1870	Stra	1	2	1	2	P	3				6	10	10	10
		SE 15.8.17	60	Un	560	Stra	1	1	1		M					1	9		9

Name	Sec.	Legal Description		Assessment	District
Watson, Charles	26	NW 14.8.17	40	1180	Stra
Waugh, Mr. *		E 27.8.17	Un	560	Stra
Wells, Eddie	25	NE 12.8.17		480	Sbrg
Wells, Joseph	49	SE 12.8.17		560	Sbrg
Wright, A.	30	NE 26.8.17	60 CE	910	Stra
Wright, F.	22	S 18.8.17	95 Un CE	1705	Stra
Wright, James	25	NW 13.8.17	CE	480	Stra
Wright, John	23	W 34.8.17	35 CE	1060	Stra

TOTALS

| | Total Assessment | NO. IN FAMILY | | | | | NO. OF ANIMALS | | | | | | | |
| | | MALES | | FEMALES | | | | | | | | | | |
		Married	Single	Married	Single	Total	Horses	Mules	Bulls	Oxen	Cows	Cows Under 3 years	Sheep	Pigs
Township 7, Range 17	92,331	42	60	31	52	185	81	2	1	16	68	65		181
Township 7, Range 18	79,455	29	43	26	26	124	87	2	1	27	42	50		140
Township 7, Range 19	54,555	32	53	23	25	133	49			32	29	23	1	92
Township 8, Range 17	81,488	27	82	25	35	169	92	6	2	42	62	57		170
Township 8, Range 18	76,550	29	48	29	38	144	67			15	42	61	10	135
Township 8, Range 19	71,400	18	44	21	16	99	51	2		22	39	32		93
	$455,779	177	330	155	192	854	427	12	4	154	282	288	11	811

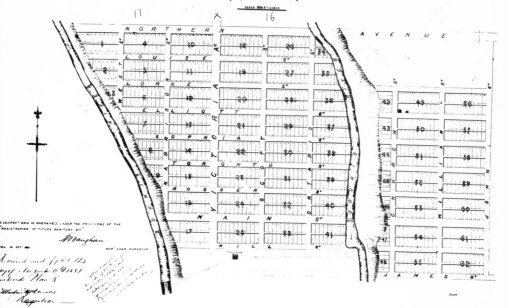

SOURIS CITY RATEPAYERS 1886
(from Oakland assessment roll of that year)

Coleman, E. R.	Lots 3, 4 & 5, Block 54
Drummond Bros.	Lots 13 & 16, Block 21
	Lots 3, 4 & 5, Block 51
	Lots 14 & 18, Block 53
Elliott, Jabez	Lots 1 & 2, Block 45
Hall, T. W.	Lot 6, Block 51
Harman, W. B.	Lots 17 & 18, Block 19
Kinley, R.	E½ of Lot 19, Block 53
	Lot 4, Block 53
McKenzie, D. L.	Lot 3, Block 45
Nichol, Thos.	Lot 5, Block 44
	Block 48 (?)
Westfield, J.	Lots 9 & 10, Block 61

251

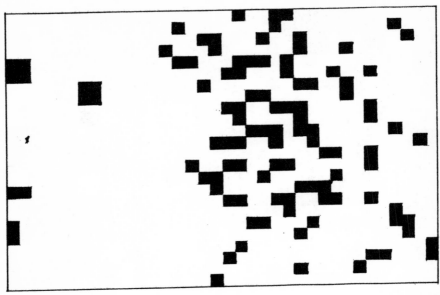

Extent of Settlement in Oakland 1881

1882

1886

1888

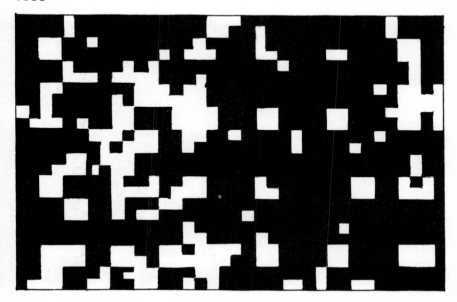

Index